Available Light

Available Light

Anthropological Reflections
on Philosophical Topics

Clifford Geertz

PRINCETON UNIVERSITY PRESS

PRINCETON AND OXFORD

Third printing, and first paperback printing, 2001
Paperback ISBN 0-691-08956-6

The Library of Congress has cataloged the cloth edition of this book as follows

Geertz, Clifford.
  Available light : anthropological reflections on philosophical topics / Clifford
Geertz.
    p. cm.
  Articles previously published chiefly 1983–1999.
  Includes bibliographical references and index.
  ISBN 0-691-04974-2 (CL : acid-free paper)
  1. Ethnology.   2. Philosophy.   3. Pluralism (Social sciences).   I. Title.

GN345 .G46 2000
306—dc21   99-054958

British Library Cataloging-in-Publication Data is available

This book has been composed in Goudy with Bernhard Tango display

Printed on acid-free paper. ∞

www.pup.princeton.edu

Printed in the United States of America

10 9 8 7 6 5 4

for

Joan Scott,

Albert Hirschman,

and Michael Walzer

colleagues

Contents ∞

Preface ∞

As befits two disciplines, neither of which is clearly defined and both of which address themselves to the whole of human life and thought, anthropology and philosophy are more than a little suspicious of one another. The anxiety that comes with a combination of a diffuse and miscellaneous academic identity and an ambition to connect just about everything with everything else and get, thereby, to the bottom of things leaves both of them unsure as to which of them should be doing what. It is not that their borders overlap, it is that they have no borders anyone can, with any assurance, draw. It is not that their interests diverge, it is that nothing, apparently, is alien to either of them.

Beyond their normally oblique and implicit competition for the last word and the first, the two fields share a number of other characteristics that trouble their relations with one another and make cooperation between them unnecessarily difficult. Most especially, both of them are porous and imperiled, fragile and under siege. They find themselves, these days, repeatedly invaded and imposed upon by interlopers claiming to do their job in a more effective manner than they themselves, trapped in inertial rigidities, are able to do it.

For philosophy this is an old story. Its history consists of one after another of its protectorates and principalities—mathematics, physics, biology, psychology, latterly even logic and epistemology—breaking away to become independent, self-governing special sciences. For anthropology, this contraction of imperium under separatist pressure is more recent and less orderly, but it is no less severe.

Having carved out, from the mid-nineteenth century on, a special place for itself as the study of culture, "that complex whole including . . . beliefs, morals, laws, customs . . . acquired by man as a member of society," it now finds various cooked-up and johnny-come-lately disciplines, semidisciplines, and marching societies (gender studies, science studies, queer studies, media studies, ethnic studies, postcolonial studies, loosely grouped, the final insult, as "cultural studies"), crowding into the space it has so painstakingly, and so bravely, cleared and weeded and begun to work. Whether as an ancient and honored holding company whose holdings, and honor, are slowly slipping away or as an intellectual high adventure spoiled by poachers, parvenus, and hangers-on, the sense of dispersal and dissolution, of "end-ism," grows by the day. Not a particularly felicitous situation for generous interaction and the combining of forces.

Yet, the attempt to so interact and so combine remains well worth making. Not only are the fears exaggerated and the suspicions ungrounded (neither field is about to go away quite yet, and they are less opposed in either style or temper than their louder champions like to imagine), but the stirred up and trackless postmodern seas they are now indeed alike passing through makes them, more and more, in active need of one another. The end is not nigh, or anywhere near, for either enterprise. But aimlessness, a baffled wandering in search of direction and rationale, is.

My own interest in effecting a connection, or strengthening one, or, thinking of Montaigne or Montesquieu, perhaps reviving one, stems not from any interest in altering my professional identity, with which I am as comfortable as could be expected after fifty years struggling to establish it, nor in widening it out to some sort of higher-order thinker-without-portfolio. I am an ethnographer, and a writer about ethnography, from beginning to end; and I don't do systems. But it probably is related, somehow or other, to the fact that, as I explain in the opening chapter, I started out "in philosophy" but gave it up, after an indecently short time, to ground my thought more directly, as I thought, in the world's variety. The sorts of issues I was concerned with then, and which I wanted to pursue empirically rather than only conceptually—the role of ideas in behavior, the meaning of meaning, the judgment of judgment—

persist, broadened and reformulated, and I trust substantialized, in my work on Javanese religion, Balinese states, and Moroccan bazaars, on modernization, on Islam, on kinship, on law, on art, and on ethnicity. And it is these concerns and issues that are reflected, a bit more explicitly, in the "reflections" here assembled.

Paradoxically, relating the sort of work I do—ferreting out the singularities of other peoples' ways-of-life—to that philosophers, or at least the sort of philosophers who interest me, do—examining the reach and structure of human experience, and the point of it all—is in many ways easier today than it was in the late forties when I imagined myself headed for a philosopher's career. This is, in my view, mainly a result of the fact that there has been, since then, a major shift in the way in which philosophers, or the bulk of them anyway, conceive their vocation, and that shift has been in a direction particularly congenial to those, like myself, who believe that the answers to our most general questions—why? how? what? whither?—to the degree they have answers, are to be found in the fine detail of lived life.

The main figure making this shift possible, if not causing it, is, again in my view, that posthumous and mind-clearing insurrectionist, "The Later Wittgenstein." The appearance in 1953, two years after his death, of *Philosophical Investigations*, and the transformation of what had been but rumors out of Oxbridge into an apparently endlessly generative text, had an enormous impact upon my sense of what I was about and what I hoped to accomplish, as did the flow of "Remarks," "Occasions," "Notebooks," and "*Zettel*" that followed it out of the *Nachlass* over the next decades. In this I was hardly alone among people working in the human sciences trying to find their way out of their stoppered fly-bottles. But I was surely one of the more thoroughly preadapted to receive the message. If it is true, as has been argued, that the writers we are willing to call master are those who seem to us finally to be saying what we feel we have long had on the tip of our tongue but have been ourselves quite unable to express, those who put into words what are for us only inchoate motions, tendencies, and impulses of mind, then I am more than happy to acknowledge Wittgenstein as my master. Or one of them, anyway. That he would return the favor and acknowledge me as his pupil is, of course, more than unlikely; he did not much like to think that he was agreed with or understood.

However that may be, his attack upon the idea of a private language, which brought thought out of its grotto in the head into the public square where one could look at it, his notion of a language game, which provided a new way of looking at it once it arrived there—as a set of practices—and his proposal of "forms of life" as (to quote one commentator) the "complex of natural and cultural circumstances which are presupposed in . . . any particular understanding of the world," seem almost custom designed to enable the sort of anthropological study I, and others of my ilk, do. They were, of course, along with their accompaniments and corollaries— "following a rule," "don't look for the meaning, look for the use," "a whole cloud of philosophy condensed into a drop of grammar," "saying and showing," "family resemblance," "a picture held us captive," "seeing-as," "stand not quite there," "back to the rough ground," "aspect blindness," "my spade is turned"—not so designed, but they were part of a merciless, upending critique of philosophy. But it was a critique of philosophy that rather narrowed the gap between it and going about in the world trying to discover how in the midst of talk people—groups of people, individual people, people as a whole—put a distinct and variegated voice together.

The way in which the gap was narrowed, or perhaps only located and described, is suggested by what, for a working anthropologist, is the most inviting of the tags just listed: "Back to the rough ground!" "We have got," Wittgenstein wrote, "on to slippery ice where there is no friction and so in a certain sense conditions are ideal, but also, just because of that, we are unable to walk. We want to walk: so we need *friction*. Back to the rough ground!" (*PI*, 107). The notion that anthropology (though, of course, not only anthropology) is exploring the rough ground on which it is possible for thought, Wittgenstein's or anyone else's, to gain traction is for me not only a compelling idea in itself; it is the idea, unfocused and unformulated, that led me to migrate into the field, in both senses of "field," in the first place. Wearied of slipping about on Kantian, Hegelian, or Cartesian iceflows, I wanted to walk.

Or walkabout. In moving across places and peoples, restlessly seeking out contrasts and constancies for whatever insight they might provide into any enigma that might appear, one produces less a position, a steady, accumulating view on a fixed budget of issues, than a series of positionings—assorted arguments to assorted ends. This leaves a great deal of blur and uncertainty in place; perhaps most of it. But in this, too, we are following Wittgenstein: One might ask, he writes, "'is a blurred concept a *concept* at all?'—Is an indistinct photograph a picture of a person at all? Is it even always an advantage to replace an indistinct picture by a sharp one? Isn't the indistinct one exactly what we need?" (*PI*, 71).

Whether it is or it isn't, and whomever the "we" might be, what follows below is a diverse and only partially ordered set of commentaries, examples, critiques, ruminations, assessments, and inquiries having to do with matters and persons—"relativism," "mind," "knowledge" "selfhood," Taylor, Rorty, Kuhn, James—at least arguably "philosophical." After a more or less introductory opening chapter reviewing the vagrant advance of my professional career, prepared for the American Council of Learned Society's "A Life of Learning" series, the next three chapters address moral anxieties that have arisen in carrying out fieldwork, certain sorts of so-called antirelativist arguments recently popular in anthropology, and a critique of some defenses of cultural parochialism in moral philosophy. Chapter V, "The State of Art," collects five extemporary pieces on present moral and epistemological controversies in and around anthropology. That is followed by more systematic considerations of the work of Charles Taylor, Thomas Kuhn, Jerome Bruner, and William James, prepared for symposia in their honor. Chapter X, "Culture, Mind, Brain . . . ," is yet one more consideration of the (possible) relations between what (supposedly) goes on in our heads and what (apparently) goes on in the world. And, finally, "The World in Pieces" is concerned with the questions raised for political theory by the recent upsurge in "ethnic conflict."

As for acknowledgments, which usually appear at about this point, I have, by now, so many people to thank that I am unwilling to risk leaving someone out by essaying a list; anyway, most of them have been thanked before. I have, instead, simply dedicated the book to my co-conspirators in the School of Social Science at the Institute for Advanced Study, where most everything in it first was written and discussed, rewritten and rediscussed, and where we have together created a place and an attitude worth defending. To prevent deep reading, by them or anyone else, they are listed in order of their distance down the corridor from my office.

Princeton
August 1999

Acknowledgments ∞

Chapter I: Given as the Charles Homer Haskins Lecture of the American Council of Learned Societies, Philadelphia, 1999.

Chapter II: Copyright © 1968 by the Antioch Review, Inc. First appeared in the *Antioch Review*, Vol. 28, No. 2. Reprinted by permission of the Editors.

Chapter III: Given as the Distinguished Lecture, annual meeting of the American Anthropological Association, Chicago, 1983; originally published in *The American Anthropologist* 86(2): 263–278, 1984. Reprinted by permission of the American Anthropological Association.

Chapter IV: Given as the Tanner Lecture in Human Values, University of Michigan, Ann Arbor, 1985; originally published in *Tanner Lectures on Human Values*, vol. 7, Salt Lake City: University of Utah Press, 1986, pp. 253–275.

Chapter V: Sections originally published in, respectively, *Times Literary Supplement*, June 5, 1985; *The New York Review of Books*, November 30, 1995; *The New York Review of Books*, October 22, 1998; *New Literary History* 21 (1990): 321–335; *The Yale Journal of Criticism* 5 (1993): 129–135. Reprinted with permission from *The New York Review of Books*. Copyright © 1995–8 NYREV, Inc.

Chapter VI: Originally published in James Tully and Daniel M. Weinstock, eds., *Philosophy in an Age of Pluralism*, Cambridge: Cambridge University Press, 1995, pp. 83–95. Reprinted with the permission of Cambridge University Press.

Chapter VII: Originally published in *Common Knowledge*, 6, 1 (1997): 1–5.

Chapter VIII: Given as the William James Lecture, Harvard Divinity School, 1998; originally published in *Raritan: A Quarterly Review*, Vol. 18, No. 3 (Winter 1999): 1–19. Reprinted by permission.

Chapter IX: Forthcoming in D. Bakhurst and S. Shanker, eds., *Language, Culture, Self: The Philosophical Psychology of Jerome Bruner*, London: Sage Publications. A part was originally published in *The New York Review of Books*, April 10, 1997.

Chapter X: Previously unpublished. Given at the inaugural symposium, Fernand de Saussure Foundation, Archamps/Geneva, 1999.

Chapter XI: Given as Annual Lecture in Modern Philosophy, Institut für die Wissenschaften vom Menschen, Vienna, 1995; originally published (in English) in *FOCAAL* 23 (1998): 91–117.

Available Light

I ∞

Passage and Accident:
A Life of Learning

Overture

It is a shaking business to stand up in public toward the end of an improvised life and call it learned. I didn't realize, when I started out, after an isolate childhood, to see what might be going on elsewhere in the world, that there would be a final exam. I suppose that what I have been doing all these years is piling up learning. But, at the time, it seemed to me that I was trying to figure out what to do next, and hold off a reckoning: reviewing the situation, scouting out the possibilities, evading the consequences, thinking through the thing again. You don't arrive at many conclusions that way, or not any that you hold to for very long, so summing it all up before God and Everybody is a bit of a humbug. A lot of people don't quite know where they are going, I suppose; but I don't even know, for certain, where I have been. But all right already. I've tried virtually every other literary genre at one time or another. I might as well try *Bildungsroman*.

The Bubble

I have, in any case, learned at least one thing in the course of patching together a scholarly career: it all depends on the timing. I entered the academic world at what has to have been the best time to enter it in the whole course of its history; at least in the United States, possibly altogether. When I emerged from the U.S. Navy in 1946, having been narrowly saved by The Bomb from being obliged to invade Japan, the great boom in American higher education was just getting underway, and I have ridden the wave all the way through, crest after crest, until today, when it seems at last, like me, to be finally subsiding. I was twenty. I wanted to get away from California, where I had an excess of relatives but no family. I wanted to be a novelist, preferably famous. And, most fatefully, I had the G.I. Bill.

Or, more exactly, *we* had the G.I. Bill: millions of us. As has been many times retailed—there was even a television special on the subject a year or so ago, and there is a book about it called, not inappropriately, *When Dreams Come True*—the flood of determined veterans, nearly two and a half million of us, onto college campuses in the half decade immediately following 1945 altered, suddenly and forever, the whole face of higher education in this country. We were older, we had been through something our classmates and our teachers, for the most part, had not, we were in a hurry, and we were wildly uninterested in the rites and masquerades of under-graduate life. Many of us were married; most of the rest of us, myself included, soon would be. Perhaps most importantly, we transformed the class, the ethnic, the religious, and even to some degree the racial composition of the national student body. And at length, as the wave moved through the graduate schools, we transformed the professoriate too. Between 1950 and 1970, the number of doctorates awarded annually increased five-fold, from about six thousand a year to about thirty thousand. (In 1940 it had been three thousand. No wonder the sixties happened!) That was perhaps not what William Randolph Hearst and the American Legion, who mobilized popular support for the Bill, precisely had in mind. But even at the time, we knew we were the vanguard of something large and consequential: the degreeing of America.

Having grown up rural in the Great Depression, I had not sup-posed I would be going to college, so that when the possibility sud-denly presented itself, I had no idea how to respond to it. After drifting around San Francisco most of the summer "readjusting" myself to a civilian existence, also at the government's expense, I asked a high school English teacher, an old-style leftist and waterfront agitator who had first suggested to me that I might become a writer—like Steinbeck, say, or Jack London—what I should do. He said (approximately): "You should go to Antioch College. It has a system where you work half the time and study half the time." That sounded promising, so I sent in an application he happened to have around, was accepted within a week or two, and went confidently off to see what was cooking, happening, or going down in southern Ohio. (As I say, this was another time. I am not sure I even knew that applications were sometimes rejected, and I had no plan B. Had I been turned down, I probably would have gone to work for the telephone company, tried to write in the evenings, forgotten the whole thing, and we should all have been spared the present occasion.)

Antioch, between 1946 and 1950, was, at first glance, the very model of that most deeply American, and to my mind most thoroughly admirable, of educational institutions—the small, small town, vaguely Christian, even more vaguely populist, liberal arts college. With fewer than a thousand students, only about half of them on campus at a time (the other half were off working somewhere, in Chicago, New York, Detroit, and the like), seventy-five or eighty live-in, on-call, faculty members, and wedged in between the woods and the railroad tracks in Yellow Springs, Ohio (population 2,500), it looked, all lattice arbors and brick chimneys, as though it had been set up on an MGM back lot for Judy and Mickey, or perhaps Harold Lloyd, to play out the passage from home— fumbling at sex, attempting alcohol, driving about in open cars, conning fuddled professors, trying on outrageous selves. There was some of that, but the place was a good deal more serious, not to say grave, than either its looks or its location suggested. Utopian, experimental, nonconformist, painfully earnest, desperately intense, and filled with political radicals and aesthetic free spirits (or were they aesthetic radicals and political free spirits?), it was countercultural before its time—a cast of mind and presentation that the influx of GI's, unwilling to take anything from anybody under any circumstances ever again, powerfully reinforced.

Let loose in this disorderly field of moralized self-fashioning (the reigning ethos of the place was Quaker, that most interior of iron cages; the reigning attitude, Jewish, all irony, impatience, and auto-critique; the combination, a sort of noisy introspection, passing curious), I simply took just about every course that in any way looked as though it might interest me, come in handy, or do my character some good, which is the definition, I suppose—certainly it was Antioch's—of a liberal education. As I wanted to be a writer, I thought, absurdly, of course, that I should major in English. But I found even that constraining, and so switched to philosophy, toward whose requirements virtually any class I happened into—musicology, for example, or fiscal policy—could be counted. As for the "work" side of the "work-study" program, and the alarming question it raised—what sort of business enterprise has a slot for an apprentice *littérateur?*—I thought, even more absurdly, that I should get into journalism as an enabling occupation, something to support me until I found my voice; a notion quickly put to rest by a stint as a copy-boy on the, then as now, crazed and beggarly *New York Post*. The result of all this searching, sampling, and staying loose (though, as I noted, I did manage to get married in the course of it all) was that, when I came to graduate, I had no more sense of what I might do to get on in the world than I had had when I entered. I was still readjusting.

But, as Antioch, for all its bent toward moral strenuousness and the practical life, was neither a seminary nor a trade school, that was hardly the point. What one was supposed to obtain there, and what I certainly did obtain, was a feeling for what Hopkins called "all things counter, original, spare, strange"—for the irregularity of what happens, and the rarity of what lasts. This was, after all, "the ignoble fifties," when, the story has it, the public square was empty, everyone was absorbed in witchhunts and selfish pursuits, and all was gray upon gray, when it wasn't suburban technicolor. But that is not how I remember it. How I remember it is as a time of Jamesian intensity, a time when, given the sense that everything could disappear in a thermonuclear moment, becoming someone upon whom nothing was lost was a far more urgent matter than laying plans and arranging ambitions. One might be lost or helpless, or racked with ontological anxiety; but one could try, at least, not to be obtuse.

However that may be, as the place was, alas, graduating me, it was necessary to depart and go elsewhere. The question was: where, elsewhere? With nothing substantial in sight in the way of a job (none of the people I had worked for wanted ever to see me again), I thought it expedient to take shelter in graduate school, and my wife, Hildred, another displaced English major unprepared for "the real world," thought she might do so as well. But, once again, I didn't know how to go about accomplishing this, and as I had used up my G.I. Bill, I was—we were—again without resources. So I replayed my '46 scenario and asked another unstandard academic, a charismatic, disenchanted philosophy professor named George Geiger, who had been Lou Gehrig's backup on the Columbia baseball team and John Dewey's last graduate student, what I should do. He said (also approximately): "Don't go into philosophy; it has fallen into the hands of Thomists and technicians. You should try anthropology."

As Antioch had no courses in that subject, I had shown no interest in it, and neither of us knew anything much about what it consisted of, this was a somewhat startling proposal. Geiger, it transpired, had been in contact with Clyde Kluckhohn, a professor of anthropology at Harvard who was engaged with some colleagues in developing an experimental, interdisciplinary department there called "Social Relations," in which cultural anthropology was conjoined not with archaeology and physical anthropology as was, and unfortunately still is, normally the case, but with psychology and sociology. That, he said, would be just the place for me.

Perhaps. I had no particular argument against it. But what clinched the matter was that (this is the part you may have some trouble believing) the American Council of Learned Societies had just instituted an also experimental first-year graduate fellowship program. The fellowships were to be awarded, one per institution, by a selected faculty member at a liberal arts college to his or her most promising student. Geiger (or "Mr. Geiger," as I still must call him, though he died last year at ninety-four, teaching practically to the end, beautifully unreconciled to time or fashion) was the Council's man at Antioch. He thought me, he said, no more unpromising than anyone else around, so if I wanted the fellowship I could have it. As the stipend was unusually generous for the times, indeed, for any times, it could support both myself and Hildred not just for one year but for two. So we applied to SocRel (and, again, nowhere else), were admitted, and, after another strange summer in San Francisco, trying to pick up pieces that would have been better left dropped, went off to Cambridge (Mass.) to become vocationalized.

I have written elsewhere, in another exercise in this sort of crafted candor and public self-concealment, about the enormous, unfocused, almost millenarian exhilaration that attended the social relations department in the 1950s, and what we who were there then were pleased to call its Project—the construction of "A Common Language for the Social Sciences." Bliss was it in that dawn; but the golden age was, as is the case with the assertive and the nonconforming, as well as with the exciting, in academia, all-too-brief. Founded in 1946 as a gathering of fugitives from traditional departments made restless with routinism by the derangements of the war, the social relations department began to lose its air by the 1960s, when rebelliousness took less intramural directions, and it was dissolved, with apparently only residual regret and not much ceremony, in 1970. But at full throttle, it was a wild and crazy ride, if you cared for that sort of thing and could contrive not to fall off at the sharper turns.

My stay in the department was, in one sense, quite brief—two hectic years in residence learning the attitude; one, no less hectic, on the staff, transmitting the attitude ("stand back, the Science is starting!") to others. But in another sense, as I was in and out of the place for a decade, writing a thesis, pursuing research projects, studying for orals ("How do they break horses among the Blackfoot?"), it was quite long. After a year being brought up to speed, not only in anthropology, but in sociology, social psychology, clinical psychology, and statistics, by the dominant figures in those fields (Kluckhohn, Talcott Parsons, Gordon Allport, Henry Murray, Frederick Mosteller, and Samuel Stouffer), another checking out what the other insurrectionists about the place were plotting (Jerome Bruner, Alex Inkeles, David Schneider, George Homans, Barrington

Moore, Eron Vogt, Pitrim Sorokin . . .), I found myself, along with my wife, facing that most brutal and inescapable—then, anyway; things have slipped a bit since—fact of the anthropological life: fieldwork.

And once again, I caught the wave. An interdisciplinary research team, handsomely funded by the Ford Foundation in the open-handed way that foundation funded ambitious, off-beat enterprises in its heroic, early days before its namesake's namesake discovered what was happening, was being organized under the combined, if rather uncertain, auspices of the social relations department, the even more newly formed, more obscurely funded, and more mysteriously intended Center for International Studies at MIT and Gadjah Mada, the revolutionary university setting up shop in a sultan's palace in just-independent Indonesia—a grand consortium of the visionary, the ominous, and the inchoate. The team was composed of two psychologists, a historian, a sociologist, and five anthropologists, all of them Harvard graduate students. They were to go to central Java to carry out, in cooperation with a matching group from Gadjah Mada, a long-term intensive study of a small, upcountry town. Hildred and I, who had hardly begun to think seriously, amid all our rushing to catch up on things, about where we might do fieldwork, were asked one afternoon by the team's faculty director (who, in the event, deserted the enterprise, mysteriously claiming illness) whether we would consider joining the project—she, to study family life, I, to study religion. As improbably and as casually as we had become anthropologists, and just about as innocently, we became Indonesianists.

And so it goes: the rest is postscript, the working out of a happenstance fate. Two and a half years living with a railroad laborer's family in Java's volcano-ringed rice bowl, the Brantas River plain, while the country raced, via free elections, toward cold war convulsion and impassive killing fields. Return to Cambridge to write a thesis on Javanese religious life under the direction of Cora DuBois, an eminent Southeast Asianist who had been appointed while I was away as the first woman professor in the department (and the second, I think, in all of Harvard). Return to Indonesia, this time to Bali and Sumatra and further political melodrama, culminating in revolt and civil war. A year recuperating at the newly founded Center for Advanced Study in the Behavioral Sciences, with the likes of Thomas Kuhn, Meyer Fortes, Roman Jakobson, W.V.O. Quine, Edward Shils, George Miller, Ronald Coase, Melford Spiro, David Apter, Fred Eggan, and Joseph Greenberg. A year at Berkeley, as the sixties ignited. Ten at Chicago, as they blew up—part of the time teaching, part of the time directing the Committee for the Comparative Study of New Nations, a multidisciplinary research project on the postcolonial states of Asia and Africa, part of the time off in an ancient walled town in the Moroccan Middle Atlas, studying bazaars, mosques, olive growing, and oral poetry and supervising students' doctoral research. And finally (as I am seventy-three, and unretired, it surely must be finally), nearly thirty years at the Institute for Advanced Study in Princeton, struggling to keep an unconventional School of Social Science going in the face of—how shall I put it?—a certain institutional timorousness and self-conceit. And all of this, in the same form and the same rhythm that I have by now, I am sure, wearied you with to the point of skepticism: a moment of confusion and uncertainty of direction, an unlooked for opportunity dropped carelessly at my feet, a change of place, task, self, and intellectual ambience. A charmed life, in a charmed time. An errant career, mercurial, various, free, instructive, and not all that badly paid.

The question is: Is such a life and such a career available now? In the Age of Adjuncts? When graduate students refer to themselves as "the pre-unemployed"? When few of them are willing to go off for years to the bush and live on taro (or even the equivalent in the Bronx or Bavaria), and the few who are willing find funding scarce for such irrelevance? Has the bubble burst? The wave run out?

It is difficult to be certain. The matter is *sub judice*, and aging scholars, like aging parents and retired athletes, tend to see the present as the past devitalized, all loss and faithlessness and falling away. But there does seem to be a fair amount of malaise about, a sense that things are tight and growing tighter, an academic underclass is forming, and it is probably not altogether wise just now to take unnecessary chances, strike new directions, or offend the powers. Tenure is harder to get (I understand it takes *two* books now, and God knows how many letters, many of which I have, alas, to write), and the process has become so extended as to exhaust the energies and dampen the ambitions of those caught up in it. Teaching loads are heavier; students are less well prepared; administrators, imagining themselves CEOs, are absorbed with efficiency and the bottom line. Scholarship is thinned and merchandized, and flung into hyperspace. As I say, I do not know how much of this is accurate, or, to the degree that it is accurate, how much it represents but a passing condition, soon to right itself; how much an inevitable retrenchment from an abnormal, unsustainable high, the smoothing of a blip; how much a sea-change, an alteration, rich and strange, in the structure of chances and possibilities. All I know is that, up until just a few years ago, I blithely, and perhaps a bit fatuously, used to tell students and younger colleagues who asked how to get ahead in our odd occupation that they should stay loose, take risks, resist the cleared path, avoid careerism, go their own way, and that if they did so, if they kept at it and remained alert, optimistic, and loyal to the truth, my experience was that they could get away with murder, could do as they wish, have a valuable life, and nonetheless prosper. I don't do that any more.

Changing the Subject

Everyone knows what cultural anthropology is about: it's about culture. The trouble is that no one is quite sure what culture is. Not only is it an essentially contested concept, like democracy, religion, simplicity, or social justice; it is a multiply defined one, multiply employed, ineradicably imprecise. It is fugitive, unsteady, encyclopedic, and normatively charged, and there are those, especially those for whom only the really real is really real, who think it vacuous altogether, or even dangerous, and would ban it from the serious discourse of serious persons. An unlikely idea, it would seem, around which to try to build a science. Almost as bad as matter.

Coming into anthropology from a humanities background, and especially from one in literature and philosophy, I saw the concept of culture looming immediately large, both as a way into the mysteries of the field and as a means for getting oneself thoroughly lost in them. When I arrived at Harvard, Kluckhohn was engaged, along with the then dean of the discipline, recently retired from Berkeley, Alfred Kroeber, in preparing what they hoped would be a definitive, message-from-headquarters compilation of the various definitions of "culture" appearing in the literature from Arnold and Tylor forward, of which they found 171, sortable into thirteen categories, and I, supposedly at home among elevated concepts, was conscripted to read over what they had done and suggest changes, clarifications, reconsiderations, and so on. I can't say that this exercise led, for me or for the profession generally, to a significant reduction of semantic anxiety, or to a decline in the birthrate of new definitions; rather the opposite, in fact. But it did plunge me, brutally and without much in the way of guide or warning, into the heart of what I would later learn to call my field's problematic.

The vicissitudes of "culture" (the *mot*, not the *chose*—there is no *chose*), the battles over its meaning, its use, and its explanatory worth, were in fact only beginning. In its ups and downs, its drift toward and away from clarity and popularity over the next half-century, can be seen both anthropology's lumbering, arrhythmic line of march and my own. By the 1950s, the eloquence, energy, breadth of interest, and sheer brilliance of such writers as Kroeber and Kluckhohn, Ruth Benedict, Robert Redfield, Ralph Linton, Geoffrey Gorer, Franz Boas, Bronislaw Malinowski, Edward Sapir, and, most spectacularly, Margaret Mead—who was everywhere, in the press, at lecterns, before congressional committees, heading projects, founding committees, launching crusades, advising philanthropists, guiding the perplexed, and, not least, pointing out to her colleagues wherein they were mistaken—made the anthropological idea of culture at once available to, well, the culture, and so diffuse and all-embracing as to seem like an all-seasons explanation for anything human beings might contrive to do, imagine, say, be, or believe. Everyone knew that the Kwakiutl were megalomanic, the Dobu paranoid, the Zuni poised, the Germans authoritarian, the Russians violent, the Americans practical and optimistic, the Samoans laid-back, the Navaho prudential, the Tepotzlanos either unshakably unified or hopelessly divided (there were two anthropologists who studied them, one the student of the other), and the Japanese shame-driven; and everyone knew they were that way because their culture (each one had one, and none had more than one) made them so. We were condemned, it seemed, to working with a logic and a language in which concept, cause, form, and outcome had the same name.

I took it as my task, then—though in fact no one actually assigned it to me, and I am not sure to what degree it was a conscious decision—to cut the idea of culture down to size, to turn it into a less expansive affair. (I was, admittedly, hardly alone in this ambition. Discontent with haze and handwaving was endemic in my generation.) It seemed urgent, it still seems urgent, to make "culture" into a delimited notion, one with a determinate application, a definite sense, and a specified use—the at least somewhat focused subject of an at least somewhat focused science.

This proved hard to do. Leaving aside the question of what it takes to count as a science, and whether anthropology has any hope of ever qualifying as one, a question that has always seemed factitious to me—call it a study if it pleases you, a pursuit, an inquiry—the intellectual materials necessary to such an effort were simply not available or, if available, unrecognized as such. That the effort was made, again not just by myself, but by a wide range of quite differently minded, that is, differently dissatisfied, people, and that it had a certain degree of success, is a sign not only that some received ideas of "culture"—that it is learned behavior, that it is superorganic, that it shapes our lives as a cake-mold shapes a cake or gravity our movements, that it evolves as Hegel's absolute evolves, under the direction of ingenerate laws toward a perfected integrity—had begun to lose their force and persuasion. It is also a sign that an abundance of new, more effective varieties of what Coleridge called speculative instruments were coming to hand. It turned out to be, almost entirely, tools made elsewhere, in philosophy, linguistics, semiotics, history, psychology, sociology, and the cognitive sciences, as well as to some degree in biology and literature, that enabled anthropologists, as time went on, to produce less panoptical, and less inertial, accounts of culture and its workings. We needed, it seemed, more than one idea, or a hundred and seventy-one versions of the same idea.

It was, in any case, with such an accumulation of proleptic worries and semi-notions that I departed, after less than a year of preparation, and most of that linguistic, to Java in 1952, to locate and describe, perhaps even to go so far as to explain, something called "religion" in a remote and rural subdistrict five hundred miles south-southeast of Jakarta. Again, I have retailed elsewhere the practical difficulties involved in this, which were enormous (I damn near died, for one thing), but largely overcome. The important point, so far as the development of my take on things is concerned, is that field research, far from sorting things out, scrambled them further. What in a Harvard classroom had been a methodological dilemma, a conundrum to puzzle over, was, in a bend-in-the-road Javanese town, trembling in the midst of convulsive change, an immediate predicament, a world to engage. Perplexing as it was, "Life Among the Javans" was rather more than a riddle, and it took rather more than categories and definitions, and rather more also than classroom cleverness and a way with words, to find one's way around in it.

What made the "Modjokuto Project," as we decided to call it in the usual, unavailing effort to disguise identities ("Modjokuto" means "Middletown," a conceit I was dubious of then and have grown no fonder of since), particularly disruptive of accepted phrasings and standard procedures was that it was, if not the first, surely one of the earliest and most self-conscious efforts on the part of anthropologists to take on not a tribal group, an island settlement, a disappeared society, a relic people, nor even a set-off, bounded small community of herders or peasants, but a whole, ancient and inhomogeneous, urbanized, literate, and politically active society—a civilization, no less—and to do so not in some reconstructed, smoothed-out "ethnographical present" in which everything could be fitted to everything else in just-so timelessness, but in all its ragged presence and historicity. A folly perhaps; but if so, it is one that has been succeeded by a stream of others that has rendered a vision of culture designed for the (supposedly) seclusive Hopi, primordial Aborigines, or castaway Pygmies futile and obsolete. Whatever Java was, or Indonesia, or Modjokuto, or later, when I got there, Morocco, it wasn't "a totality of behavior patterns . . . lodged in [a] group," to quote one of those lapidary definitions from the Kroeber-Kluckhohn volume.

The years in Modjokuto, both then and later as I kept returning, struggling to keep up with things, turned out not to consist of locating bits of Javanese culture deemed "religious," marking them off from other bits called, no more helpfully, "secular," and subjecting the whole to functional analysis: "Religion" holds society together, sustains values, maintains morale, keeps public conduct in order, mystifies power, rationalizes inequality, justifies unjust deserts, and so on—the reigning paradigm, then and since. It turned out to be a matter of gaining a degree of familiarity (one never gets more than that) with the symbolic contrivances by means of which individuals imagined themselves as persons, as actors, sufferers, knowers, judges, as, to introduce the exposing phrase, participants in a form of life. It was these contrivances, carriers of meaning and bestowers of significance (communal feasts, shadowplays, Friday prayers, marriage closings, political rallies, mystical disciplines, popular dramas, court dances, exorcisms, Ramadan, rice plantings, burials, folk tales, inheritance laws), that enabled the imaginings and actualized them, that rendered them public, discussable, and, most consequentially, susceptible of being critiqued and fought over, on occasion revised. What had begun as a survey of (this has to be in quotes) "the role of ritual and belief in society," a sort of comparative mechanics, changed as the plot thickened and I was caught up in it, into a study of a particular instance of meaning-making and the complexities that attended it.

There is no need to go further here with the substance of either the study or the experience. I wrote a seven-hundred-page thesis (Professor DuBois was appalled), squashed down to a four-hundred-page book, retailing the outcome. The point is the lessons, and the lessons were:

1. Anthropology, at least of the sort I profess and practice, involves a seriously divided life. The skills needed in the classroom or at the desk and those needed in the field are quite

different. Success in the one setting does not insure success in the other. And vice versa.

2. The study of other peoples' cultures (and of one's own as well, but that brings up other issues) involves discovering who they think they are, what they think they are doing, and to what end they think they are doing it, something a good deal less straightforward than the ordinary canons of Notes and Queries ethnography, or for that matter the glossy impressionism of pop art "cultural studies," would suggest.

3. To discover who people think they are, what they think they are doing, and to what end they think they are doing it, it is necessary to gain a working familiarity with the frames of meaning within which they enact their lives. This does not involve feeling anyone else's feelings, or thinking anyone else's thoughts, simple impossibilities. Nor does it involve going native, an impractical idea, inevitably bogus. It involves learning how, as a being from elsewhere with a world of one's own, to live with them.

Again, the rest is postscript. Over the next forty years, or nearly so, I spent more than ten in the field, developing and specifying this approach to the study of culture, and the other thirty (I have not done very much teaching, at least since I moved to the Institute) attempting to communicate its charms in print.

There is, in any case, apparently something to the idea of *Zeitgeist*, or at least to that of mental contagion. One thinks one is setting bravely off in an unprecedented direction and then looks up to find all sorts of people one has never even heard of headed the same way. The linguistic turn, the hermeneutical turn, the cognitive revolution, the aftershocks of the Wittgenstein and Heidegger earthquakes, the constructivism of Thomas Kuhn and Nelson Goodman, Benjamin, Foucault, Goffman, Lévi-Strauss, Suzanne Langer, Kenneth Burke, developments in grammar, semantics, and the theory of narrative, and latterly in neural mapping and the somaticization of emotion all suddenly made a concern with meaning-making an acceptable preoccupation for a scholar to have. These various departures and novelties did not, of course, altogether comport, to put it mildly; nor have they proved of equal usefulness. But they provided the ambience, and, again, the speculative instruments, to make the existence of someone who saw human beings as, quoting myself paraphrasing Max Weber, "suspended in webs of meaning they themselves have spun" a good deal easier. For all my determination to go my own way, and my conviction that I had, I was, all of a sudden, an odd man in.

After Java there was Bali, where I tried to show that kinship, village form, the traditional state, calendars, law, and, most infamously, the cockfight could be read as texts, or, to quiet the literalminded, "text-analogues"—enacted statements of, in another exposing phrase, particular ways of being in the world. Then there was Morocco and a similar approach to marabouts, city design, social identity, monarchy, and the arabesque exchanges of the cycling market. At Chicago, where I had by then begun to teach and agitate, a more general movement, stumbling and far from unified, in these directions got underway and started to spread. Some, both there and elsewhere, called this development, at once theoretical and methodological, "symbolic anthropology." But I, regarding the whole thing as an essentially hermeneutic enterprise, a bringing to light and definition, not a metaphrase or a decoding, and uncomfortable with the mysterian, cabalistic overtones of "symbol," preferred "interpretive anthropology." In any case, "symbolic" or "interpretive" (some even preferred "semiotic"), a budget of terms, some mine, some other people's, some reworked from earlier uses, began to emerge, around which a revised conception of what I, at least, still called "culture" could be built: "thick description," "model-of/model-for," "sign system," "*epistemé*," "ethos," "paradigm," "criteria," "horizon," "frame," "world," "language games," "interpretant," "*sinnzusamenhang*," "trope," "*sjuzet*," "experience-near," "illocutionary," "discursive formation," "defamiliarization," "competence/performance," "*fictiō*," "family resemblance," "heteroglossia," and, of course, in several of its innumerable, permutable senses, "structure." The turn toward meaning, however denominated and however expressed, changed both the subject pursued and the subject pursuing it.

Not that all this happened without the usual quota of fear and loathing. After the turns, there came the wars: the culture wars, the science wars, the value wars, the history wars, the gender wars, the wars of the paleos and the posties. Except when driven beyond distraction, or lumbered with sins I lack the wit to commit, I, myself, am shy of polemic; I leave the rough stuff to those who Lewis Namier so finely dismissed as persons more interested in themselves than their work. But as the temperature rose and rhetoric with it, I found myself in the middle of howling debates, often enough the bemused focus of them ("did *I* say *that?*"), over such excited questions as whether the real is truly real and the true really true. Is knowledge possible? Is the good a matter of opinion? Objectivity a sham? Disinterestedness bad faith? Description domination? Is it power, pelf, and political agendas all the way down? Between old debenture holders, crying that the sky is falling because relativists have taken factuality away, and advanced personalities, cluttering the landscape with slogans, salvations, and strange devices, as well as a great deal of unrequired writing, these last years in the human sciences have been, to say the least, full of production values. Whatever is happening to the American mind, it certainly isn't closing.

Is it, then, flying apart? In its anthropological precincts there seem to be, at the moment, a curious lot of people who think so. On all sides one hears laments and lamentations about the lost unity of the field, about insufficient respect for the elders of the tribe, about the lack of an agreed agenda, a distinct identity, and a common purpose, about what fashion and controversy are doing to mannerly discourse. For my part, I can only say, realizing that I am sometimes held responsible—the vogue word is "complicit"—for the fact both that things have gone much too far and that they haven't gone nearly far enough, that I remain calm and unfazed; not so much above the battle, as beside it, skeptical of its very assumptions. The unity, the identity, and the agreement were never there in the first place, and the idea that they were is the kind of folk belief to which anthropologists, of all people, ought to be resistant. And as for not going far enough, rebelliousness is an overpraised virtue; it is important to say something and not just threaten to say something, and there are better things to do with even a defective inheritance than trash it.

So where am I now, as the millennium approaches me, scythe in hand? Well, I am not going back into the field anymore, at least not for extended stays. I spent my sixtieth birthday crouched over a slit-trench latrine in "Modjokuto" (well, not the *whole* day, but you know what I mean), wondering what in hell I was doing there at my age, with my bowels. I enjoyed fieldwork immensely (yes, I know, not all the time), and the experience of it did more to nourish my soul, and indeed to create it, than the academy ever did. But when it's over, it's over. I keep writing; I've been at it too long to stop, and anyway I have a couple of things I still haven't said. As for anthropology, when I look at what at least some of the best among the oncoming generations are doing or want to do, in the face of all the difficulties they face in doing it and the ideological static that surrounds almost all adventurous scholarship in the humanities and social sciences these days, I am, to choose my words carefully, sanguine enough of mind. As long as someone struggles somewhere, as the battle cry from my own Wobbly youth had it, no voice is wholly lost. There is a story about Samuel Beckett that captures my mood as I close out an improbable career. Beckett was walking with a friend across the lawn of Trinity College, Dublin, one warm and sunny April morning. The friend said, ah, isn't it now a fine and glorious day, to which Beckett readily assented; it was, indeed, a fine and glorious day. "A day like this," the friend went on, "makes you glad you were ever born." And Beckett said: "Oh, I wouldn't go so far as that."

Waiting Time

In his direct and plainspoken contribution to this series of fablings and auto-obituaries a couple of years ago, so different in tone and aspiration to my own, the cliometrical economic historian, Robert Fogel, concludes by saying that he is working these days on "the possibility of creating life-cycle intergenerational data sets" that will permit him and his research team to "study the impact of socio-economic and biomedical stress early in life on the rate of onset of chronic disease, on the capacity to work at middle and late ages, and on 'waiting time' until death." (He is, I hear from other sources, now weighing rat placentas toward that end.) I am not certain—uncharacteristically, Professor Fogel neglects to give his cutting points—whether I still qualify for the "late ages" or not. But in any case, the "waiting time" category ("Gogo: I can't go on like this. Didi: That's what you think.") and the onset of disabling diseases— Felix Randall, the farrier's, "fatal four disorders / fleshed there, all contended"—cannot be very far away; and as either White remarked to Thurber or Thurber remarked to White, the claw of the old seapuss gets us all in the end.

I am, as I imagine you can tell from what I've been saying, and the speed at which I have been saying it, not terribly good at waiting, and I will probably turn out not to handle it at all well. As my friends and co-conspirators age and depart what Stevens called "this vast inelegance," and I, myself, stiffen and grow uncited, I shall surely be tempted to intervene and set things right yet once more. But that, doubtless, will prove unavailing, and quite possibly comic. Nothing so ill-befits a scholarly life as the struggle not to leave it, and—Frost, this time, not Hopkins—"no memory of having starred / can keep the end from being hard." But for the moment, I am pleased to have been given the chance to contrive my own fable and plead my own case before the necrologists get at me. No one should take what I have been doing here as anything more than that.

II ∞

Thinking as a Moral Act: Ethical Dimensions of Anthropological Fieldwork in the New States

When I try to sum up what, above all else, I have learned from grappling with the sprawling prolixities of John Dewey's work, what I come up with is the succinct and chilling doctrine that thought is conduct and is to be morally judged as such. It is not the notion that thinking is a serious matter that seems to be distinctive of this last of the New England philosophers; all intellectuals regard mental productions with some esteem. It is the argument that the reason thinking is serious is that it is a social act, and that one is therefore responsible for it as for any other social act. Perhaps even more so, for, in the long run, it is the most consequential of social acts.

In short, Dewey brings thinking out into the public world where ethical judgment can get at it. To some, this seems to debase it terribly, to turn it into a thing, a weapon, a possession or something equally ordinary. Revolutionary moralists—for that, finally, amid all his awarkwardness of expression, is what Dewey was—are never much liked, particularly by those, in this case practitioners of the intellectual trades, whom they so severely call to account. They are almost always attacked, as he has been, as undermining established practices and corrupting the young. Yet, for better or worse, they usually have their effect: the practices, if not undermined, are at least shaken; the youth, if not corrupted, are at least disquieted. Since Dewey, it has been much more difficult to regard thinking as an abstention from action, theorizing as an alternative to commitment, and the intellectual life as a kind of secular monasticism, excused from accountability by its sensitivity to the Good.

Nowhere has this been more true than in the social sciences. As these sciences have developed technically, the question of their moral status has become increasingly pressing. Yet, from Deweyian point of view, most of the debates stimulated by this concern have been somewhat lacking in point, for they rarely have been based on any circumstantial examination of what such research is as a form of conduct. Humanists cry that the social scientists are barbarizing the world and grabbing off all the grants, social scientists that they are saving it—or anyway are going to shortly, if only their grants are increased. But the moral quality of the experience of working social scientists, the ethical life they lead while pursuing their inquiries, is virtually never discussed except in the most general terms. This should be a searching investigation of a central aspect of modern consciousness. Unfortunately, it has descended into an exchange of familiar opinions between cultural game wardens, like Jacques Barzun, and scientistic fundamentalists, like B. F. Skinner, concerning the terrible or wonderful effects the systematic study of human life has had, is having, or is going to have sooner than we think.

Yet, the impact of the social sciences upon the character of our lives will finally be determined more by what sort of moral experience they turn out to embody than by their merely technical effects or by how much money they are permitted to spend. As thought is conduct, the results of thought inevitably reflect the quality of the kind of human situation in which they were obtained. The methods and theories of social science are not being produced by computers but by men and women; and, for the most part, by men and women operating not in laboratories but in the same social world to which the methods apply and the theories pertain. It is this which gives the whole enterprise its special character. Most social scientific research involves direct, intimate, and more or less disturbing encounters with the immediate details of contemporary life, encounters of a sort which can hardly help but affect the sensibilities of the persons who practice it. And, as any discipline is what the persons who practice it make it, these sensibilities become as embedded in its constitution as do those of an age in its culture. An assessment of the moral implications of the scientific study of human life which is going to consist of more than elegant sneers or mindless celebrations must begin with an inspection of social scientific research as a variety of moral experience.

To propose, after such a preamble, my own experience as a fit subject for review may seem to suggest a certain pretentiousness. Certainly the risk of attitudinizing is not to be lightly dismissed. Discussing one's moral perceptions in public is always an invitation to cant and, what is worse, to entertain the conception that there is something especially noble about having been refined enough simply to have had them. Even the confirmed self-hater prides himself, as Nietzsche once pointed out, on his moral sensitivity in discerning so acutely what a wretch he is.

Yet, if I do propose to discuss here a few of the ethical dimensions of my own research experience, it is not because I consider them unique or special. Rather, I suspect them of being common to the point of universality among those engaged in similar work, and therefore representative of something more than themselves or myself. Even more important, as my work has had to do with the New States of Asia and Africa (or, more precisely, with two of them, Indonesia and Morocco), and with the general problem of the modernization of traditional societies, it is perhaps particularly apposite to an assessment of social research as a form of conduct and the implications to be drawn for social science as a moral force. Whatever else one may say of such inquiry, one can hardly claim that it is focused on trivial issues or abstracted from human concerns.

It is not, of course, the only sort of work social scientists are doing, nor even the only sort anthropologists are doing. Other insights would be derived, other lessons drawn, from inspecting other sorts; and a general evaluation of the impact of social science on our culture will have to take account of them all. It is to contribute toward putting the debate over the moral status of social science on firmer ground, and not to propose my own experiences or my own line of work as canonical, that the following scattered and necessarily somewhat personal reflections are directed

∽

One of the more disquieting conclusions to which thinking about the new states and their problems has led me is that such thinking is rather more effective in exposing the problems than it is in uncovering solutions for them. There is a diagnostic and a remedial side to our scientific concern with these societies, and the diagnostic seems, in the very nature of the case, to proceed infinitely faster than the remedial. Therefore, one result of very extended, very thorough, periods of careful research is usually a much keener realization that the new states are indeed in something of a fix. The emotion this sort of reward for patient labors produces is rather like that I imagine Charlie Brown to feel when, in one "Peanuts" strip, Lucy says to him: "You know what the trouble with you is Charlie Brown? The trouble with you is you're you." After a panel of wordless appreciation of the cogency of this observation, Charlie asks: "Well, whatever can I do about that?" and Lucy replies: "I don't give advice. I just point out the roots of the problem."

The roots of the problem in the new states are rather deep, and social research often serves little more than to demonstrate just how deep they are. When it comes to giving advice, what has been discovered usually seems to be more useful in pointing out ways in which the present unbearable situation could be worsened (and probably will be) rather than ways in which it might be ameliorated. Francis Bacon's aphorism seems to me distinctly less axiomatic by the day: Knowledge—at least the sort of knowledge I have been able to dig up—does not always come to very much in the way of power.

All this is not a mere attack of sentimental pessimism on my part; it is a stubbornly objective aspect of social research in the new states. In evidence of this assertion, let me discuss for a moment a problem which is fundamental, not only in Indonesia and Morocco, where I have encountered it, but in virtually all the new states: agrarian reform.

This problem appears in quite different, even contrasting, forms in Indonesia and Morocco, for reasons which are at once ecological, economic, historical, and cultural. But, in either place, to analyze it systematically is not only to appreciate for the first time just how great a problem it really is, but to uncover the factors which make it so recalcitrant; and these factors turn out to be very similar in the two places. In particular, there is in both situations a radical short-run incompatibility between the two economic goals which together comprise what agrarian reform in the long run consists of: technological progress and improved social welfare. Less abstractly, a radical increase in agricultural production and a significant reduction of rural un- (or under-) employment seem for the moment to be directly contradictory ambitions.

In Indonesia, and particularly in its Javanese heartland where (ca. 1960) the population densities run up to over 1,500 per square mile, this contradiction expresses itself in terms of an extraordinarily labor-intensive, but, on the whole, highly productive mode of exploitation. The countless third- and quarter-acre rice terraces which blanket Java, Bali, and certain regions of Sumatra and the Celebes are worked almost as though they were gardens—or, perhaps more exactly, greenhouse tanks. Virtually everything is done by hand. Very simple (and very ingenious) tools are used. Hordes of laborers drawn from the enormous rural population work with extreme care and thoroughness.

Whether you want to call these workers "underemployed" or not depends on definitions. Certainly, most of them make some contribution to the high per acre output; with equal certainty, they would be better employed elsewhere if there were an elsewhere to employ them and if there were mechanized means at hand to accomplish their agricultural tasks. There are not, however. And it is here that the rub comes: technological progress of any serious scope (i.e., aside from marginal changes like increased fertilizing and improved seed selection) means the massive displacement of rural labor, and this is unthinkable under present conditions. As a Dutch economist once remarked, with modern technology the agricultural work of Java could be done with 10 percent of the present work force, but that would leave the other 90 percent starving.

At this point, someone who remembers what became of Malthus' dire forebodings concerning Europe always appears to say, "Industrialization!" But how is industrialization to be financed in a country where the huge peasantry itself consumes the overwhelming bulk of what it produces, and what exports exist largely go toward securing the subsistence of the urban masses? And how, even if it can be financed, can it possibly be of such a scope (and in these days of automation, of such a sort) to absorb more than a minute fraction of the labor a true agricultural revolution in Java would release?

In essence, faced with a choice between maintaining employment and increasing production per worker, the Javanese peasant "chooses" (an absurdly voluntaristic word to use in this context) to maintain employment regardless of the level of welfare. In fact, he has been making that "choice" at virtually every juncture for at least a hundred years. It is hard to see what else he could have done under the circumstances or what else he can do now.

Admittedly, the situation is not as unrelievedly black as all this. I simplify for argument and emphasis. There are some things (improved educational levels, awakened popular aspiration, new seeds) to be entered on the other side of the ledger. But it is hardly cheery. There is the close connection between the labor-absorbing technology and the intricate village social system. There is the thorough interlocking of the processes of land parcelization, multiple cropping, and share tenancy which makes each of them that much more difficult to reverse. There is the ever-increasing emphasis on subsistence crops and the consequent decline of animal husbandry and mixed farming. Wherever you turn, the arteries are hardened.

The Moroccan situation presents on the surface a quite different picture, but not, when closely examined, a very much brighter one. Though the population is growing with alarming rapidity, its sheer bulk is not yet the towering problem it is in Indonesia. Rather than a highly labor-intensive, but highly productive, exploitation pattern, there is a split between large-scale (often *very* large-scale—

2,500 acres and more) modern farmers and very small-scale four- and five-acre traditional dirt farmers. The first are highly mechanized and, for the most part, quite productive. The second not only are not mechanized, but the level of their traditional technology is, unlike that of Java, very low. Since they are working marginal lands in what is at best (again in contrast to Java) an extremely difficult ecological setting, they are signally unproductive. A statistical epitome, even if it is only approximate, communicates the situation with sufficient brutality: about one-half of 1 percent of the rural population—some 5,000 large farmers—cultivates (1965) about 7 percent of the country's land, contributes about 15 percent of its total agricultural product, and accounts for about 60 percent of its agricultural (30 percent of total) export income.

The image is thus classic and clear. And so is the dilemma it presents. On the one hand, a continuation of large-scale, well-to-do farmers alongside impoverished, small-scale ones is, over and above its social injustice, not one that is likely to endure very long in the postcolonial world, and indeed has now already begun to be altered. On the other, a disappearance of such farmers and their replacement by small peasants threatens, at least initially and perhaps for a very long time, a fall in agricultural output and foreign exchange earnings which a country approaching a demographic crisis at full gallop and plagued by the usual balance-of-payments problems cannot very well regard with equanimity.

As in a situation like the Indonesian, the first response is to think of industrialization, so in a situation of this sort it is to think of land reform. But though land reform can remove the large farmers, it cannot in itself make good modern farmers out of poor traditional ones. In fact, as it tends, given popular pressures, to involve extensive parcelization and consequent decapitalization of the large farms, it amounts to a step in the Indonesian direction of choosing higher levels of rural employment over economic rationalization. This sort of "choice" is, for all its welfare attractions, a most dubious one, given a physical setting where advanced techniques are necessary not just to prevent the decline of output but to avoid a progressive deterioration of the environment to levels for all intents and purposes irreversible.

But so, equally, is its reverse dubious: the maintenance of an enclave of prosperous farmers (or as is now increasingly the case, highly mechanized, elite-run state farms) in the midst of an expanding mass of improverished rural proletarians. In Indonesia, the Marxists have been somewhat hard put to locate their familiar class enemies so as to pin the blame for peasant poverty on them; kulaks are in short supply. But in Morocco, their arguments have more than a surface plausibility. The Moroccan situation is revolutionary enough. The only problem is that it is difficult to see how the revolution could lead to anything but declining levels of living and a wholesale mortgaging of future possibilities to some quite short-run, and quite marginal, gains for a small percentage of the present rural population. The calculation is, admittedly, extremely rough, but if, as has been estimated, 60 percent of the rural population owns no land and the large farmers own about two million acres, then redistributing their lands in, say, ten-acre parcels would reduce the propertyless population by about 3 percent—the annual rate of demographic increase.

Again, the situtation is actually neither so thoroughly bleak nor so simple. A more balanced discussion would have to mention the serious efforts being made to raise the technological level of peasant agriculture, the relatively high degree of realism of Moroccan governmental policies, and so forth. But my point here is merely that, in Morocco as in Indonesia, the task of aligning the need for maintaining and increasing agricultural production and the need for maintaining and increasing agricultural employment is an extraordinarily difficult one. The twin aims of genuine agrarian reform—technological progress and improved social welfare—pull very strongly against one another; and the more deeply one goes into the problem, the more apparent this unpleasant fact becomes.

But my intent here is not to preach despair, a despair I do not in fact feel, but to suggest something of what the moral situation embodied in the sort of work I do is like. The imbalance between an ability to find out what the trouble is, or at least something of what the trouble is, and an ability to find out what might be done to alleviate it is not confined, in new state research, to the area of agrarian reform; it is pervasive. In education, one comes up against the clash between the need to maintain "standards" and the need to expand opportunities; in politics, against the clash between the need for rational leadership and effective organization and the need to involve the masses in the governmental process and to protect individual liberty; in religion, against the clash between the need to prevent spiritual exhaustion and the need to avoid the petrification of obsolete attitudes. And so on. Like the problem of aligning production and employment, these dilemmas are hardly unique to the new states. But they are, in general, graver, more pressing, and less tractable there. To continue the medical image, the sort of moral atmosphere in which someone occupationally committed to thinking about the new states finds himself often seems to me not entirely incomparable to that of the cancer surgeon who spends most of his effort delicately exposing severe pathologies he is not equipped to do anything about.

∞

All this is, however, on a rather impersonal, merely professional level; and one meets it, more or less well, by conjuring up the usual vocational stoicism. However ineffective a scientific approach to social problems may be, it is more effective than the available alternatives: cultivating one's garden, thrashing about wildly in the dark, or lighting candles to the Madonna. But there is another moral peculiarity of fieldwork experience in the new states which is rather more difficult to neutralize because, so much more personal, it strikes rather closer to home. It is difficult to formulate it very well for someone who has not experienced it, or even, for that matter, for oneself. I shall try to communicate it in terms of a notion of a special sort of irony—"anthropological irony."

Irony rests, of course, on a perception of the way in which reality derides merely human views of it, reduces grand attitudes and large hopes to self-mockery. The common forms of it are familiar enough. In dramatic irony, deflation results from the contrast between what the character perceives the situation to be and what the audience knows it to be; in historical irony, from the inconsistency between the intentions of sovereign personages and the natural outcomes of actions proceeding from those intentions. Literary irony rests on a momentary conspiracy of author and reader against the stupidities and self-deceptions of the everyday world; Socratic, or pedagogical, irony rests on intellectual dissembling in order to parody intellectual pretension.

But the sort of irony which appears in anthropological fieldwork, though no less effective in puncturing illusion, is not quite like any of these. It is not dramatic, because it is double-edged: the actor sees through the audience as clearly as the audience through the actor. It is not historical, because it is acausal: it is not that one's actions produce, through the internal logic of events, results the reverse of what was intended by them (though this sometimes happens too), but that one's predictions of what other people will do, one's social expectations, are constantly surprised by what, independently of one's own behavior, they actually do. It is not literary, because not only are the parties not in league, but they are in different moral universes. And it is not Socratic, because it is not intellectual pretension which is parodied, but the mere communication of thought—and not by intellectual dissembling, but by an all-too-earnest, almost grim, effort at understanding.

In fieldwork, the manifestation of serious misapprehensions as to what the situation is almost always begins on the informants' side of the encounter, though, unfortunately for the investigator's self-esteem, it doesn't end there. The first indications, having to do with blunt demands for material help and personal services, though always tricky to handle, are fairly easily adjusted to. They never disappear, and they never cease to tempt the anthropologist into the easy (and useless) trinkets-and-beads way out of establishing relationships with the natives or of quieting guilt over being a prince among paupers. But they soon become routine, and after awhile one even develops a certain resignation toward the idea of being viewed, even by one's most reliable friends, as much as a source of income as a person. One of the psychological fringe benefits of anthropological research—at least I think it's a benefit—is that it teaches you how it feels to be thought of as a fool and used as an object, and how to endure it.

Much more difficult to come to terms with, however, is another very closely related sort of collision between the way I typically see things and the way most of my informants do; more difficult, because it concerns not just the immediate content of the relationship between us but the broader meaning of that content, its symbolic overtones. For all but completely traditional informants (and one finds very few of those anymore), I represent an exemplification, a walking display case, of the sort of life-chances they themselves will soon have, or if not themselves, then surely their children. As my earlier remarks about problems and solutions indicate, I am rather less certain about this than they are, and the result, from the point of view of my own reactions, is what I think of as "the touching faith problem." It is not altogether comfortable to live among people who feel themselves suddenly heir to vast possibilities they surely have every right to possess but will in all likelihood not get.

Nor does the fact that you seem in their eyes to have already been gifted with such a heritage (as, in fact, though not to the degree they usually imagine, you actually have) ease the situation any. You are placed, willy-nilly, in a moral posture somewhat comparable to that of the bourgeois informing the poor to be patient, Rome wasn't built in a day. One does not actually proffer this sort of homily; at least not more than once. But the posture is inherent in the situation, irrespective of what one does, thinks, feels, or wishes, by virtue of the fact that the anthropologist is a member, however marginal, of the world's more privileged classes; and yet, unless he (she) is either incredibly naïve or wildly self-deceiving (or, as sometimes happens, both), he can hardly bring himself to believe that the informant, or the informant's children, are on the immediate verge of joining him as members of this transcultural elite. It is this radical asymmetry in view of what the informant's (and beyond him, his country's) life-chances really are, especially when it is combined with an agreement on what they should be, which colors the fieldwork situation with that very special moral tone I think of as ironic.

It is ironic in the first place because the social institutions of which the anthropologist is supposedly such an exemplary product, and which he (she) consequently values rather highly, do not seem to be the royal roads to well-being for his informants that they were for him: he is a display case for goods which are, despite their surface resemblances to local products, not actually available on domestic markets. This is especially noticeable with respect to education where the touching faith problem appears in its most acute form. The notion that schools are magic wands which will in themselves transform the life-chances of a Moroccan or Indonesian child into those of an American, a French, or a Dutch child is widespread. For a small minority of the already well-positioned it can and does. But for the great majority it can but change completely uneducated children into slightly educated ones. This is, in itself, no mean achievement. The rapid spread of popular education is one of the more encouraging phenomena on the generally unencouraging new state scene, and if it demands illusions to sustain it then we shall have to have the illusions. But for people with grander ideas, ideas stimulated by the manic optimism of radical nationalism, this sort of marginal advance is very much not what they have in mind. Similar confusions of hopes for possibilities center around civil service employment, ownership of machines, and residence in large cities; and with respect to the country as a whole, around economic planning, popular suffrage, and third-force diplomacy. These institutions and instrumentalities have their place in any genuine attempt at social reconstruction; indeed, such reconstruction is, in all likelihood, impossible without them. But they are not the miracle workers they are reputed to be. The so-called revolution of rising expectations shows a fair promise of culminating in a revolution of rising disappointments, a fact which the anthropologist, who will be after all going home to suburbia in a year or so, can permit himself to see rather more clearly than his all-too-engagé informants. They, at best, can allow themselves, uneasily and half-consciously, only to suspect it.

Such a sense that one sees the relationship between oneself and one's informants with an unclouded eye would be more comforting, however, were it not for another twist to the whole situation which puts this supposed fact in rather serious doubt. For, if the anthropologist is indeed largely irrelevant to the informants' fates and governed by interests which, save in the most glancing of ways, do not touch theirs, on what grounds has one the right to expect them to accept and help one? One is placed, in this sort of work, among necessitous people hoping for radical improvements in their conditions of life that do not seem exactly imminent; moreover, one is a type benefactor of just the sort of improvements they are looking for, also obliged to ask them for charity—and what is almost worse, having them give it. This ought to be a humbling, thus elevating, experience; but most often it is simply a disorienting one. All the familiar rationalizations having to do with science, progress, philanthropy, enlightenment, and selfless purity of dedication ring false, and one is left, ethically disarmed, to grapple with a human relationship which must be justified over and over again in the most immediate of terms. Morally, one is back on a barter level; one's currency is unnegotiable, one's credits have all dissolved. The only thing one really has to give in order to avoid mendicancy (or—not to neglect the trinkets-and-beads approach—bribery) is oneself. This is an alarming thought; and the initial response to it is the appearance of a passionate wish to become personally valuable to one's informants—i.e., a friend—in order to maintain self-respect. The notion that one has been marvelously successful in doing this is the investigator's side of the touching faith coin: one believes in cross-cultural communion (one calls it "rapport") as one's subjects believe in tomorrow. It is no wonder that so many anthropologists leave the field seeing tears in the eyes of their informants that, I feel quite sure, are not really there.

I do not wish to be misunderstood here. No more than I feel that significant social progress in the new states is impossible do I feel that genuine human contact across cultural barriers is impossible. Had I not seen a certain amount of the first and experienced, now and then, a measure of the second, my work would have been insupportable. What I am pointing to, in either case, is an enormous pressure on both the investigator and the subjects to regard these goals as near when they are in fact far, assured when they are merely wished for, and achieved when they are at best approximated. This pressure springs from the inherent moral asymmetry of the fieldwork situation. It is therefore not wholly avoidable but is part of the ethically ambiguous character of that situation as such. In a way which is in no sense adventitious, the relationship between an anthropologist and an informant rests on a set of partial fictions half seen-through.

So long as they remain only partial fictions (thus partial truths) and but half seen-through (thus half-obscured), the relationship progresses well enough. The anthropologist is sustained by the scientific value of the data being gathered, and perhaps by a certain relief in merely discovering that the task is not altogether Sisyphean after all. As for the informant, his or her interest is kept alive by a whole series of secondary gains: a sense of being an essential collaborator in an important, if but dimly understood, enterprise; a pride in one's own culture and in the expertness of one's knowledge of it; a chance to express private ideas and opinions (and retail gossip) to a neutral outsider; as well, again, as a certain amount of direct or indirect material benefit of one sort or another. And so on—the rewarding elements are different for almost each informant. But if the implicit agreement to regard one another, in the face of some very serious indications to the contrary, as members of the same cultural universe breaks down, none of these more matter-of-fact incentives can keep the relationship going very long. It either gradually expires in an atmosphere of futility, boredom, and generalized disappointment or, much less often, collapses suddenly into a mutual sense of having been deceived, used, and rejected. When this happens the anthropologist sees a loss of rapport: one has been jilted. The informant sees a revelation of bad faith: one has been humiliated. And they are shut up once more in their separate, internally coherent, uncommunicating worlds.

Let me give an example. When I was in Java, one of my better informants was a young clerk in his early thirties, who, though he had been born in the small country town I was studying and had lived there all his life, had larger aspirations; he wanted to be a writer. In fact, he was one. While I was there he wrote and produced a play, based on his sister's recent divorce, in which, partly for verisimilitude but rather more for revenge (her unfortunate ex-husband still lived in the town), the sister played herself. The plot amounted to a sort of Javanese *Doll's House*: an educated girl (she had been to junior high school) wishes to escape the bounds of the traditional wife role; her husband refuses to permit her to do so, so she walks out on him—except that, art being an improvement on life, in the play she shoots him instead. Aside from this curious work, he wrote a large number of other (unpublished) stories and (unproduced) plays, most of which took their general outlines from traditional tales in which he was, for all his surface modernism, very much interested and very knowledgeable. His work with me had mainly to do with such materials—myths, legends, spells, etc.—and he was a good informant: industrious, intelligent, accurate, enthusiastic. We got along quite well until an odd incident having to do with my typewriter occurred, after which he refused even to greet me in the street, much less to work with me.

He had been borrowing the typewriter now and again to type his works up in hunt-and-peck fashion, preparing a sort of manuscript edition of them. As time went on, he borrowed it more and more, until he seemed to have it most of the time, which, as I had no other, was inconvenient. I decided, therefore, to try to bring the borrowing down to more moderate levels. One day, when he dispatched, as usual, his little brother to borrow the machine for an afternoon, I sent back a note saying that I was sorry but I needed it for some work of my own. This was the first time I had issued such a refusal. Within ten minutes, the younger brother was back carrying a note which, not mentioning the typewriter or my refusal at all, merely said that my informant, owing to a pressing engagement, would be unable (also for the first time) to make the scheduled appointment we had for the following day. He would try, however, to make the next one, three days hence if he could. I interpreted this, quite correctly, as a tit for my tat, and, fearful as ever of a loss of rapport, I made what was a stupid and, so far as our relationship was concerned, fatal error. Instead of just letting the incident pass, I answered the note, saying I was sorry he would be unable to make our appointment, I hoped I had not affronted him in any way, and I could spare the typewriter after all as I was going to go out into the paddies instead. Three hours later, back came the younger brother, the typewriter, and a very long (typewritten) note, the burden of which was that: (1) of course he had not been affronted, after all it was *my* typewriter; (2) he was very sorry, but it now turned out that not only would he be unable to make our next appointment, but the press of his literary work unfortunately made it impossible for him to find the time to come any more at all. I made some feeble efforts to repair the situation—rendered even more feeble by my sense of having behaved like an ass—but it was too late. He went back to copying his works in longhand and I found a new informant—a hospital worker, who, practicing a certain amount of amateur medicine among his neighbors, was more interested in my drug supply than my typewriter—to work with on mythic materials.

A mere quibble, ridiculously overblown? A comical misunderstanding aggravated by abnormally thin skins and stupid errors of tact? Certainly. But why did such a molehill become such a mountain? Why did we have such difficulty with so simple a matter as borrowing and lending a typewriter? Because, of course, it was not a typewriter—or, at least, not only a typewriter—which was being borrowed and lent, but a complex of claims and concessions only dimly recognized. Borrowing it, my informant was, tacitly, asserting his demand to be taken seriously as an intellectual, a "writer"—i.e., a peer; lending it, I was, tacitly, granting that demand. Lending it, I was, tacitly, interpreting our relationship as one of personal friendship—i.e., admitting myself to the inner circle of his moral community; borrowing it, he was, still tacitly, accepting that interpretation. We both knew, I am sure, that these agreements could be only partial: we were not really colleagues and not really comrades. But while our relationship persisted, they were at least partial, were to some degree real, which given the facts of the situation—that he was as far from being an inglorious Milton as I was from being a Javanese—was something of an accomplishment. But when I refused the use of the symbol of our unspoken pact to regard, by a kind of mutual suspension of disbelief, our two cultural worlds as one, his suspicion, always lingering, that I did not take his "work" as seriously as I took my own, broke into consciousness. When he in turn refused to come to our next appointment, my fear, also always there, that he saw me as but an inconsequent stranger to whom he was attached by only the most opportunistic of considerations, broke into mine. Its true anatomy apparently exposed, the relationship collapsed in bitterness and disappointment.

Such an end to anthropologist-informant relationships is hardly typical: usually the sense of being members, however temporarily, insecurely, and incompletely, of a single moral community can be maintained even in the face of the wider social realities which press in at almost every moment to deny it. It is this fiction—fiction, not falsehood—that lies at the heart of successful anthropological field research; and, because it is never completely convincing for any of the participants, it renders such research, considered as a form of conduct, continuously ironic. To recognize the moral tension, the ethical ambiguity, implicit in the encounter of anthropologist and informant, and to still be able to dissipate it through one's actions and one's attitudes, is what encounter demands of both parties if it is to be authentic, if it is to actually happen. And to discover that is to discover also something very complicated and not altogether clear about the nature of sincerity and insincerity, genuineness and hypocrisy, honesty and self-deception. Fieldwork is an educational experience all around. What is difficult is to decide what has been learned.

∞

There are, of course, many more ethical dimensions of fieldwork than the two I have been able to discuss here: the imbalance between the ability to uncover problems and the power to solve them, and the inherent moral tension between investigator and subject. Nor, as the fact that I have been able to discuss them perhaps indicated, are these two necessarily the most profound. But even the mere revelation that they, and others like them, exist may contribute toward dispelling a few popular illusions about what, as conduct, social science is. In particular, the widespread notion that social scientific research consists of an attempt to discover hidden wires with which to manipulate cardboard persons should have some doubt cast upon it. It is not just that the wires do not exist and the persons are not cardboard; it is that the whole enterprise is directed not toward the impossible task of controlling history but toward the only quixotic one of widening the role of reason in it.

It is the failure to see this—not only on the part of those who are hostile to social science on principle (what principle is a deeper question), but on the part of many of its most ardent apologists—which has rendered much of the discussion over its moral status pointless. The fact is that social science is neither a sinister attack upon our culture, nor the means of its final deliverance; it is merely part of that culture. From the point of view of moral philosophy, the central question to ask about social science is not the one which would-be Platonic Guardians from either side are forever asking: Will it sink us or save us? It will, almost certainly, do neither. The central question to ask is, What does it tell us about the values by which we—all of us—in fact live? The need is to put social science not in the dock, which is where our culture belongs, but on the witness stand.

Whether, when this is done, it will turn out to be a witness for the prosecution or the defense is, I suppose, an open question. But it is clear that its testimony will, like that of any witness, be more pertinent to certain matters than to others. In particular, such an inquiry should clarify what sort of social behavior scientific thinking about human affairs is, and should do so in a way in which philosophical analyses of ethical terms, the logic of personal decision or the sources of moral authority—in themselves, all useful endeavors—cannot. Even my glancing examination of a few fragments of my own experience offers some leads in this direction—in exposing what "detachment," "relativism," "scientific method," and the like mean not as shibboleths and slogans but as concrete acts performed by particular persons in specific social contests. Discussing them as such, as aspects of a métier, will not put an end to dispute, but it may help to make it profitable.

The nature of scientific detachment—disinterestedness, if one can still use that term—is a good example. The popular stereotype of the white-coated laboratory technician, as antiseptic emotionally as sartorially, is but the expression of a general notion that such detachment consists in a kind of neurotic affectlessness put to use. Like a eunuch in a harem, a scientist is a functionary with a useful defect; and, like a eunuch, correspondingly dangerous because of an insensibility to subcerebral (often called "human") concerns. I don't know much about what goes on in laboratories; but in anthropological fieldwork, detachment is neither a natural gift nor a manufactured talent. It is a partial achievement laboriously earned and precariously maintained. What little disinterestedness one manages to attain comes not from failing to have emotions or neglecting to perceive them in others, nor yet from sealing oneself into a moral vacuum. It comes from a personal subjection to a vocational ethic.

This is, I realize, not an original discovery. What needs explanation is why so many people are so terribly eager to deny it and to insist instead that, at least while practicing, social scientists are unmoved by moral concern altogether—not disinterested, but uninterested. With respect to outside critics, perhaps academic vested interests will explain the bulk of the cases, and ignorance carefully preserved most of the rest. But when the same protestations are made by many social scientists themselves—"I don't give advice, I just point out the roots of the problem"—it is perhaps necessary to look a little deeper, to the difficulties inherent in sustaining a scientific ethic not just at a writing desk or on a lecture platform, but in the very midst of everyday social situations, to the difficulties of being at one and the same time an involved actor and a detached observer.

The outstanding characteristic of anthropological fieldwork as a form of conduct is that it does not permit any significant separation of the occupational and extra-occupational spheres of one's life. On the contrary, it forces this fusion. One must find one's friends among one's informants and one's informants among one's friends; one must regard ideas, attitudes, and values as so many cultural facts and continue to act in terms of those which define one's own commitments; one must see society as an object and experience it as a subject. Everything anyone says, everything anyone does, even the mere physical setting, has both to form the substance of one's personal existence and to be taken as grist for one's analytical mill. At home, the anthropologist goes comfortably off to the office to ply a trade like everyone else. In the field, the anthropologist has to learn to live and think at the same time.

As I have suggested, this learning process can advance only so far, even under the best of conditions, which anyhow never obtain. The anthropologist inevitably remains more alien than he desires and less cerebral than he imagines. But it does enforce, day in and day out, the effort to advance it, to combine two fundamental orientations toward reality—the engaged and the analytic—into a single attitude. It is this attitude, not moral blankness, which we call detachment or disinterestedness. And whatever small degree of it one manages to attain comes not by adopting an I-am-a-camera ideology or by enfolding oneself in layers of methodological armor, but simply by trying to do, in such an equivocal situation, the scientific work one has come to do. And as the ability to look at persons and events (and at oneself) with an eye at once cold and concerned is one of the surest signs of maturity in either an individual or a people, this sort of research experience has rather deeper, and rather different, moral implications for our culture than those usually proposed.

A professional commitment to view human affairs analytically is not in opposition to a personal commitment to view them in terms of a particular moral perspective. The professional ethic rests on the personal and draws its strength from it; we force ourselves to see out of a conviction that blindness—or illusion—cripples virtue as it cripples people. Detachment comes not from a failure to care, but from a kind of caring resilient enough to withstand an enormous tension between moral reaction and scientific observation, a tension which only grows as moral perception deepens and scientific understanding advances. The flight into scientism, or, on the other side, into subjectivism, is but a sign that the tension cannot any longer be borne, that nerve has failed and a choice has been made to suppress either one's humanity or one's rationality. These are the pathologies of science, not its norm.

In this light, the famous value relativism of anthropology is not the moral Pyrrhonism it has often been accused of being, but an expression of faith that to attempt to see human behavior in terms of the forces which animate it is an essential element in understanding it, and that to judge without understanding constitutes an offense against morality. Values are indeed values, and facts, alas, indeed facts. But to engage in that style of thinking called social scientific is to attempt to transcend the logical gap that separates them by a pattern of conduct, which, enfolding them into a unitary experience, rationally connects them. The call for the application of "the scientific method" to the investigation of human affairs is a call for a direct confrontation of that divorce between sense and sensibility which has been rightly diagnosed to be the malady of our age and to the ending of which John Dewey's lifework, imperfect like any other, was unconditionally dedicated.

III ∞

Anti Anti-Relativism

A scholar can hardly be better employed than in destroying a fear. The one I want to go after is cultural relativism. Not the thing itself, which I think merely there, like Transylvania, but the dread of it, which I think unfounded. It is unfounded because the moral and intellectual consequences that are commonly supposed to flow from relativism—subjectivism, nihilism, incoherence, Machiavellianism, ethical idiocy, esthetic blindness, and so on—do not in fact do so and the promised rewards of escaping its clutches, mostly having to do with pasteurized knowledge, are illusory.

To be more specific, I want not to defend relativism, which is a drained term anyway, yesterday's battle cry, but to attack anti-relativism, which seems to me broadly on the rise and to represent a streamlined version of an antique mistake. Whatever cultural relativism may be or originally have been (and there is not one of its critics in a hundred who has got that right), it serves these days largely as a specter to scare us away from certain ways of thinking and toward others. And, as the ways of thinking away from which we are being driven seem to me to be more cogent than those toward which we are being propelled, and to lie at the heart of the anthropological heritage, I would like to do something about this. Casting out demons is a praxis we should practice as well as study.

My through-the-looking-glass title is intended to suggest such an effort to counter a view rather than to defend the view it claims to be counter to. The analogy I had in mind in choosing it—a logical one, I trust it will be understood, not in any way a substantive one—is what, at the height of the cold war days (you remember them) was called "anti anti-communism." Those of us who strenuously opposed the obsession, as we saw it, with the Red Menace were thus denominated by those who, as they saw it, regarded the Menace as the primary fact of contemporary political life, with the insinuation—wildly incorrect in the vast majority of cases—that, by the law of the double negative, we had some secret affection for the Soviet Union.

Again, I mean to use this analogy in a formal sense; I don't think relativists are like communists, anti-relativists are like anti-communists, and that anyone (well . . . hardly anyone) is behaving like Senator McCarthy. One could construct a similar parallelism using the abortion controversy. Those of us who are opposed to increased legal restrictions on abortion are not, I take it, pro-abortion, in the sense that we think abortion a wonderful thing and hold that the greater the abortion rate the greater the well-being of society; we are "anti anti-abortionists" for quite other reasons I need not rehearse. In this frame, the double negative simply doesn't work in the usual way; and therein lies its rhetorical attractions. It enables one to reject something without thereby committing oneself to what it rejects. And this is precisely what I want to do with anti-relativism.

So lumbering an approach to the matter, explaining and excusing itself as it goes, is necessary because, as the philosopher-anthropologist John Ladd has remarked, "all the common definitions of . . . relativism are framed by opponents of relativism . . . they are absolutist definitions."[1] (Ladd, whose immediate focus is Edward Westermarck's famous book, is speaking of "ethical relativism" in particular, but the point is general: for "cognitive relativism" think of Israel Scheffler's attack on Thomas Kuhn; for "aesthetic relativism," Wayne Booth's on Stanley Fish.)[2] And, as Ladd also says, the result of this is that relativism, or anything that at all looks like relativism under such hostile definitions, is identified with nihilism.[3] To suggest that "hard rock" foundations for cognitive, esthetic, or moral judgments may not, in fact, be available, or anyway that those one is being offered are dubious, is to find oneself accused of disbelieving in the existence of the physical world, thinking pushpin as good as poetry, regarding Hitler as just a fellow with unstandard tastes, or even, as I myself have recently been—God save the mark— "[having] no politics at all."[4] The notion that someone who does not hold your views holds the reciprocal of them, or simply hasn't got any, has, whatever its comforts for those afraid reality is going to go away unless we believe very hard in it, not conduced to much in the way of clarity in the anti-relativist discussion, but merely to far too many people spending far too much time describing at length what it is they do *not* maintain than seems in any way profitable.

All this is of relevance to anthropology because, of course, it is by way of the idea of relativism, grandly ill-defined, that it has most disturbed the general intellectual peace. From our earliest days, even when theory in anthropology—evolutionary, diffusionist, or *elementargedankenisch*—was anything but relativistic, the message that we have been thought to have for the wider world has been that, as they see things differently and do them otherwise in Alaska or the D'Entrecasteaux, our confidence in our own seeings and doings and our resolve to bring others around to sharing them are rather poorly based. This point, too, is commonly ill-understood. It has not been anthropological theory, such as it is, that has made our field seem to be a massive argument against absolutism in thought, morals, and esthetic judgment; it has been anthropological data: customs, crania, living floors, and lexicons. The notion that it was Boas, Benedict, and Melville Herskovits, with a European assist from Westermarck, who infected our field with the relativist virus, and Kroeber, Kluckhohn, and Redfield, with a similar assist from Lévi-Strauss, who have labored to rid us of it, is but another of the myths that bedevil this whole discussion. After all, Montaigne could draw relativistic, or relativistic-looking, conclusions from the fact, as he heard it, that the Caribs didn't wear breeches; he did not have to read *Patterns of Culture*. Even earlier on, Herodotus, contemplating "certain Indians of the race called Callatians," among whom men were said to eat their fathers, came, as one would think he might, to similar views.

The relativist bent, or more accurately the relativist bent anthropology so often induces in those who have much traffic with its materials, is thus in some sense implicit in the field as such; in cultural anthropology perhaps particularly, but in much of archaeology, anthropological linguistics, and physical anthropology as well. One cannot read too long about Nayar matriliny, Aztec sacrifice, the Hopi verb, or the convolutions of the hominid transition and not begin at least to consider the possibility that, to quote Montaigne again, "each man calls barbarism whatever is not his own practice . . . for we have no other criterion of reason than the example and idea of the opinions and customs of the country we live in."[5] That notion, whatever its problems, and however more delicately expressed, is not likely to go entirely away unless anthropology does.

It is to this fact, progressively discovered to be one as our enterprise has advanced and our findings grown more circumstantial, that both relativists and anti-relativists have, according to their sensibilities, reacted. The realization that news from elsewhere about ghost marriage, ritual destruction of property, initiatory fellatio, royal immolation, and nonchalant adolescent sex naturally inclines the mind to an "other beasts other mores" view of things has led to arguments, outraged, desperate, and exultant by turns, designed to persuade us either to resist that inclination in the name of reason, or to embrace it on the same grounds. What looks like a debate about the broader implications of anthropological research is really a debate about how to live with them.

Once this fact is grasped, and "relativism" and "anti-relativism" are seen as general responses to the way in which what Kroeber once called the centrifugal impulse of anthropology—distant places, distant times, distant species . . . distant grammars—affects our sense of things, the whole discussion comes rather better into focus. The supposed conflict between Benedict's and Herskovits's call for tolerance and the untolerant passion with which they called for it turns out not to be the simple contradiction so many amateur logicians have held it to be, but the expression of a perception, caused by thinking a lot about Zunis and Dahomeys, that, the world being so full of a number of things, rushing to judgment is more than a mistake, it's a crime. Similarly, Kroeber's and Kluckhohn's pan-cultural verities—Kroeber's were mostly about messy creatural matters like delirium and menstruation, Kluckhohn's about messy social ones like lying and killing within the in-group—turn out not to be just the arbitrary, personal obsessions they so much look like, but the expression of a much vaster concern, caused by thinking a lot about *anthropōs* in general, that if something isn't anchored everywhere nothing can be anchored anywhere. Theory here—if that is what these earnest advices as to how we must look at things if we are to be accounted decent should be called—is rather more an exchange of warnings than an analytical debate. We are being offered a choice of worries.

What the relativists, so-called, want us to worry about is provincialism—the danger that our perceptions will be dulled, our intellects constricted, and our sympathies narrowed by the overlearned and overvalued acceptances of our own society. What the anti-relativists, self-declared, want us to worry about, and worry about and worry about, as though our very souls depended upon it, is a kind of spiritual entropy, a heat death of the mind, in which everything is as significant, thus as insignificant, as everything else: anything goes, to each his own, you pays your money and you takes your choice, I know what I like, not in the south, *tout comprendre, c'est tout pardonner.*

As I have already suggested, I myself find provincialism altogether the more real concern so far as what actually goes on in the world. (Though even there, the thing can be overdone: "You might as well fall flat on your face," one of Thurber's marvelous "morals" goes, "as lean too far over backward.") The image of vast numbers of anthropology readers running around in so cosmopolitan a frame of mind as to have no views as to what is and isn't true, or good, or beautiful, seems to me largely a fantasy. There may be some genuine nihilists out there, along Rodeo Drive or around Times Square, but I doubt very many have become such as a result of an excessive sensitivity to the claims of other cultures; and at least most of the people I meet, read, and read about, and indeed I myself, are all-too-committed to something or other, usually parochial. "'Tis the eye of childhood that fears a painted devil": anti-relativism has largely concocted the anxiety it lives from.

∞

But surely I exaggerate? Surely anti-relativists, secure in the knowledge that rattling gourds cannot cause thunder and that eating people is wrong, cannot be so excitable? Listen, then, to William Gass, novelist, philosopher, *précieux*, and pop-eyed observer of anthropologists' ways:

Anthropologists or not, we all used to call them "natives"—those little, distant, jungle and island people—and we came to recognize the unscientific snobbery in that. Even our more respectable journals could show them naked without offense, because their pendulous or pointed breasts were as inhuman to us as the udder of a cow. Shortly we came to our senses and had them dress. We grew to distrust our own point of view, our local certainties, and embraced relativism, although it is one of the scabbier whores; and we went on to endorse a nice equality among cultures, each of which was carrying out its task of coalescing, conversing, and structuring some society. A large sense of superiority was one of the white man's burdens, and that weight, released, was replaced by an equally heavy sense of guilt.

No more than we might expect a surgeon to say "Dead and good riddance" would an anthropologist exclaim, stepping from the culture just surveyed as one might shed a set of working clothes, "What a lousy way to live!" Because, even if the natives were impoverished, covered with dust and sores; even if they had been trodden on by stronger feet till they were flat as a path; even if they were rapidly dying off; still, the observer could remark how frequently they smiled, or how infrequently their children fought, or how serene they were. We can envy the Zuni their peaceful ways and the Navaho their "happy heart."

It was amazing how mollified we were to find that there was some functional point to food taboos, infibulation, or clitoridectomy; and if we still felt morally squeamish about human sacrifice or headhunting, it is clear we were still squeezed into a narrow modern European point of view, and had no sympathy, and didn't—couldn't—understand. Yet when we encountered certain adolescents among indolent summery seaside tribes who were allowed to screw without taboo, we wondered whether this enabled them to avoid the stresses of our own youth, and we secretly hoped it hadn't.

Some anthropologists have untied the moral point of view, so sacred to Eliot and Arnold and Emerson, from every mooring (science and art also float away on the stream of Becoming), calling any belief in objective knowledge "fundamentalism," as if it were the same as benighted Biblical literalism; and arguing for the total mutability of man and the complete sociology of what under such circumstances could no longer be considered knowledge but only *doxa*, or "opinion."[6]

This overheated vision of "the anthropological point of view," rising out of the mists of caricatured arguments ill-grasped to start with (it is one of Gass's ideas that Mary Douglas is some sort of skeptic, and Benedict's satire, cannier than his, has escaped him altogether), leaves us with a fair lot to answer for. But even from within the profession, the charges, though less originally expressed, as befits a proper science, are hardly less grave. Relativism ("[T]he position that all assessments are assessments relative to some standard or other, and standards derive from cultures"), I. C. Jarvie remarks,

> has these objectionable consequences: namely, that by limiting critical assessment of human works it disarms us, dehumanises us, leaves us unable to enter into communicative interaction; that is to say, unable to criticize cross-culturally, cross-subculturally; ultimately, relativism leaves no room for criticism at all. . . . [B]ehind relativism nihilism looms.[7]

More in front, scarecrow and leper's bell, it sounds like, than behind: certainly none of us, clothed and in our right minds, will rush to embrace a view that so dehumanizes us as to render us incapable of communicating with anybody. The heights to which this beware of the scabby whore who will cut off your critical powers sort of thing can aspire is indicated, to give one last example, by Paul Johnson's ferocious book on the history of the world since 1917, *Modern Times*, which, opening with a chapter called "A Relativistic World" (Hugh Thomas's review of the book in the *TLS* was more aptly entitled "The Inferno of Relativism"), accounts for the whole modern disaster—Lenin and Hitler, Amin, Bokassa, Sukarno,

Mao, Nasser, and Hammarskjöld, Structuralism, the New Deal, the Holocaust, both world wars, 1968, inflation, Shinto militarism, OPEC, and the independence of India—as outcomes of something called "the relativist heresy."[8] "A great trio of German imaginative scholars," Nietzsche, Marx, and (with a powerful assist—our contribution—from Frazer) Freud, destroyed the nineteenth century morally as Einstein, banishing absolute motion, destroyed it cognitively, and Joyce, banishing absolute narrative, destroyed it esthetically:

> Marx described a world in which the central dynamic was economic interest. To Freud the principal thrust was sexual. . . . Nietzsche, the third of the trio, was also an atheist . . . [and he] saw [the death of God] as . . . an historical event, which would have dramatic consequences. . . . Among the advanced races, the decline and ultimately the collapse of the religious impulse would leave a huge vacuum. The history of modern times is in great part the history of how that vacuum [has] been filled. Nietzsche rightly perceived that the most likely candidate would be what he called "The Will to Power." . . . In place of religious belief, there would be secular ideology. Those who had once filled the ranks of the totalitarian clergy would become totalitarian politicians. . . . The end of the old order, with an unguided world adrift in a relativistic universe, was a summons to such gangster statesmen to emerge. They were not slow to make their appearance.[9]

After this there is perhaps nothing much else to say, except perhaps what George Stocking says, summarizing others—"cultural relativism, which had buttressed the attack against racialism, [can] be perceived as a sort of neo-racialism justifying the backward techno-economic status of once colonized peoples."[10] Or what Lionel Tiger says, summarizing himself: "the feminist argument [for "the social non-necessity . . . of the laws instituted by patriarchy"] reflects the cultural relativism that has long characterized those social sciences which rejected locating human behavior in biological processes."[11] Mindless tolerance, mindless intolerance; ideological promiscuity, ideological monomania; egalitarian hypocrisy, egalitarian simplisticism—all flow from the same infirmity. Like Welfare, The Media, The Bourgeoisie, or The Ruling Circles, Cultural Relativism causes everything bad.

Anthropologists, plying their trade and in any way reflective about it, could, for all their own sort of provincialism, hardly remain unaffected by the hum of philosophical disquiet rising everywhere around them. (I have not even mentioned the fierce debates brought on by the revival of political and moral theory, the appearance of deconstructionist literary criticism, the spread of nonfoundationalist moods in metaphysics and epistemology, and the rejection of whiggery and method-ism in the history of science.) The fear that our emphasis on difference, diversity, oddity, discontinuity, incommensurability, uniqueness, and so on—what William Empson called "the gigan-/-tic anthropological circus riotiously/[Holding] open all its booths"—might end leaving us with little more to say than that elsewhere things are otherwise and culture is as culture does has grown more and more intense.[12] So intense, in fact, that it has led us off in some all-too-familiar directions in an attempt, ill-conceived, so I think, to still it.

One could ground this last proposition in a fair number of places in contemporary anthropological thought and research—from Harrisonian "Everything That Rises Must Converge" materialism to Popperian "Great Divide" evolutionism. ("We Have Science . . . or Literacy, or Intertheoretic Competition, or the Cartesian Conception of Knowledge . . . but They Have Not.")[13] But I want to concentrate here on two of central importance, or anyway popularity, right now: the attempt to reinstate a context-independent concept of "Human Nature" as a bulwark against relativism, and the attempt to reinstate, similarly, a similar one of that other old friend, "The Human Mind."

Again, it is necessary to be clear so as not to be accused, under the "if you don't believe in my God you must believe in my Devil" assumption I mentioned earlier, of arguing for absurd positions—radical, culture-is-all historicism, or primitive, the-brain-is-a-blackboard empiricism—which no one of any seriousness holds, and quite possibly, a momentary enthusiasm here and there aside, ever has held. The issue is not whether human beings are biological organisms with intrinsic characteristics. Men can't fly and pigeons can't talk. Nor is it whether they show commonalities in mental functioning wherever we find them. Papuans envy, Aborigines dream. The issue is, what are we to make of these undisputed facts as we go about explicating rituals, analyzing ecosystems, interpreting fossil sequences, or comparing languages.

∞

These two moves toward restoring culture-free conceptions of what we amount to as basic, sticker-price *homo* and essential, no additives *sapiens* take a number of quite disparate forms, not in much agreement beyond their general tenor, naturalist in the one case, rationalist in the other. On the naturalist side there is, of course, sociobiology, evolutionary psychology, and other hyper-adaptationist orientations. But there are also perspectives growing out of psychoanalysis, ecology, neurology, display-and-imprint ethology, some kinds of developmental theory, and some kinds of Marxism. On the rationalist side there is, of course, the new intellectualism one associates with structuralism and other hyper-logicist orientations. But there are also perspectives growing out of generative linguistics, experimental psychology, artificial intelligence research, ploy and counterploy microsociology, some kinds of developmental theory, and some kinds of Marxism. Attempts to banish the specter of relativism whether by sliding down The Great Chain of Being or edging up it—the dog beneath the skin, a mind for all cultures—do not comprise a single enterprise, massive and coordinate, but a loose and immiscible crowd of them, each pressing its own cause and in its own direction. The sin may be one, but the salvations are many.

It is for this reason, too, that an attack, such as mine, upon the efforts to draw context-independent concepts of "Human Nature" or "The Human Mind" from biological, psychological, linguistic, or for that matter cultural (HRAF and all that) inquiries should not be mistaken for an attack upon those inquiries as research programs. Whether or not sociobiology is, as I think, a degenerative research program destined to expire in its own confusions, and neuroscience a progressive one (to use Imre Lakatos's useful epithets) on the verge of extraordinary achievements, anthropologists will be well-advised to attend to, with various shades of mixed, maybe, maybe not, verdicts for structuralism, generative grammar, ethology, AI, psychoanalysis, ecology, microsociology, Marxism, or developmental psychology in between, is quite beside the point.[14] It is not, or anyway not here, the validity of the sciences, real or would-be, that is at issue. What concerns me, and should concern us all, are the axes that, with an increasing determination bordering on the evangelical, are being busily ground with their assistance.

As a way into all this on the naturalist side we can look for a moment at a general discussion widely accepted—though, as it consists largely of pronouncements, it is difficult to understand why—as a balanced and moderate statement of the position: Mary Midgeley's *Beast and Man, The Roots of Human Nature*. In the Pilgrim's Progress, "once I was blind but now I see" tonalities that have become characteristic of such discourses in recent years, Midgeley writes:

> I first entered this jungle myself some time ago, by slipping out over the wall of the tiny arid garden cultivated at that time under the name of British Moral Philosophy. I did so in an attempt to think about human nature and the problem of evil. The evils in the world, I thought are real. That they are so is neither a fancy imposed on us by our own culture, nor one created by our will and imposed on the world. Such suggestions are bad faith. What we abominate is not optional. Culture certainly varies the details, but then we can criticize our culture. What standard [note the singular] do we use for this? What is the underlying structure of human nature which culture is designed to complete and express? In this tangle of questions I found some clearings being worked by Freudian and Jungian psychologists, on principles that seemed to offer hope but were not quite clear to me. Other areas were being mapped by anthropologists, who seemed to have some interest in my problem, but who were inclined . . . to say that what human beings had in common was not in the end very important: that the key to all the mysteries [lay] in culture. This seemed to me shallow. . . . I [finally] came upon another clearing, this time an

expansion of the borders of traditional zoology, made by people [Lorenz, Tinbergen, Eibes-Eibesfeldt, Desmond Morris] studying the natures of other species. They had done much work on the question of what such a *nature* was—recent work in the tradition of Darwin, and indeed of Aristotle, bearing directly on problems in which Aristotle was already interested, but which have become peculiarly pressing today.[15]

The assumptions with which this declaration of conscience is riddled—that fancies imposed on us by cultural judgments (that the poor are worthless? that Blacks are subhuman? that women are irrational?) are inadequately substantial to ground real evil; that culture is icing, biology, cake; that we have no choice as to what we shall hate (hippies? bosses? eggheads? . . . relativists?); that difference is shallow, likeness, deep; that Lorenz is a straightforward fellow and Freud a mysterious one—may perhaps be left to perish of their own weight. One garden has been but exchanged for another. The jungle remains several walls away.

More important is what sort of garden this "Darwin meets Aristotle" one is. What sort of abominations are going to become unoptional? What sort of facts unnatural?

Well, mutual admiration societies, sadism, ingratitude, monotony, and the shunning of cripples, among other things—at least when they are carried to excess:

> Grasping this point ["that what is *natural* is never just a condition or activity . . . but a certain *level* of that condition or activity proportionate to the rest of one's life"] makes it possible to cure a difficulty about such concepts as *natural* which has made many people think them unusable. Besides their strong sense, which recommends something, they have a weak sense, which does not. In the weak sense, sadism is natural. This just means that it occurs; we should recognize it. . . . But in a strong and perfectly good sense, we may call sadistic behavior *unnatural*—meaning that a policy based on this natural impulse, and extended through somebody's life into organized activity, is, as [Bishop] Butler said, "contrary to the whole constitution of human nature." . . . That consenting adults

should bite each other in bed is in all senses natural; that schoolteachers should bully children for their sexual gratification is not. There is something wrong with this activity beyond the actual injury that it inflicts. . . . Examples of this wrong thing—of unnaturalness—can be found which do not involve other people as victims; for instance, extreme narcissism, suicide, obsessiveness, incest, and exclusive mutual admiration societies. "It is an unnatural life" we say, meaning that its center has been misplaced. Further examples, which do involve victimizing others, are redirected aggression, the shunning of cripples, ingratitude, vindictiveness, parricide. All these things are *natural* in that there are well-known impulses toward them which are parts of human nature. . . . But redirected aggression and so on can properly be called *unnatural* when we think of nature in the fuller sense, not just as an assembly of parts, but as an organized whole. They are parts which will ruin the shape of that whole if they are allowed in any sense to take it over.[16]

Aside from the fact that it legitimates one of the more popular sophisms of intellectual debate nowadays, asserting the strong form of an argument and defending the weak one (sadism is natural as long as you don't bite too deep), this little game of concept juggling (natural may be unnatural when we think of nature "in the fuller sense") displays the basic thesis of all such Human Nature arguments: virtue (cognitive, esthetic, and moral alike) is to vice as fitness is to disorder, normality to abnormality, well-being to sickness. The task for man, as for his lungs or his thyroid, is to function properly. Shunning cripples can be dangerous to your health.

Or as Stephen Salkever, a political scientist and follower of Midgeley's, puts it:

Perhaps the best developed model or analogue for an adequate functionalist social science is that provided by medicine. For the physician, physical features of an individual organism become intelligible in the light of a basic conception of the problems confronting this self-directed physical system and in the light of a general sense of healthy or well-functioning state of the organism relative to those problems. To understand a patient is to understand him or her as being more or less healthy relative to some stable and objective standard of physical well-being, the kind of standard the Greeks called *aretè*. This word is now ordinarily translated "virtue," but in the political philosophy of Plato and Aristotle it refers simply to the characteristic or definitive excellence of the subject of any functional analysis.[17]

Again, one can look almost anywhere within anthropology these days and find an example of the revival of this "it all comes down to" (genes, species being, cerebral architecture, psycho-sexual constitution . . .) cast of mind. Shake almost any tree and a selfish altruist or a biogenetic structuralist is likely to fall out.

But it is better, I think, or at least less disingenuous, to have for an instance neither a sitting duck nor a self-destructing artifact. And so let me examine, very briefly, the views, most especially the recent views, of one of our most experienced ethnographers and influential theorists, as well as one of our most formidable polemicists: Melford Spiro. Purer cases, less shaded and less circumspect, and thus all the better to appall you with, could be found. But in Spiro we are at least not dealing with some marginal phenomenon—a Morris or an Ardrey—easily dismissed as an enthusiast or a popularizer, but with a major figure at, or very near, the center of the discipline.

Spiro's more important recent forays into "down deep" in the *Homo* anthropology—his rediscovery of the Freudian family romance, first in his own material on the kibbutz and then in Malinowski's on the Trobriands—are well-known and will be, I daresay, as convincing or unconvincing to their readers as psychoanalytic theory of a rather orthodox sort is in general. But my concern is, again, less with that than with the Here Comes Everyman antirelativism he develops on the basis of it. And to get a sense for that, an article of his summarizing his advance from past confusions to present clarities will serve quite well. Called "Culture and Human Nature," it catches a mood and a drift of attitude much more widely spread than its rather beleaguered, no longer avant-garde theoretical perspective.[18]

Spiro's paper is, as I mentioned, again cast in the "when a child I spake as a child but now that I am grown I have put away childish things" genre so prominent in the anti-relativist literature generally. (Indeed, it might better have been titled, as another southern California–based anthropologist—apparently relativism seems a clear and present danger out that way—called the record of his deliverance, "Confessions of a Former Cultural Relativist.")[19]

Spiro begins his apologia with the admission that when he came into anthropology in the early 1940s he was preadapted by a Marxist background and too many courses in British philosophy to a radically environmentalist view of man, one that assumed a *tabula rasa* view of mind, a social determinist view of behavior, and a cultural relativist view of, well . . . culture, and then traces his field trip history as a didactic, parable for our times, narrative of how he came not just to abandon these ideas but to replace them by their opposites. In Ifaluk, he discovered that a people who showed very little social aggression could yet be plagued by hostile feelings. In Israel, he discovered that children "raised in [the] totally communal and cooperative system" of the kibbutz and socialized to be mild, loving, and noncompetitive nevertheless resented attempts to get them to share goods and when obliged to do so grew resistant and hostile. And in Burma, he discovered that a belief in the impermanence of sentient existence, Buddhist nirvana and nonattachment, did not result in a diminished interest in the immediate materialities of daily life.

> In short, [my field studies] convinced me that many motivational dispositions are culturally invariant [and] many cognitive orientations [are so] as well. These invariant dispositions and orientations stem . . . from pan-human biological and cultural constants, and they comprise that universal human nature which, together with received anthropological opinion, I had formerly rejected as yet another ethnocentric bias.[20]

Whether or not a portrait of peoples from Micronesia to the Middle East as angry moralizers deviously pursuing hedonic interests will altogether still the suspicion that some ethnocentric bias yet clings to Spiro's view of universal human nature remains to be seen.

What doesn't remain to be seen, because he is quite explicit about them, are the kinds of ideas, noxious products of a noxious relativism, such a recourse to medical functionalism is designed to cure us of:

> [The] concept of cultural relativism . . . was enlisted to do battle against racist notions in general, and the notion of primitive mentality, in particular. . . . [But] cultural relativism was also used, at least by some anthropologists, to perpetuate a kind of inverted racism. That is, it was used as a powerful tool of cultural criticism, with the consequent derogation of Western culture and of the mentality which it produced. Espousing the philosophy of primitivism . . . the image of primitive man was used . . . as a vehicle for the pursuit of personal utopian quests, and/or as a fulcrum to express personal discontent with Western man and Western society. The strategies adopted took various forms, of which the following are fairly representative. (1) Attempts to abolish private property, or inequality, or aggression in Western societies have a reasonably realistic chance of success since such states of affairs may be found in many primitive societies. (2) Compared to at least some primitives, Western man is uniquely competitive, warlike, intolerant of deviance, sexist, and so on. (3) Paranoia is not necessarily an illness, because paranoid thinking is institutionalized in certain primitive societies; homosexuality is not deviant because homosexuals are the cultural cynosures of some primitive societies; monogamy is not viable because polygamy is the most frequent form of marriage in primitive societies.[21]

Aside from adding a few more items to the list, which promises to be infinite, of unoptional abominations, it is the introduction of the idea of "deviance," conceived as a departure from an inbuilt norm, like an arrhythmic heartbeat, not as a statistical oddity, like fraternal polyandry, that is the really critical move amid all this huffing and puffing about "inverted racism," "utopian quests," and "the philosophy of primitivism." For it is through that idea, The Lawgiver's Friend, that Midgeley's transition between the natural natural (aggression, inequality) and the unnatural natural (paranoia, homosexuality) gets made. Once that camel's nose has been pushed inside, the tent—indeed, the whole riotous circus crying all its booths—is in serious trouble.

Just how much trouble can perhaps be more clearly seen from Robert Edgerton's companion piece to Spiro's in the same volume, "The Study of Deviance, Marginal Man or Everyman?"[22] After a useful, rather eclectic, review of the study of deviance in anthropology, psychology, and sociology, including again his own quite interesting work with American retardates and African intersexuals, Edgerton too comes, rather suddenly as a matter of fact—a cartoon light bulb going on—to the conclusion that what is needed to make such research genuinely productive is a context-independent conception of human nature—one in which "genetically encoded potentials for behavior that we all share" are seen to "underlie [our universal] propensity for deviance." Man's "instinct" for self-preservation, his flight/fight mechanism, and his intolerance of boredom are instanced; and, in an argument I, in my innocence, had thought gone from anthropology, along with euhemerism and primitive promiscuity, it is suggested that, if all goes well on the science side, we may, in time, be able to judge not just individuals but entire societies as deviant, inadequate, failed, unnatural:

> More important still is our inability to test any proposition about the relative adequacy of a society. Our relativistic tradition in anthropology has been slow to yield to the idea that there could be such a thing as a deviant society, one that is contrary to human nature. . . . Yet the idea of a deviant society is central to the alienation tradition in sociology and other fields and it poses a challenge for anthropological theory. Because we know so little about human nature . . . we cannot say whether, much less how, any society has failed. . . . Nevertheless, a glance at any urban newspaper's stories of rising rates of homicide, suicide, rape and other violent crimes should suffice to suggest that the question is relevant not only for theory, but for questions of survival in the modern world.[23]

With this the circle closes; the door slams. The fear of relativism, raised at every turn like some mesmeric obsession, has led to a position in which cultural diversity, across space and over time, amounts to a series of expressions, some salubrious, some not, of a settled, underlying reality, the essential nature of man, and anthropology amounts to an attempt to see through the haze of those expressions to the substance of that reality. A sweeping, schematic, and content-hungry concept, conformable to just about any shape that comes along, Wilsonian, Lorenzian, Freudian, Marxian, Benthamite, Aristotelian ("one of the central features of Human Nature," some anonymous genius is supposed to have remarked, "is a separate judiciary") becomes the ground upon which the understanding of human conduct, homicide, suicide, rape . . . the derogation of Western culture, comes definitively to rest. Some gods from some machines cost, perhaps, rather more than they come to.

∞

About that other conjuration "The Human Mind," held up as a protective cross against the relativist Dracula, I can be somewhat more succinct; for the general pattern, if not the substantial detail, is very much the same. There is the same effort to promote a privileged language of "real" explanation ("nature's own vocabulary," as Richard Rorty, attacking the notion as scientistic fantasy, has put it); and the same wild dissensus as to just which language—Shannon's? Saussure's? Piaget's?—that in fact is.[24] There is the same tendency to see diversity as surface and universality as depth. And there is the same desire to represent one's interpretations not as constructions brought to their objects—societies, cultures, languages—in an effort, somehow, somewhat to comprehend them, but as quiddities of such objects forced upon our thought.

There are, of course, differences as well. The return of Human Nature as a regulative idea has been mainly stimulated by advances in genetics and evolutionary theory, that of the Human Mind by ones in linguistics, computer science, and cognitive psychology. The inclination of the former is to see moral relativism as the source of all our ills, that of the latter is to pin the blame on conceptual relativism. And a partiality for the tropes and images of therapeutic discourse (health and illness, normal and abnormal, function and disfunction) on the one side is matched by a penchant for those of epistemological discourse (knowledge and opinion, fact and illusion, truth and falsity) on the other. But they hardly count, these differences, against the common impulse to final analysis, we have now arrived at Science, explanation. Wiring your theories into something called the Structure of Reason is as effective a way to insulate them from history and culture as building them into something called the Constitution of Man.

So far as anthropology as such is concerned, however, there is another difference, more or less growing out of these, which, while also (you should excuse the expression) more relative than radical, does act to drive the two sorts of discussions in somewhat divergent, even contrary, directions, namely, that where the Human Nature tack leads to bringing back one of our classical conceptions into the center of our attention—"social deviance"—the Human Mind tack leads to bringing back another—"primitive (*sauvage*, primary, preliterate) thought." The anti-relativist anxieties that gather in the one discourse around the enigmas of conduct, gather in the other around those of belief.

More exactly, they gather around "irrational" (or "mystical," "prelogical," "affective," or, particularly nowadays, "noncognitive") beliefs. Where it has been such unnerving practices as headhunting, slavery, caste, and footbinding which have sent anthropologists rallying to the grand old banner of Human Nature under the impression that only thus could taking a moral distance from them be justified, it has been such unlikely conceptions as witchcraft substance, animal tutelaries, god-kings, and (to foreshadow an example I will be getting to in a moment) a dragon with a golden heart and a horn at the nape of its neck which have sent them rallying to that of the Human Mind under the impression that only thus could adopting an empirical skepticism with respect to them be defended. It is not so much how the other half behaves that is so disquieting, but—what is really rather worse—how it thinks.

There are, again, a fairly large number of such rationalist or neo-rationalist perspectives in anthropology of varying degrees of purity, cogency, coherence, and popularity, not wholly consonant one with another. Some invoke formal constancies, usually called cognitive universals; some, developmental constancies, usually called cognitive stages; some, operational constancies, usually called cognitive processes. Some are structuralist, some are Jungian, some are Piagetian, some look to the latest news from MIT, Bell Labs, or Carnegie-Mellon. All are after something steadfast: Reality reached, Reason saved from drowning.

What they share, thus, is not merely an interest in our mental functioning. Like an interest in our biological makeup, that is un-controversially A Good Thing, both in itself and for the analysis of culture; and if not all the supposed discoveries in what is coming to be called, in an aspiring sort of way, "cognitive science" turn out in the event genuinely to be such, some doubtless will, and will alter significantly not only how we think about how we think but how we think about what we think. What, beyond that, they share, from Claude Lévi-Strauss to Rodney Needham, something of a distance, and what is not so uncontroversially beneficent, is a foundationalist view of Mind. That is, a view which sees it—like "The Means of Production" or "Social Structure" or "Exchange" or "Energy" or "Culture" or "Symbol" in other, bottom-line, the-buck-stops-here approaches to social theory (and of course like "Human Nature")—as the sovereign term of explanation, the light that shines in the relativist darkness.

That it is the fear of relativism, the anti-hero with a thousand faces, that provides a good part of the impetus to neo-rationalism, as it does to neo-naturalism, and serves as its major justification, can be conveniently seen from the excellent collection of anti-relativist exhortations—plus one unbuttoned relativist piece marvelously de-signed to drive the others to the required level of outrage—edited by Martin Hollis and Steven Lukes, *Rationality and Relativism*.[25] A product of the so-called rationality debate that Evans-Pritchard's chicken stories, among other things, seem to have induced into British social science and a fair part of British philosophy ("Are there absolute truths that can be gradually approached over time through rational processes? Or are all modes and systems of thought equally valid if viewed from within their own internally consistent frames of reference?"), the book more or less covers the Reason in Danger! waterfront.[26] "The temptations of relativism are perennial and pervasive," the editors' introduction opens, like some Cromwellian call to the barricades: "[The] primrose path to relativism . . . is paved with plausible contentions."[27]

The three anthropologists in the collection all respond with enthusiasm to this summons to save us from ourselves. Ernest Gellner argues that the fact that other people do not believe what we, the Children of Galileo, believe about how reality is put together is no argument against the fact that what we believe is not the correct, "One True Vision."[28] And especially as others, even Himalayans, seem to him to be coming around, he thinks it almost certain that it is. Robin Horton argues for a "cognitive common core," a culturally universal, only trivially variant, "primary theory" of the world as filled with middle-sized, enduring objects, interrelated in terms of a "push-pull" concept of causality, five spatial dichotomies (left/right, above/below, etc.), a temporal trichotomy (before/at the same time/ after) and two categorical distinctions (human/nonhuman, self/ other), the existence of which insures that "Relativism is bound to fail whilst Universalism may, some day, succeed."[29]

But it is Dan Sperber, surer of his rationalist ground (Jerry Fodor's computational view of mental representations) than either of these, and with a One True Vision of his own ("there is no such thing as a non-literal fact"), who develops the most vigorous attack.[30] Relativism, though marvelously mischievous (it makes "ethnography . . . inexplicable, and psychology immensely difficult"), is not even an indefensible position, it really doesn't qualify as a position at all. Its ideas are semi-ideas, its beliefs semi-beliefs, its propositions semi-propositions. Like the gold-hearted dragon with the horn at the base of his neck that one of his elderly Dorze informants innocently, or perhaps not quite so innocently, invited him to track down and kill (wary of nonliteral facts, he declined), such "relativist slogans" as "peoples of different cultures live in different worlds" are not, in fact, factual beliefs. They are half-formed and indeterminate representations, mental stopgaps, that result when, less circumspect than computers, we try to process more information than our inherent conceptual capacities permit. Useful, sometimes, as place holders until we can get our cognitive powers up to speed, occasionally fun to toy with while we are waiting, even once in a while "sources of suggestion in [genuine] creative thinking," they are not, these academic dragons with plastic hearts and no horn at all, matters even their champions take as true, for they do not really understand, nor can they, what they mean. They are hand-wavings—more elaborate or less—of a, in the end, conformist, false-profound, misleading, "hermeneutico-psychedelic," self-serving sort:

> The best evidence against relativism is . . . the very activity of
> anthropologists, while the best evidence for relativism [is] in
> the writings of anthropologists. . . . In retracing their steps [in
> their works], anthropologists transform into unfathomable gaps
> the shallow and irregular cultural boundaries they had not
> found so difficult to cross [in the field], thereby protecting their
> own sense of identity, and providing their philosophical and lay
> audience with just what they want to hear.[31]

In short, whether in the form of hearty common sense (never mind about liver gazing and poison oracles, we have after all got things more or less right), wistful ecumenicalism (despite the variations in more developed explanatory schemes, juju or genetics, at base everyone has more or less the same conception of what the world is like), or aggressive sciencism (there are things which are really ideas, such as "propositional attitudes" and "representational beliefs," and there are things that only look like ideas, such as "there's a dragon down the road" and "peoples of different cultures live in different worlds"), the resurrection of the Human Mind as the still point of the turning world defuses the threat of cultural relativism by disarming the force of cultural diversity. As with "Human Nature," the deconstruction of otherness is the price of truth. Perhaps, but it is not what either the history of anthropology, the materials it has assembled, or the ideals that have animated it would suggest; nor is it only relativists who tell their audiences what they would like to hear. There are some dragons—"tigers in red weather"—that deserve to be looked into.

∽

Looking into dragons, not domesticating or abominating them, nor drowning them in vats of theory, is what anthropology has been all about. At least, that is what it has been all about, as I, no nihilist, no subjectivist, and possessed, as you can see, of some strong views as to what is real and what is not, what is commendable and what is not, what is reasonable and what is not, understand it. We have, with no little success, sought to keep the world off balance; pulling out rugs, upsetting tea tables, setting off firecrackers. It has been the office of others to reassure; ours to unsettle. Australopithecenes, Tricksters, Clicks, Megaliths—we hawk the anomalous, peddle the strange. Merchants of astonishment.

We have, no doubt, on occasion moved too far in this direction and transformed idiosyncrasies into puzzles, puzzles into mysteries, and mysteries into humbug. But such an affection for what doesn't fit and won't comport, reality out of place, has connected us to the leading theme of the cultural history of "Modern Times." For that history has indeed consisted of one field of thought after another having to discover how to live on without the certainties that launched it. Brute fact, natural law, necessary truth, transcendent beauty, immanent authority, unique revelation, even the in-here self facing the out-there world have all come under such heavy attack as to seem by now lost simplicities of a less strenuous past. But science, law, philosophy, art, political theory, religion, and the stubborn in-sistences of common sense have contrived nonetheless to continue. It has not proved necessary to revive the simplicities.

It is, so I think, precisely the determination not to cling to what once worked well enough and got us to where we are and now doesn't quite work well enough and gets us into recurrent stalemates that makes a science move. As long as there was nothing around much faster than a marathon runner, Aristotle's physics worked well enough, Eleatic paradoxes notwithstanding. So long as technical in-strumentation could get us but a short way down and a certain way out from our sense-delivered world, Newton's mechanics worked well enough, action-at-a-distance perplexities notwithstanding. It was not relativism—Sex, the Dialectic and the Death of God—that did in absolute motion, Euclidean space, and universal causation. It was wayward phenomena, wave packets and orbital leaps, before which they were helpless. Nor was it Relativism—Hermeneutico-

Psychedelic Subjectivism—that did in (to the degree they *have* been done in) the Cartesian *cogito*, the Whig view of history, and "the moral point of view so sacred to Eliot and Arnold and Emerson." It was odd actualities—infant betrothals and nonillusionist paintings—that embarrassed their categories.

In this move away from old triumphs become complacencies, one-time breakthroughs transformed to roadblocks, anthropology has played, in our day, a vanguard role. We have been the first to insist on a number of things: that the world does not divide into the pious and the superstitious; that there are sculptures in jungles and paintings in deserts; that political order is possible without centralized power and principled justice without codified rules; that the norms of reason were not fixed in Greece, the evolution of morality not consummated in England. Most important, we were the first to insist that we see the lives of others through lenses of our own grinding and that they look back on ours through ones of their own. That this led some to think the sky was falling, solipsism was upon us, and intellect, judgment, even the sheer possibility of communication had all fled is not surprising. The repositioning of horizons and the decentering of perspectives has had that effect before. The Cardinal Bellarmines you have always with you; and as someone has remarked of the Polynesians, it takes a certain kind of mind to sail out of the sight of land in an outrigger canoe.

But that is, at least at our best and to the degree that we have been able, what we have been doing. And it would be, I think, a large pity if, now that the distances we have established and the elsewheres we have located are beginning to bite, to change our sense of sense and our perception of perception, we should turn back to old songs and older stories in the hope that somehow only the superficial need alter and that we shan't fall off the edge of the world. The objection to anti-relativism is not that it rejects an it's-all-how-you-look-at-it approach to knowledge or a when-in-Rome approach to morality, but that it imagines that they can only be defeated by placing morality beyond culture and knowledge beyond both. This, speaking of things which must needs be so, is no longer possible. If we wanted home truths, we should have stayed at home.

Notes

1. J. Ladd, "The Poverty of Absolutism," in *Edward Westermarck: Essays on His Life and Works*, Acta Philosophica Fennica (Helsinki) 34 (1982): 158–180.

2. I. Scheffler, *Science and Subjectivity*, Indianapolis: Bobbs-Merrill, 1967; W. Booth, "A New Strategy for Establishing a Truly Democratic Criticism," *Daedalus* 112 (1983): 193–214.

3. Ladd, "The Poverty of Absolutism," p. 158.

4. P. Rabinow, "Humanism as Nihilism: The Bracketing of Truth and Seriousness in American Cultural Anthropology," in N. Haan et al., eds., *Social Science as Moral Inquiry*, New York: Columbia University Press, 1983, p. 70.

5. M. de Montaigne, *Les Essais de Michel de Montaigne*, P. Villery, ed., Paris: Universitaires de France, 1978, p. 205. See T. Todorov, "Montaigne. Essays in Reading," in G. Defaux, ed., *Yale French Studies*, vol. 64, New Haven: Yale University Press, 1983, pp. 113–114, for a general discussion of Montaigne's relativism similar to mine.

6. W. Gass, "Culture, Self, and Style," *Syracuse Scholar* 2 (1981): 54–68.

7. I. Jarvie, "Rationalism and Relativism," *British Journal of Sociology* 34 (1983): 45, 46.

8. P. Johnson, *Modern Times*, New York: Harper & Row, 1983; for Thomas's review, "The Inferno of Relativism," *Times Literary Supplement*, July 8, p. 178.

9. Johnson, *Modern Times*, p. 48.

10. G. Stocking, "Afterword: A View from the Center," *Ethnos* 47 (1982): 176.

11. L. Tiger and J. Sepher, *Women in the Kibbutz*, New York: Harcourt Brace-Jovanovich, 1975, p. 16.

12. Quoted, to opposite purposes, in C. Kluckhohn, "Education, Values and Anthropological Relativity," in C. Kluckhohn, ed., *Culture and Behavior*, New York: Free Press, 1962.

13. For materialism, see M. Harris, *The Rise of Anthropological Theory*, New York: Crowell, 1968; for "science" and "The Big Ditch," E. Gellner, *Spectacles and Predicaments*, Cambridge: Cambridge University Press, 1979; for "intertheoretic competition," R. Horton, "Tradition and Modernity Revisited," in M. Hollis and S. Lukes, eds., *Rationality and Relativism*, Cambridge: MIT Press, 1982, pp. 201–260; for "the Cartesian Conception of Knowledge," S. Lukes, "Relativism in Its Place," in Hollis and Lukes, eds., *ibid.*, pp. 261–305, cf. B. Williams, *Descartes: The Project of Pure Inquiry*, Harmondsworth, England: Penguin, 1978; for Popper, from whom all these blessings flow, K. Popper, *Conjectures and Refutations: The Growth of Scientific Knowledge*, London: Routledge and Kegan Paul, 1963, and K. Popper, *Objective Knowledge: An Evolutionary Approach*, Oxford: Clarendon Press, 1972.

14. For "progressive" and "degenerative" research programs, see I. Lakatos, *The Methodology of Scientific Research*, Cambridge: Cambridge University Press, 1976.

15. M. Midgeley, *Beast and Man: The Roots of Human Nature*, Ithaca: Cornell University Press, 1978, pp. xiv–xv; italics in original.

16. *Ibid.*, pp. 79–80; italics in original. The "monotony" example occurs in a footnote ("Monotony is itself an abnormal extreme").

17. S. Salkever, "Beyond Interpretation: Human Agency and the Slovenly Wilderness," in Haan et al., eds., *Social Science*, p. 210.

18. M. Spiro, "Culture and Human Nature," in G. Spindler, ed., *The Making of Psychological Anthropology*, Berkeley: University of California Press, 1978, pp. 330–360.

19. H. Baggish, "Confessions of a Former Cultural Relativist," in E. Angeloni, ed., *Anthropology 83/84*, Guilford, Conn.: Dushkin Publishing, 1983. For another troubled discourse on "the relativism problem" from that part of the world ["I set out what I think a reasonable point of view to fill the partial void left by ethical relativism, which by the 1980s seems more often to be repudiated than upheld"), see E. Hatch, *Culture and Morality: The Relativity of Values in Anthropology*, New York: Columbia University Press, 1983, quotation at p. 12.

20. Spiro, "Culture and Human Nature," pp. 349–350.

21. *Ibid.*, p. 336.

22. R. Edgerton, "The Study of Deviance, Marginal Man or Everyman?" in Spindler, ed., *The Making of Psychological Anthropology*, pp. 444–471.

23. *Ibid.*, p. 470.

24. R. Rorty, "Method and Morality," in Haan et al., eds., *Social Science*, pp. 155–176; cf. R. Rorty, *Philosophy and the Mirror of Nature*, Princeton: Princeton University Press, 1979.

25. There are also some more moderate, split-the-difference pieces, by Ian Hacking, Charles Taylor, and Lukes, but only the first of these seems genuinely free of cooked-up alarms.

26. The parenthetical quotations are from the book jacket, which for once reflects the contents.

27. Hollis and Lukes, eds., *Rationality and Relativism*, p. 1.

28. E. Gellner, in *ibid.*

29. R. Horton, in *ibid.*

30. D. Sperber, "Apparently Irrational Beliefs," in *ibid.*, pp. 149–180.

31. *Ibid.*, p. 180.

IV

The Uses of Diversity

Anthropology, my *fröhliche Wissenschaft*, has been fatally involved over the whole course of its history (a long one, if you start it with Herodotus; rather short, if you start it with Tylor) with the vast variety of ways in which men and women have tried to live their lives. At some points, it has sought to deal with that variety by capturing it in some universalizing net of theory: evolutionary stages, pan-human ideas or practices, or transcendental forms (structures, archetypes, subterranean grammars). At others, it has stressed particularity, idiosyncrasy, incommensurability—cabbages and kings. But recently it has found itself faced with something new: the possibility that the variety is rapidly softening into a paler, and narrower, spectrum. We may be faced with a world in which there simply aren't any more headhunters, matrilinealists, or people who predict the weather from the entrails of a pig. Difference will doubtless remain—the French will never eat salted butter. But the good old days of widow burning and cannibalism are gone forever.

In itself, as a professional issue, this process of the softening of cultural contrast (assuming it is real) is perhaps not so disturbing. Anthropologists will simply have to learn to make something of subtler differences, and their writings may grow more shrewd if less spectacular. But it raises a broader issue, moral, aesthetic, and cognitive at once, that is much more troubling, and that lies at the center of much current discussion about how it is that values are to be justified: what I will call, just to have something that sticks in the mind, The Future of Ethnocentrism.

I shall come back to some of those more general discussions after a bit, for it is toward them that my overall concern is directed; but as a way into the problem I want to begin with the presentation of an argument, unusual I think and more than a little disconcerting, which the French anthropologist Claude Lévi-Strauss develops at the beginning of his recent collection of essays, contentiously entitled (contentiously, at least, for an anthropologist) *The View from Afar—Le regard éloigné.*[1]

∞

Lévi-Strauss's argument arose in the first place in response to a UNESCO invitation to deliver a public lecture to open The International Year to Combat Racism and Racial Discrimination, which, in case you missed it, was 1971. "I was chosen," he writes,

> because twenty years earlier I had written [a pamphlet called] "Race and History" for UNESCO [in which] I had stated a few basic truths. . . . [In] 1971, I soon realized that UNESCO expected me [simply] to repeat them. But twenty years earlier, in order to serve the international institutions, which I felt I had to support more than I do today, I had somewhat overstated my point in the conclusion to "Race and History." Because of my age perhaps, and certainly because of reflections inspired by the present state of the world, I was now disgusted by this obligingness and was convinced that, if I was to be useful to UNESCO and fulfill my commitment honestly, I should have to speak in complete frankness.[2]

As usual, that turned out not to be altogether a good idea, and something of a farce followed. Members of the UNESCO staff were dismayed that "I had challenged a catechism [the acceptance of which] had allowed them to move from modest jobs in developing countries to sanctified positions as executives in an international institution."[3] The then director general of UNESCO, another determined Frenchman, unexpectedly took the floor so as to reduce Lévi-

Strauss's time to speak and thus force him to make the "improving" excisions that had been suggested to him. Lévi-Strauss, *incorrigible*, read his entire text, apparently at high speed, in the time left.

All that aside, a normal day at the UN, the problem with Lévi-Strauss's talk was that in it "I rebelled against the abuse of language by which people tend more and more to confuse racism . . . with attitudes that are normal, even legitimate, and in any case, unavoidable"—that is, though he does not call it that, ethnocentrism.[4]

Ethnocentrism, Lévi-Strauss argues in that piece, "Race and Culture," and, somewhat more technically in another, "The Anthropologist and the Human Condition," written about a decade further on, is not only not in itself a bad thing, but, at least so long as it does not get out of hand, rather a good one. Loyalty to a certain set of values inevitably makes people "partially or totally insensitive to other values" to which other people, equally parochial, are equally loyal.[5] "It is not at all invidious to place one way of life or thought above all others or to feel little drawn to other values." Such "relative incommunicability" does not authorize anyone to oppress or destroy the values rejected or those who carry them. But, absent that, "it is not at all repugnant":

> It may even be the price to be paid so that the systems of values of each spiritual family or each community are preserved and find within themselves the resources necessary for their renewal. If . . . human societies exhibit a certain optimal diversity beyond which they cannot go, but below which they can no longer descend without danger, we must recognize that, to a large extent, this diversity results from the desire of each culture to resist the cultures surrounding it, to distinguish itself from them—in short to be itself. Cultures are not unaware of one another, they even borrow from one another on occasion; but, in order not to perish, they must in other connections remain somewhat impermeable toward one another.[6]

It is thus not only an illusion that humanity can wholly free itself from ethnocentrism, "or even that it will care to do so"; it would not be a good thing if it did do so. Such a "freedom" would lead to a world "whose cultures, all passionately fond of one another, would aspire only to celebrate one another, in such confusion that each would lose any attraction it could have for the others and its own reason for existing."[7]

Distance lends, if not enchantment, anyway indifference, and thus integrity. In the past, when so-called primitive cultures were only very marginally involved with one another—referring to themselves as "The True Ones," "The Good Ones," or just "The Human Beings," and dismissing those across the river or over the ridge as "earth monkeys" or "louse eggs," that is, not, or not fully, human—cultural integrity was readily maintained. A "profound indifference to other cultures was . . . a guarantee that they could exist in their own manner and on their own terms."[8] Now, when such a situation clearly no longer obtains, and everyone, increasingly crowded on a small planet, is deeply interested in everyone else, and in everyone else's business, the possibility of the loss of such integrity, because of the loss of such indifference, looms. Ethnocentrism can perhaps never entirely disappear, being "consubstantial with our species," but it can grow dangerously weak, leaving us prey to a sort of moral entropy:

> We are doubtless deluding ourselves with a dream when we think that equality and fraternity will some day reign among human beings without compromising their diversity. However, if humanity is not resigned to becoming the sterile consumer of values that it managed to create in the past . . . capable only of giving birth to bastard works, to gross and puerile inventions, [then] it must learn once again that all true creation implies a certain deafness to the appeal of other values, even going so far as to reject them if not denying them altogether. For one cannot fully enjoy the other, identify with him, and yet at the same time remain different. When integral communication with the other is achieved completely, it sooner or later spells doom for both his and my creativity. The great creative eras were those in which communication had become adequate for mutual stimulation by remote partners, yet was not so frequent

or so rapid as to endanger the indispensable obstacles between individuals and groups or to reduce them to the point where overly facile exchanges might equalize and nullify their diversity.[9]

Whatever one thinks of all this, or however surprised one is to hear it coming from an anthropologist, it certainly strikes a contemporary chord. The attractions of "deafness to the appeal of other values" and of a relax-and-enjoy-it approach to one's imprisonment in one's own cultural tradition are increasingly celebrated in recent social thought. Unable to embrace either relativism or absolutism—the first because it disables judgment, the second because it removes it from history—our philosophers, historians, and social scientists turn toward the sort of we-are-we and they-are-they *imperméabilité* Lévi-Strauss recommends. Whether one regards this as arrogance made easy, prejudice justified, or as the splendid, here-stand-I honesty of Flannery O'Connor's "when in Rome do as you done in Milledgeville," it clearly puts the question of The Future of Ethnocentrism—and of cultural diversity—in rather a new light. Is drawing back, distancing elsewhere, The View from Afar, really the way to escape the desperate tolerance of UNESCO cosmopolitanism? Is the alternative to moral entropy moral narcissism?

∞

The forces making for a warmer view of cultural self-centeredness over the last twenty-five or thirty years are multiple. There are those "state of the world" matters to which Lévi-Strauss alludes, and most especially the failure of most Third World countries to live up to the thousand-flowers hopes for them current just before and just after their independence struggles. Amin, Bokassa, Pol Pot, Khomeini at the extremes, Marcos, Mobuto, Sukarno, and Mrs. Gandhi less extravagantly, have put something of a chill on the notion that there are worlds elsewhere to which our own compares clearly ill. There is the successive unmasking of the Marxist utopias—the Soviet Union, China, Cuba, Vietnam. And there is the weakening of the Decline of the West pessimism induced by world war, world depression, and the loss of empire. But there is also, and I think not least important, the rise in awareness that universal consensus—trans-national, trans-cultural, even trans-class—on normative matters is not in the offing. Everyone—Sikhs, Socialists, Positivists, the Irish—is not going to come around to a common opinion concerning what is decent and what is not, what is just and what is not, what is beautiful and what is not, what is reasonable and what is not; not soon, perhaps not ever.

If one abandons (and of course not everyone, perhaps not even most everyone, has) the idea that the world is moving toward essential agreement on fundamental matters, or even, as with Lévi-Strauss, that it should, then the appeal of relax-and-enjoy-it ethnocentrism naturally grows. If our values cannot be disentangled from our history and our institutions and nobody else's can be disentangled from theirs, then there would seem to be nothing for it but to follow Emerson and stand on our own feet and speak with our own voice. "I hope to suggest," Richard Rorty writes in a recent piece (marvelously entitled "Postmodernist Bourgeois Liberalism"), "how [we postmodernist bourgeois liberals] might convince our society that loyalty to itself is loyalty enough . . . that it need be responsible only to its own traditions."[10] What an anthropologist in search of "the consistent laws underlying the observable diversity of beliefs and institutions"[11] arrives at from the side of rationalism and high science, a philosopher, persuaded that "there is no 'ground' for [our] loyalties and convictions save the fact that the beliefs and desires and emotions which buttress them overlap those of lots of other members of the group with which we identify for purposes of moral and political deliberation" arrives at from the side of pragmatism and prudential ethics.[12]

The similarity is even greater despite the very different starting points from which these two savants depart (Kantianism without a transcendental subject, Hegelianism without an absolute spirit), and the even more different ends toward which they tend (a trim world of transposable forms, a disheveled one of coincident discourses), because Rorty, too, regards invidious distinctions between groups as not only natural but essential to moral reasoning:

[The] naturalized Hegelian analogue of [Kantian] "intrinsic human dignity" is the comparative dignity of a group with which a person identifies herself. Nations or churches or movements are, on this view, shining historical examples not because they reflect rays emanating from a higher source, but because of contrast-effects—comparison with worse communities. Persons have dignity not as an interior luminescence, but because they share in such contrast-effects. It is a corollary of this view that the moral justification of the institutions and practices of one's group—e.g., of the contemporary bourgeoisie—is mostly a matter of historical narratives (including scenarios about what is likely to happen in certain future contingencies), rather than of philosophical meta-narratives. The principal backup for historiography is not philosophy but the arts. which serve to develop and modify a group's self-image by, for example, apotheosizing its heroes, diabolizing its enemies, mounting dialogues among its members, and refocusing its attention.[13]

Now, as a member of both these intellectual traditions myself, of the scientific study of cultural diversity by profession and of postmodern bourgeois liberalism by general persuasion, my own view, to get round now to that, is that an easy surrender to the comforts of merely being ourselves, cultivating deafness and maximizing gratitude for not having been born a Vandal or an Ik, will be fatal to both. An anthropology so afraid of destroying cultural integrity and creativity, our own and everyone else's, by drawing near to other people, engaging them, seeking to grasp them in their immediacy and their difference, is destined to perish of an inanition for which no manipulations of objectivized data sets can compensate. Any moral philosophy so afraid of becoming entangled in witless relativism or transcendental dogmatism that it can think of nothing better to do with other ways of going at life than to make them look worse than our own is destined merely to conduce (as someone has said of the writings of V. S. Naipaul, perhaps our leading adept at constructing such "contrast-effects") toward making the world safe for condescension. Trying to save two disciplines from themselves at once may seem like hubris. But when one has double citizenships one has double obligations.

⬤⬤

Their different demeanors and their different hobby-horses notwithstanding (and I confess myself very much closer to Rorty's messy populism than to Lévi-Strauss's fastidious mandarinism—in itself, perhaps, but a cultural bias of my own), these two versions of to-each-his-own morality rest, in part anyway, on a common view of cultural diversity: namely, that its main importance is that it provides us with, to use a formula of Bernard Williams's, alternatives to us as opposed to alternatives for us. Other beliefs, values, ways of going on, are seen as beliefs we would have believed, values we would have held, ways we would have gone on, had we been born in some other place or some other time than that in which we actually were.

So, indeed, we would have. But such a view seems to make both rather more and rather less of the fact of cultural diversity than it should. Rather more, because it suggests that to have had a different life than one has in fact had is a practical option one has somehow to make one's mind up about (should I have been a Bororo? am I not fortunate not to have been a Hittite?); rather less, because it obscures the power of such diversity, when personally addressed, to transform our sense of what it *is* for a human being, Bororo, Hittite, Structuralist, or Postmodern Bourgeois Liberal, to believe, to value, or to go on: what it is like, as Arthur Danto has remarked, echoing Thomas Nagel's famous question about the bat, "to think the world is flat, that I look irresistible in my Poiret frocks, that the Reverend Jim Jones would have saved me through his love, that animals have no feeling or that flowers do—or that punk is where it's at."[14] The trouble with ethnocentrism is not that it commits us to our own commitments. We are, by definition, so committed, as we are to having our own headaches. The trouble with ethnocentrism is that it impedes us from discovering at what sort of angle, like Forster's Cavafy, we stand to the world; what sort of bat we really are.

This view—that the puzzles raised by the fact of cultural diversity have more to do with our capacity to feel our way into alien sensibilities, modes of thought (punk rock and Poiret frocks) we do not possess, and are not likely to, than they do with whether we can escape preferring our own preferences—has a number of implications which bode ill for a we-are-we and they-are-they approach to things cultural. The first of these, and possibly the most important, is that those puzzles arise not merely at the boundaries of our society, where we would expect them under such an approach, but, so to speak, at the boundaries of ourselves. Foreignness does not start at the water's edge but at the skin's. The sort of idea that both anthropologists since Malinowski and philosophers since Wittgenstein are likely to entertain that, say, Shi'is, being other, present a problem, but, say, soccer fans, being part of us, do not, or at least not of the same sort, is merely wrong. The social world does not divide at its joints into perspicuous we's with whom we can empathize, however much we differ *with* them, and enigmatical they's, with whom we cannot, however much we defend to the death their right to differ *from* us. The wogs begin long before Calais.

Both recent anthropology of the From the Native's Point of View sort (which I practice) and recent philosophy of the Forms of Life sort (to which I adhere) have been made to conspire, or to seem to conspire, in obscuring this fact by a chronic misapplication of their most powerful and most important idea: the idea that meaning is socially constructed.

The perception that meaning, in the form of interpretable signs—sounds, images, feelings, artifacts, gestures—comes to exist only within language games, communities of discourse, intersubjective systems of reference, ways of worldmaking; that it arises within the frame of concrete social interaction in which something is a something for a you and a me, and not in some secret grotto in the head; and that it is through and through historical, hammered out in the flow of events, is read to imply (as, in my opinion, neither Malinowski nor Wittgenstein—nor for that matter Kuhn or Foucault—meant it to imply) that human communities are, or should be, semantic monads, nearly windowless. We are, says Lévi-Strauss, passengers in the trains which are our cultures, each moving on its own track, at its own speed, and in its own direction. The trains rolling alongside, going in similar directions and at speeds not too different from our own are at least reasonably visible to us as we look out from our compartments. But trains on an oblique or parallel track which are going in an opposed direction are not. "[We] perceive only a vague, fleeting, barely identifiable image, usually just a momentary blur in our visual field, supplying no information about itself and merely irritating us because it interrupts our placid contemplation of the landscape which serves as the backdrop to our daydreaming"[15] Rorty is more cautious and less poetic, and I sense less interested in other people's trains, so concerned is he where his own is going, but he speaks of a more or less accidental "overlap" of belief systems between "rich North American bourgeois" communities and others that "[we] need to talk with" as enabling "whatever conversation between nations may still be possible."[16] The grounding of feeling, thought, and judgment in a form of life—which indeed is the only place, in my view, as it is in Rorty's, that they can be grounded—is taken to mean that the limits of my world are the limits of my language, which is not exactly what the man said.

What he said, of course, was that the limits of my language are the limits of my world, which implies not that the reach of our minds, of what we can say, think, appreciate, and judge, is trapped within the borders of our society, our country, our class, or our time, but that the reach of our minds, the range of signs we can manage somehow to interpret, is what defines the intellectual, emotional, and moral space within which we live. The greater that is, the greater we can make it become by trying to understand what flat earthers or the Reverend Jim Jones (or Iks or Vandals) are all about, what it is like to be them, the clearer we become to ourselves, both in terms of what we see in others that seems remote and what we see that seems reminiscent, what attractive and what repellent, what sensible and what quite mad; oppositions that do not align in any simple way, for there are some things quite appealing about bats, some quite repugnant about ethnographers.

It is, Danto says in that same article I quoted a moment ago, "the gaps between me and those who think differently than I—

which is to say everyone, and not simply those segregated by differences in generations, sex, nationality, sect, and even race—[that] define the real boundaries of the self."[17] It is the asymmetries, as he also says, or nearly, between what we believe or feel and what others do, that make it possible to locate where we now are in the world, how it feels to be there, and where we might or might not want to go. To obscure those gaps and those asymmetries by relegating them to a realm of repressible or ignorable difference, mere unlikeness, which is what ethnocentrism does and is designed to do (UNESCO universalism obscures them—Lévi-Strauss is quite right about that—by denying their reality altogether), is to cut us off from such knowledge and such possibility: the possibility of quite literally, and quite thoroughly, changing our minds.

☞

The history of any people separately and all peoples together, and indeed of each person individually, has been a history of such a changing of minds, usually slowly, sometimes more rapidly; or if the idealist sound of that disturbs you (it ought not, it is not idealist, and it denies neither the natural pressures of fact nor the material limits of will), of sign systems, symbolic forms, cultural traditions. Such changes have not necessarily been for the better, perhaps not even normally. Nor have they led to a convergence of views, but rather to a mingling of them. What, back in his blessed Neolithic, was indeed once something at least rather like Lévi-Strauss's world of integral societies in distant communication has turned into something rather more like Danto's postmodern one of clashing sensibilities in inevadable contact. Like nostalgia, diversity is not what it used to be; and the sealing of lives into separate railway carriages to produce cultural renewal or the spacing of them out with contrast-effects to free up moral energies are romantical dreams, not undangerous.

The general tendency that I remarked in opening for the cultural spectrum to become paler and more continuous without becoming less discriminate (indeed, it is probably becoming more discriminate as symbolic forms split and proliferate), alters not just its bearing on moral argument but the character of such argument it-self. We have become used to the idea that scientific concepts change with changes in the sorts of concerns to which scientists address themselves—that one does not need the calculus to deter-mine the velocity of a chariot or quantal energies to explain the swing of a pendulum. But we are rather less aware that the same thing is true of the speculative instruments of moral reasoning. Ideas which suffice for Lévi-Strauss's magnificent differences do not for Danto's troubling asymmetries; and it is the latter with which we find ourselves increasingly faced.

More concretely, moral issues stemming from cultural diversity (which are, of course, far from being all the moral issues there are) that used to arise, when they arose at all, mainly between soci-eties—the "customs contrary to reason and morals" sort of thing on which imperialism fed—now increasingly arise within them. Social and cultural boundaries coincide less and less closely—there are Japanese in Brazil, Turks on the Main, and West Indian meets East in the streets of Birmingham—a shuffling process which has of course been going on for quite some time (Belgium, Canada, Leb-anon, South Africa—and the Caesars' Rome was not all that homo-geneous), but which is, by now, approaching extreme and near uni-versal proportions. The day when the American city was the main model of cultural fragmentation and ethnic tumbling is quite gone; the Paris of *nos ancêtres les gaulois* is getting to be about as polygot, and as polychrome, as Manhattan, and Paris may yet have a North African mayor (or so, anyway, many of *les gaulois* fear) before New York has a Hispanic one.

This rising within the body of a society, inside the boundaries of a "we," of wrenching moral issues centered around cultural diversity, and the implications it has for our general problem, "the future of ethnocentrism," can perhaps be made rather more vivid with an example; not a made-up, science-fiction one about water on anti-worlds or people whose memories interchange while they are asleep, of which philosophers have recently grown rather too fond, in my opinion, but a real one, or at least one represented to me as real by the anthropologist who told it to me: The Case of the Drunken Indian and the Kidney Machine.

The case is simple, however knotted its resolution. The extreme shortage, due to their great expense, of artificial kidney machines led, naturally enough, to the establishment a few years ago of a queuing process for access to them by patients needing dialysis in a government medical program in the southwestern United States directed, also naturally enough, by young, idealistic doctors from major medical schools, largely northeastern. For the treatment to be effective, at least over an extended period of time, strict discipline as to diet and other matters is necessary on the part of the patients. As a public enterprise, governed by antidiscrimination codes, and anyway, as I say, morally motivated, queuing was organized in terms not of the power to pay but simply severity of need and order of application, a policy which led, with the usual twists of practical logic, to the problem of the drunken Indian.

The Indian, after gaining access to the scarce machine, refused, to the great consternation of the doctors, to stop, or even control, his drinking, which was prodigious. His position, under some sort of principle like that of Flannery O'Connor's I mentioned earlier of remaining oneself whatever others might wish to make of you, was: I am indeed a drunken Indian, I have been one for quite some time, and I intend to go on being one for as long as you can keep me alive by hooking me up to this damn machine of yours. The doctors, whose values were rather different, regarded the Indian as blocking access to the machine by others on the queue, in no less desperate straits, who could, as they saw it, make better use of its benefits—a young, middle-class type, say, rather like themselves, destined for college and, who knows, medical school. As the Indian was already on the machine by the time the problem became visible they could not quite bring themselves (nor, I suppose, would they have been permitted) to take him off it; but they were very deeply upset—at least as upset as the Indian, who was disciplined enough to show up promptly for all his appointments, was resolute—and surely would have devised some reason, ostensibly medical, to displace him from his position in the queue had they seen in time what was coming. He continued on the machine, and they continued distraught, for several years until, proud, as I imagine him, grateful (though not to the doctors) to have had a somewhat extended life in which to drink, and quite unapologetic, he died.

Now, the point of this little fable in real time is not to show how insensitive doctors can be (they were not insensitive, and they had a case), or how adrift Indians have become (he was not adrift, he knew exactly where he was); nor to suggest that either the doctors' values (that is, approximately, ours), the Indian's (that is, approximately, not-ours), or some trans-parte judgment drawn from philosophy or anthropology and issued forth by one of Ronald Dworkin's herculean judges, should have prevailed. It was a hard case and it ended in a hard way; but I cannot see that either more ethnocentrism, more relativism, or more neutrality would have made things any better (though more imagination might have). The point of the fable—I'm not sure it properly has a moral—is that it is this sort of thing, not the distant tribe, enfolded upon itself in coherent difference (the Azande or the Ik that fascinate philosophers only slightly less than science fiction fantasies do, perhaps because they can be made into sublunary Martians and regarded accordingly), that best represent, if somewhat melodramatically, the general form that value conflict arising out of cultural diversity takes nowadays.

The antagonists here, if that's what they were, were not representatives of turned-in social totalities meeting haphazardly along the edges of their beliefs. Indians holding fate at bay with alcohol are as much a part of contemporary America as are doctors correcting it with machines. (If you want to see just how, at least so far as the Indians are concerned—I assume you know about doctors—you can read James Welch's shaking novel, *Winter in the Blood*, where the contrast effects come out rather oddly.) If there was any failure here, and, to be fair, it is difficult at a distance to tell precisely how much there was, it was a failure to grasp, on either side, what it was to be on the other, and thus what it was to be on one's own. No one, at least so it seems, learned very much in this episode about either themselves or about anyone else, and nothing at all, beyond the banalities of disgust and bitterness, about the character of their encounter. It is not the inability of those involved to abandon their convictions and adopt the views of others that makes this little tale seem so utterly depressing. Nor is it their lack of a disincorporated moral rule—The Greatest Good or The Difference Principle (which would seem, as a matter of fact, to give different results here)—to which to appeal. It is their inability even to conceive, amid the mystery of difference, how one might get round an all-too-genuine moral asymmetry. The whole thing took place in the dark.

∞

What tends to take place in the dark—the only things of which "a certain deafness to the appeal of other values" or a "comparison with worse communities" conception of human dignity would seem to allow—is either the application of force to secure conformity to the values of those who possess the force; a vacuous tolerance that, engaging nothing, changes nothing; or, as here, where the force is unavailable and the tolerance unnecessary, a dribbling out to an ambiguous end.

It is surely the case that there are instances where there are, in fact, the practical alternatives. There doesn't seem much to do about the Reverend Jones, once he is in full cry, but physically to stop him before he hands out the Kool-Aid. If people think punk rock is where it's at, then, at least so long as they don't play it in the subway, it's their ears and their funeral. And it *is* difficult (some bats are battier than others) to know just how one ought to proceed with someone who holds that flowers have feelings and that animals do not. Paternalism, indifference, even superciliousness, are not always unuseful attitudes to take to value differences, even to ones more consequential than these. The problem is to know when they are useful and diversity can safely be left to its connoisseurs, and when, as I think is more often the case, and increasingly so, they are not and it cannot, and something more is needed: an imaginative entry into (and admittance of) an alien turn of mind.

In our society, the connoisseur par excellence of alien turns of mind has been the ethnographer (the historian too, to a degree, and in a different way the novelist, but I want to get back on my own reservation), dramatizing oddness, extolling diversity, and breathing broadmindedness. Whatever differences in method or theory have separated us, we have been alike in that: professionally obsessed with worlds elsewhere and with making them comprehensible first to ourselves and then, through conceptual devices not so different from those of historians and literary ones not so different from those of novelists, to our readers. And so long as those worlds really were elsewhere, where Malinowski found them and Lévi-Strauss remembers them, this was, though difficult enough as a practical task, relatively unproblematical as an analytical one. We could think about "primitives" ("savages," "natives," . . .) as we thought about Martians—as possible ways of feeling, reasoning, judging, and behaving, of going on, discontinuous with our own, alternatives to us. Now that those worlds and those alien turns of mind are mostly not really elsewhere, but alternatives for us, hard nearby, instant "gaps between me and those who think differently than I," a certain readjustment in both our rhetorical habits and our sense of mission would seem to be called for.

The uses of cultural diversity, of its study, its description, its analysis, and its comprehension, lie less along the lines of sorting ourselves out from others and others from ourselves so as to defend group integrity and sustain group loyalty than along the lines of defining the terrain reason must cross if its modest rewards are to be reached and realized. This terrain is uneven, full of sudden faults and dangerous passages where accidents can and do happen, and crossing it, or trying to, does little or nothing to smooth it out to a level, safe, unbroken plain, but simply makes visible its clefts and contours. If our peremptory doctors and our intransigent Indian (or Rorty's "rich North American[s]" and "[those we] need to talk with") are to confront one another in a less destructive way (and it is far from certain—the clefts are real—that they actually can) they must explore the character of the space between them.

It is they themselves who must finally do this; there is no substitute for local knowledge here, nor for courage either. But maps and charts may still be useful, and tables, tales, pictures, and descriptions, even theories, if they attend to the actual, as well. The uses of ethnography are mainly ancillary, but they are nonetheless real; like the compiling of dictionaries or the grinding of lenses, it is, or would be, an enabling discipline. And what it enables, when it does so, is a working contact with a variant subjectivity. It places particular we's among particular they's, and they's among we's, where all, as I have been saying, already are, however uneasily. It is the great enemy of ethnocentrism, of confining people to cultural planets where the only ideas they need to conjure with are "those around here," not because it assumes people are all alike, but because it knows how profoundly they are not and how unable yet to disregard one another. Whatever once was possible and whatever may now be longed for, the sovereignty of the familiar impoverishes everyone; to the degree it has a future, ours is dark. It is not that we must love one another or die (if that is the case—Blacks and Afrikaners, Arabs and Jews, Tamils and Singhalese—we are I think doomed). It is that we must know one another, and live with that knowledge, or end marooned in a Beckett-world of colliding soliloquy.

The job of ethnography, or one of them anyway, is indeed to provide, like the arts and history, narratives and scenarios to refocus our attention; not, however, ones that render us acceptable to ourselves by representing others as gathered into worlds we don't want and can't arrive at, but ones which make us visible to ourselves by representing us and everyone else as cast into the midst of a world full of irremovable strangenesses we can't keep clear of.

Until fairly recently (the matter now is changing, in part at least because of ethnography's impact, but mostly because the world is changing) ethnography was fairly well alone in this, for history did in fact spend much of its time comforting our self-esteem and supporting our sense that we were getting somewhere by apotheosizing our heroes and diabolizing our enemies, or with keening over vanished greatness; the social comment of novelists was for the most part internal—one part of Western consciousness holding a mirror, Trollope-flat or Dostoevsky-curved, up to another; and even travel writing, which at least attended to exotic surfaces (jungles, camels, bazaars, temples) mostly employed them to demonstrate the resilience of received virtues in trying circumstances—the Englishman remaining calm, the Frenchman rational, the American innocent. Now, when it is not so alone and the strangenesses it has to deal with are growing more oblique and more shaded, less easily set off as wild anomalies—men who think themselves descended from wallabies or who are convinced they can be murdered with a side-long glance—its task, locating those strangenesses and describing their shapes, may be in some ways more difficult; but it is hardly less necessary. Imagining difference (which of course does not mean making it up, but making it evident) remains a science of which we all have need.

∞

But my purpose here is not to defend the prerogatives of a home-spun *Wissenschaft* whose patent on the study of cultural diversity, if it ever had one, has long since expired. My purpose is to suggest that we have come to such a point in the moral history of the world (a history itself of course anything but moral) that we are obliged to think about such diversity rather differently than we had been used to thinking about it. If it is in fact getting to be the case that rather than being sorted into framed units, social spaces with definite edges to them, seriously disparate approaches to life are becoming scrambled together in ill-defined expanses, social spaces whose edges are unfixed, irregular, and difficult to locate, the question of how to deal with the puzzles of judgment to which such disparities give rise takes on a rather different aspect. Confronting landscapes and still lifes is one thing; panoramas and collages quite another.

That it is the latter we these days confront, that we are living more and more in the midst of an enormous collage, seems every-where apparent. It is not just the evening news where assassinations in India, bombings in Lebanon, coups in Africa, and shootings in Central America are set amid local disasters hardly more legible and followed on by grave discussions of Japanese ways of business, Per-sian forms of passion, or Arab styles of negotiation. It is also an enormous explosion of translation, good, bad, and indifferent, from and to languages—Tamil, Indonesian, Hebrew, and Urdu—previously regarded as marginal and recondite; the migration of cui-sines, costumes, furnishings and decor (caftans in San Francisco, Colonel Sanders in Jogjakarta, barstools in Kyoto); the appearance of gamelan themes in avant-garde jazz, Indio myths in Latino novels, magazine images in African painting. But most of all, it is that the person we encounter in the greengrocery is as likely, or nearly, to come from Korea as from Iowa, in the post office from Algeria as from the Auvergne, in the bank from Bombay as from Liverpool. Even rural settings, where alikeness is likely to be more entrenched, are not immune: Mexican farmers in the Southwest, Vietnamese fishermen along the Gulf Coast, Iranian physicians in the Midwest.

I need not go on multiplying examples. You can all think of ones of your own out of your own traffickings with your own surroundings. Not all this diversity is equally consequential (Jogja cooking will survive finger-lickin'-good); equally immediate (you don't need to grasp the religious beliefs of the man who sells you postage stamps); nor does it all stem from cultural contrast of a clear-cut sort. But that the world is coming at each of its local points to look more like a Kuwaiti bazaar than like an English gentlemen's club (to instance what, to my mind—perhaps because I have never been in either one of them—are the polar cases) seems shatteringly clear. Ethnocentrism of either the louse eggs or the there-but-for-the-grace-of-culture sort may or may not be coincident with the human species; but it is now quite difficult for most of us to know just where, in the grand assemblage of juxtaposed difference, to center it. *Les milieux* are all *mixtes*. They don't make *Umwelte* like they used to do.

Our response to this, so it seems to me, commanding fact is, so it also seems to me, one of the major moral challenges we these days face, ingredient in virtually all the others we face, from nuclear disarmament to the equitable distribution of the world's resources, and in facing it counsels of indiscriminate tolerance, which are anyway not genuinely meant, and, my target here, of surrender, proud, cheerful, defensive, or resigned, to the pleasures of invidious comparison serve us equally badly; though the latter is perhaps the more dangerous because the more likely to be followed. The image of a world full of people so passionately fond of each other's cultures that they aspire only to celebrate one another does not seem to me a clear and present danger; the image of one full of people happily apotheosizing their heroes and diabolizing their enemies alas does. It is not necessary to choose, indeed it is necessary not to choose, between cosmopolitanism without content and parochialism without tears. Neither are of use for living in a collage.

To live in a collage one must in the first place render oneself capable of sorting out its elements, determining what they are (which usually involves determining where they come from and what they amounted to when they were there) and how, practically, they relate to one another, without at the same time blurring one's own sense of one's own location and one's own identity within it. Less figuratively, "understanding" in the sense of comprehension, perception, and insight needs to be distinguished from "understanding" in the sense of agreement of opinion, union of sentiment, or commonality of commitment; the *je vous ai compris* that DeGaulle uttered from the *je vous ai compris* the *pieds noirs* heard. We must learn to grasp what we cannot embrace.

The difficulty in this is enormous, as it has always been. Comprehending that which is, in some manner of form, alien to us and likely to remain so, without either smoothing it over with vacant murmurs of common humanity, disarming it with to-each-his-own indifferentism, or dismissing it as charming, lovely even, but inconsequent, is a skill we have arduously to learn, and having learnt it, always very imperfectly, to work continuously to keep alive; it is not a connatural capacity, like depth perception or the sense of balance, upon which we can complacently rely.

It is in this, strengthening the power of our imaginations to grasp what is in front of us, that the uses of diversity, and of the study of diversity, lie. If we have (as I admit I have) more than a sentimental sympathy with that refractory American Indian, it is not because we hold his views. Alcoholism is indeed an evil, and kidney machines are ill-applied to its victims. Our sympathy derives from our knowledge of the degree to which he has earned his views and the bitter sense that is therefore in them, our comprehension of the terrible road over which he has had to travel to arrive at them and of what it is—ethnocentrism and the crimes it legitimates— that has made it so terrible. If we wish to be able capaciously to judge, as of course we must, we need to make ourselves able capaciously to see. And for that, what we have already seen—the insides of our railway compartments; the shining historical examples of our nations, our churches, and our movements—is, as engrossing as the one may be and as dazzling as the other, simply not enough.

Notes

1. C. Lévi-Strauss, *The View from Afar*, trans. J. Neugroschel and P. Hoss, New York: Basic Books, 1985.
2. *Ibid.*, p. xi.
3. *Ibid.*
4. *Ibid.*, p. xii.
5. *Ibid.*
6. *Ibid.*, p. xiii.
7. *Ibid.*
8. *Ibid.*, p. 7
9. *Ibid.*, p. 23.
10. Richard Rorty, "Postmodernist Bourgeois Liberalism," *Journal of Philosophy* 80 (1983): 583–589; at 585.
11. Lévi-Strauss, *The View from Afar*, p. 35.
12. Rorty, "Postmodernist Bourgeois Liberalism," p. 586.
13. *Ibid*, pp. 586–587.
14. Arthur Danto, "Mind as Feeling; Form as Presence; Langer as Philosopher," *Journal of Philosophy* 81 (1984): 641–647.
15. Lévi-Strauss, *The View from Afar*, p. 10.
16. Rorty, "Postmodernist Bourgeois Liberalism," p. 588.
17. Danto, "Mind as Feeling," p. 647.

$\mathcal{V}$ ⠭

The State of the Art

Waddling In

One of the advantages of anthropology as a scholarly enterprise is that no one, including its practitioners, quite knows exactly what it is. People who watch baboons copulate, people who rewrite myths in algebraic formulas, people who dig up Pleistocene skeletons, people who work out decimal point correlations between toilet training practices and theories of disease, people who decode Maya hieroglyphics, and people who classify kinship systems into typologies in which our own comes out as "Eskimo" all call themselves anthropologists. So do people who analyze African drum rhythms, arrange the whole of human history into evolutionary phases culminating in Communist China or the ecology movement, or reflect largely on the nature of human nature. Works entitled (I choose a few at random) *Medusa's Hair, The Headman and I, The Red Lamp of Incest, Ceramic Theory and Cultural Process, Do Kamo, Knowledge and Passion, American School Language, Circumstantial Deliveries,* and *The Devil and Commodity Fetishism* all present themselves as anthropological, as does the work of a man which came, unbidden, into my hands a few years ago whose theory it is that the Macedonians derive originally from Scotland on the grounds that they play the bagpipe.

There are a number of results of all this, aside from a lot of fine examples of a person's reach exceeding a person's grasp; but surely the most important is a permanent identity crisis. Anthropologists are used to being asked, and asking themselves, how what they do differs from what a sociologist, historian, psychologist, or a political scientist does, and they have no ready answer, save that it most certainly does. Efforts to define the field run from insouciant "social club" arguments ("we are all somehow the same sort of people; we think the same sort of way") to plain-man institutional ones ("anyone trained in an anthropology department is an anthropologist"). But none of them seems really satisfactory. It can't be that we study "tribal" or "primitive" peoples, because by now the majority of us don't, and anyway we're not so sure any more what, if anything, a "tribe" or a "primitive" is. It can't be that we study "other societies," because more and more of us study our own, including the increasing proportion of us—Sri Lankans, Nigerians, Japanese—who belong to such "other societies." It can't be that we study "culture," "forms of life," or the "native's point of view," because, in these hermeneutical-semiotical days, who doesn't?

There is nothing particularly novel in the state of affairs. It has been around since the beginning of the field, whenever that was (Rivers? Tylor? Herder? Herodotus?), and it will doubtless be around at its end, if it has one. But it has taken on in recent years a certain sharpness and given rise to a certain anxiety not easily warded off with "It goes with the territory" attitudes. A chronic vexation, the sort that prods, has become acute; the sort that unnerves.

The initial difficulty in describing anthropology as a coherent enterprise is that it consists, most especially in the United States, but to a significant extent elsewhere in the world as well, of a collection of quite differently conceived sciences rather accidentally thrown together because they all deal somehow or other with (to quote another, earlier, title, which I suppose would now be thought sexist) *Man and His Works*. Archaeology (except classical, which has kept its borders patrolled), physical anthropology, cultural (or social) anthropology, and anthropological linguistics have formed a kind of gathering-of-fugitives consortium whose rationale has always been as obscure as its rightness has been affirmed. The "Four Fields" ideology, proclaimed in addresses and enshrined in departments, has held together an uncentered discipline of disparate visions, ill-connected researches, and improbable allies: a triumph, and a genuine one, of life over logic.

One can do only so much, however, with sentiment, habit, and broad appeals to the advantages of breadth. As the various extra-anthropological sciences upon which the various intra-anthropological ones depend advance technically, logic begins to have its revenge. Especially in the cases of physical anthropology and linguistics, the drift away from the old alliance has been marked. In the first, developments in genetics, neurology, and ethology have up-ended the old head-measuring approach to things and led more and more students interested in human evolution to think they might as well be in a biological discipline and be done with it. In the second, the advent of generative grammar has led to the construction of a new consortium with psychology, computer studies, and other high-tech enterprises impressively entitled "Cognitive Science." Even archaeology, enmeshed in paleoecology, biogeography, and systems theory, has grown rather more autonomous and may start, one of these days, to call itself something more ambitious. It puts one in mind, all this coming apart at the seams, of departed universes: philology, natural history, political economy, the Habsburg Empire. Inner differences are starting to tell.

Nevertheless, it is not this centrifugal movement, powerful as it has become, that is the main cause of the present sense of unease. History, philosophy, literary criticism, and even latterly psychology have experienced similar internal diversification, for similar reasons, and yet managed to maintain at least some general identity. The anthropology holding company will doubtless hold, if barely, for a while longer, if only because people interested in the human animal who don't care for sociobiology, or people interested in language who are unenamored of transformational grammar, can find a home there, safe from the imperialisms of entomologists and logicians. The most shaking problems are arising in the branch of the discipline which is still the largest, the most visible, and the one most usually taken by the world at large as distinguishing it (it is also the one to which I myself belong): social—cultural, sociocultural—anthropology. If there is trouble in the marches, there is even more in the capital.

The first of the difficulties here, the most felt and the most commented upon, but I doubt the most important, is the "disappearing subject" problem. Whether "Primitives" ever should have been called such in the first place, or whether there were, even by the nineteenth century, very many really "untouched" peoples in the world, there are surely hardly any groups now deserving of such characterizations. Highland New Guinea, Amazonia, maybe some parts of the Arctic or the Kalahari, are about the only places one can even find candidates for (to invoke some other obsolescent terms of art) "intact," "simple," "elementary," "sauvage" societies; and they, to the degree they exist as such, are rapidly being incorporated, as American Indians, Australian Aborigines, and African Nilotes were before them, into somebody or other's larger plans. "Primitives," even of the sort that made Boas, Mead, Malinowski, or Evans-Pritchard famous, are a bit of a wasting asset. The overwhelming proportion of social anthropologists are not these days sailing away to uncharted isles or jungle paradises, but throwing themselves into the midst of such formidable world-historical entities as India, Japan, Egypt, Greece, or Brazil.

It is not, however, the disappearance of a subject matter supposedly unique as such that has proved so shaking to the foundations of social anthropology, but another privation the involvement with societies less castaway has brought on: the loss of research isolation. Those people with pierced noses or body tattoos, or who buried their dead in trees, may never have been the solitaries we took them to be, but *we* were. The anthropologists who went off to the Talensi, the tundra, or Tikopia did it all: economics, politics, law, religion; psychology and land tenure, dance and kinship; how children were raised, houses built, seals hunted, stories told. There was no one else around, save occasionally and at a collegial distance, another anthropologist; or if there was—a missionary, a trader, a district officer, Paul Gauguin—he or she was mentally pushed aside. Small worlds, perhaps, but pretty well our oyster.

This is all no longer. When one goes to Nigeria, Mexico, China, or in my own case Indonesia and Morocco, one encounters not just "natives" and mud huts, but economists calculating Gini coefficients, political scientists scaling attitudes, historians collating documents, psychologists running experiments, sociologists counting houses, heads, or occupations. Lawyers, literary critics, architects, even philosophers, no longer content to "draw the cork out of an old conundrum/And watch the paradoxes fizz," are getting into the act. Walking barefoot through the Whole of Culture is really no longer an option, and the anthropologist who tries it is in grave danger of being descended upon in print by an outraged textualist or a maddened demographer. We are now, clearly, some sort of special science, or at least had better become one soon. The only question is, now that "Man" is a bit much as an answer, of what?

The response to this tearing question has been less to answer it than to reemphasize the "method" considered, at least since Malinowski, to be the alpha and omega of social anthropology—ethnographic fieldwork. What we do that others don't, or only occasionally and not so well, is (this vision has it) to talk to the man in the paddy or the woman in the bazaar, largely free-form, in a one thing leads to another and everything leads to everything else manner, in the vernacular and for extended periods of time, all the while observing, from very close up, how they behave. The specialness of "what anthropologists do," their holistic, humanistic, mostly qualitative, strongly artisanal approach to social research, is (so we have taught ourselves to argue) the heart of the matter. Nigeria may not be a tribe, nor Italy an island; but a craft learnt among tribes or developed on islands can yet uncover dimensions of being that are hidden from such stricter and better organized types as economists, historians, exegetes, and political theorists.

The curious thing about this effort to define ourselves in terms of a particular style of research, colloquial and offhand, entrenched in a particular set of skills, improvisatory and personal, rather than in terms of what we study, what theories we espouse, or what findings we hope to find, is that it has been more effective outside the profession than it has been within it.

The prestige of anthropology, or anyway sociocultural anthropology, has never been higher in history, philosophy, literary criticism, theology, law, or political science, even to a degree in (the hard cases) sociology, psychology, and economics, than it is right now. Claude Lévi-Strauss, Victor Turner, Mary Douglas, Eric Wolf, Marshall Sahlins, Edmund Leach, Louis Dumont, Melford Spiro, Ernest Gellner, Marvin Harris, Jack Goody, Pierre Bourdieu, myself (to essay a list I shall doubtless live to regret) are cited everywhere, by everybody, to all sorts of purposes. The "anthropological perspective" is, so far as the general intellectual is concerned, very much "in," and there is little sign that what the jargoneers call its "outreach" is doing anything but growing. Within the discipline, however, the atmosphere is less upbeat. The very identification of "the fieldwork cast of mind" as the thing that makes us different and justified our existence in a world made methodological has only intensified concern as to its scientific respectability on the one hand and its moral legitimacy on the other. Putting so many of one's eggs in a home-made basket produces a certain nervousness, rising at times to something very near to panic.

The worry on the science side has mostly to do with the question of whether researches which rely so heavily on the personal factor—this investigator, in this time; that informant, of that place—can ever be sufficiently "objective," "systematic," "reproducible," "cumulative," "predictive," "precise," or "testable" as to yield more than a collection of likely stories. Impressionism, intuitionism, subjectivism, aestheticism, and perhaps above all the substitution of rhetoric for evidence, and style for argument, seem clear and present dangers; that most dreaded state, paradigmlessness, a permanent affliction. What sort of scientists are they whose main technique is sociability and whose main instrument is themselves? What can we expect from them but charged prose and pretty theories?

As anthropology has moved to take its place as a discipline among others, a new form of an old, all-too-familiar debate, *Geistwissenschaften vs. Naturwissenschaften,* has broken out afresh, and in an especially virulent and degraded form—déjà vu all over again. Waddling in at this late date, as Forster once said of India, to find its seat among the nations, anthropology has found itself increasingly divided between those who would extend and develop its received tradition—one which rejects the historicist/scientist dichotomy in the first place and, with Weber, Tocqueville, Burckhardt, Peirce, or Montesquieu, dreams of a *science humaine*—and those, afraid of being sent away from the table as improperly dressed, who would transform the field into some sort of social physics, complete with laws, formalisms, and apodictic proofs.

In this struggle, which breaks out everywhere from academic appointments in classy places to wild-eyed "reevaluations" of classic works, and which is growing extraordinarily bitter, the paradigm hunters have most of the cards, at least in the United States, where, pronouncing themselves "mainstream," they dominate the funding sources, the professional organizations, journals, and research institutions, and are nicely preadapted to the bottom-line mentality now pervading our public life. Cornford's earnest young men (and, now, women) determined to get all the money there is going are everywhere now, even if the money that is going doesn't come to all that much.

Yet even those on the (politically) weaker side, those more inclined to a free-style view of things, are afflicted with their own variety of failure of nerve, save that it is less methodological than moral. They are not much concerned about whether "me anthropologist, you native" research is rigorous than about whether it is decent. About that, however, they are *very* concerned.

The trouble begins with uneasy reflections on the involvement of anthropological research with colonial regimes during the heyday of Western imperialism and with its aftershadows now; reflections themselves brought on by accusations, from Third World intellectuals, about the field's complicity in the division of humanity into those who know and decide and those who are known and are decided for, that are especially disturbing to scholars who have so long regarded themselves as the native's friend, and still think they understand him better than anyone else, including perhaps himself. But it hardly ends there. Driven on by the enormous engines of postmodern self-doubt—Heidegger, Wittgenstein, Gramsci, Sartre, Foucault, Derrida, most recently Bakhtin—the anxiety spreads into a more general worry about the representation of "The Other" (inevitably capitalized, inevitably singular) in ethnographic discourse as such. Is not the whole enterprise but domination carried on by other means: "Hegemony," "monologue," "*vouloir-savoir*," "*mauvaise foi*," "orientalism"? "Who are we to speak for them?"

This is hardly a question that can simply be dismissed, as it so often has been by hardened fieldworkers, as the grumbling of café or gas-station anthropologists; but one could wish it were being met with less breastbeating and lashing out at supposed failures of mind and character on the part of bourgeois social scientists, and more attempts actually to answer it. There have been some such attempts, hesitant and rather gestural, but at least as often hypochondria has passed for self-examination, and "Down with Us!" (for the malcontents are, after all, bourgeois too) for critique. The changing situation of the ethnographer, intellectual and moral alike, brought on by the movement of anthropology from the margins of the modern world toward its center, is as poorly addressed by crying havoc as it is by crying science. Mere malaise is as evasive as mere rigor, and rather more self-serving.

Yet, and yet, all may be for, if not the best, anyway the better. The Outsider view of anthropology as a powerful regenerative force in social and humane studies, now that it is at long last becoming so fully a part of them rather than a minor amusement off to the side, may be closer to the mark than the Insider view that the passage from South Sea obscurity to worldly celebrity is simply exposing anthropology's lack of internal coherence, its methodological softness, and its political hypocrisy, as well as perhaps its practical irrelevance. The need to think through, to defend, and to extend an approach to social research that takes seriously the proposition that in understanding "others," uncapitalized and plural, it is useful to go among them as they go among themselves, ad hoc and groping, is producing an extraordinary ferment. It is not perhaps entirely surprising that such ferment looks threatening to some of those caught in the middle of it—as Randall Jarrell says somewhere, the trouble with golden ages is that the people in them go about complaining that everything looks yellow. What *is* surprising is how promising, even salvational, it often looks to others.

The conjunction of cultural popularity and professional disquiet that now characterizes anthropology is neither a paradox nor a sign that a fad is being perpetrated. It is an indication that "the anthropological way of looking things," as well as (what are more or less the same thing) "the anthropological way of finding out things" and "the anthropological way of writing about things," do have something to offer the late twentieth century—and not only in social studies—not available elsewhere, and that it is full in the throes of determining what exactly that is.

The expectations on the one side may be too high—in the first flush of structuralism they undoubtedly were—and the worries on the other too overdrawn. Nevertheless, pulled in opposed directions by technical advances in allied disciplines, divided within itself along accidental ill-drawn lines, besieged from one side by resurgent scientism and from the other by an advanced form of hand-wringing, and progressively deprived of its original subject matter, its research isolation, and its master-of-all-I-survey authority, the field seems not only to stay reasonably intact but, what is more important, to extend the sway of the cast of mind that defines it over wider and wider areas of contemporary thought. We have turned out to be rather good at waddling in. In our confusion is our strength.

Culture War

Anthropology is a conflicted discipline, perpetually in search of ways to escape its condition, perpetually failing to find them. Committed, since its beginnings, to a global view of human life—social, cultural, biological, and historical at once—it keeps falling into its parts, complaining about the fact, and trying desperately, and unsuccessfully, to project some sort of new unity to replace the unity it imagines itself once to have had, but now, through the faithlessness of present practitioners, to have mindlessly cast away. The watchword is "holism," cried out at professional meetings and in general calls to arms (of which there are a very large number) in professional journals and monographs. The reality, in the research actually done and the works actually published, is enormous diversity.

And argument, endless argument. The tensions among the major subdivisions of the field—physical anthropology, archaeology, linguistic anthropology, and cultural (or social) anthropology—have been reasonably well managed by the usual mechanisms of differentiation and specialization, in which each subfield has become a fairly autonomous discipline. This has not happened without plaintive invocations of ancestral polymaths—there were giants in those days—who supposedly "did everything." But the fissures within cultural anthropology as such, the heart of the discipline, proved increasingly prominent and less easy to contain. The division into sharply opposed schools of thought—into overall approaches conceived not as methodological alternatives but as dug-in world views, moralities, and political positionings—has grown to the point where clashes are more common than conclusions and the possibility of a general consensus on anything fundamental seems remote. The wringing of hands this brings on, and the sense of loss, is considerable, and doubtless heartfelt; but it is very likely misplaced. Anthropology generally, and cultural anthropology in particular, draws the greater part of its vitality from the controversies that animate it. It is not much destined for secured positions and settled issues.

The recent debate, much celebrated in the intellectual press and on the academic circuit, between Gananath Obeyesekere and Marshall Sahlins, two of the senior and most combat-ready figures in the field, is over how we are to understand the death of that Pacific Columbus, Captain James Cook, at the hands of the Hawaiians in 1779.[1] (Columbus "discovered" America while looking for India; Cook, three centuries later, "discovered" the Sandwich Islands— and before them, encountered Australia and New Zealand—while looking for the Northwest Passage.) Angry, eloquent, and uncompromising—as well as, on occasion, bitterly funny—they push into view some of the most central and most divisive issues in anthropological study. After one reads these two having at one another up, down, and sideways for five hundred lapel-grabbing pages or so, whatever happened to Cook, and why, seems a good deal less important, and probably less determinable, than the questions they raise about how it is we are to go about making sense of the acts and emotions of distant peoples in remote times. What does "knowing" about "others" properly consist in? Is it possible? Is it good?

At the risk of a certain degree of oversimplification (but not much: neither of these warriors is given to shaded views), we can say that Sahlins is a thoroughgoing advocate of the view that there are distinct cultures, each with a "total cultural system of human action," and that they are to be understood along structuralist lines. Obeyesekere is a thoroughgoing advocate of the view that people's actions and beliefs have particular, practical functions in their lives and that those functions and beliefs should be understood along psychological lines.[2]

Sahlins's original argument, which has changed little, if at all, since he first set it forth two decades ago, is that Cook stumbled onto the beach in Hawaii (that is, the "big island" of Hawai'i proper) at the time of a great, four-month-long ceremony called the Makahiki celebrating the annual rebirth of nature, in which the central event was the arrival from his home above the sea of the god Lono, symbolized in a giant tapa cloth and birdskin image paraded clockwise about the island for a month.

The Hawaiians divided the lunar year into two periods. One was the Makahiki time when peace, the indigenous Kuali'l priests, and the fertility god, Lono, shaped their existence, and the king was immobilized. During the rest of the year, after Lono, his birdskin image turned backward, had left again, came a time of warfare when the immigrant Nahulu priests and the virility god, Ku, were dominant, and the king was active. Cook, who arrived from the right direction and in the right manner, was taken by the Hawaiians, or at least by the various priests involved, to be Lono come in the flesh, and he was consecrated as such by means of elaborate rites in the great temple of the island.

Then, for his own reasons, but again in accidental accordance with the calendar governing the Makahiki, he departed to the horizon from which he had come. Shortly after he set sail, however, a sprung mast forced him to return to the beach for repairs. This out-of-pattern move was interpreted by the Hawaiians as a cosmological disordering, one that presaged, if it were allowed to go forward, a social and political upheaval—a "structural crisis when all the social relations . . . change their signs." It led, rather quickly, to Cook's messy end: he was stabbed and clubbed to death amid hundreds of swarming Hawaiians after he came irritably ashore, firing his pistol impulsively about. Consecrated as a god by arriving in the right way at the right time, he was killed as a god—sacrificed to keep the structure intact and unreversed—because he returned to Hawaii in the wrong way at the wrong time: a historical accident caught up in a cultural form.

To all of this highly carpentered and suspiciously seamless argument, Obeyesekere gives a resounding "no!"—more apparently for moral and political reasons than for empirical ones. It is, he says, demeaning to the Hawaiians (and to him, personally, as "a Sri Lankan native and an anthropologist working in an American university"), in that it depicts them as childish, irrational savages so intoxicated with their signs and portents as to be incapable of seeing what is before their eyes, a man like any other, and incapable of reacting to him with simple practicality and ordinary common sense.

Sahlins's account is said to be ethnocentric in that it foists upon the Hawaiians the European notion that the technological superiority of Europeans leads astonished primitives, when first encountering them, to regard them as supernatural beings. And—this is what really smarts, especially to someone like Sahlins, who, like almost all anthropologists, Obeyesekere included, sees himself as a tribune for his subjects, their public defender in a world that has pushed them aside as hapless and negligible—Sahlins's argument is said to be neo-imperialist: an attempt to silence the "real voices" of the Hawaiians, and, indeed, of "natives" in general, and replace them with the voices of the very people who first conquered them, then exploited them, and now, in the scholarly, book-writing phase of the great oppression known as colonialism, occlude them.

About Sahlins's account and its claims to be based on fact, Obeyesekere writes,

> I question this "fact," which I show was created in the European imagination of the eighteenth century and after and was based on antecedent "myth models" pertaining to the redoubtable explorer cum civilizer who is a god to the "natives." To put it bluntly, I doubt that the natives created their European god; the Europeans created him for them. This "European god" is a myth of conquest, imperialism, and civilization—a triad that cannot be easily separated.

The ensuing paper war between the two anthropologists can be followed both in Obeyesekere's rambling, beat-the-snake-with-whatever-stick-is-handy brief for the prosecution (he invokes Sri Lankan terrorism, Cortés among the Aztecs, *Heart of Darkness*, and something called "symbolic psychomimesis") and in Sahlins's more smoothed and pertinacious "and-another-thing" case for the defense. (A third of Sahlins's book consists of seventeen appendices of spectacular particularity, including "Priests and Genealogies," "Calendrical Politics," "Atua in the Marquesas and Elsewhere," "Kamakau's Gods," "Lono at Hikiau.") On both sides there is a great outpouring of facts, supposed facts, and possible facts that touches on virtually everything that is known, or thought to be known, about Cook's misadventure and the conditions surrounding it.

Sahlins has something of a natural advantage in this data slinging, because, as a longstanding Oceanist of great repute, he has written extensively on Polynesian ethnohistory generally and that of Hawaii particularly. Obeyesekere's work has been almost entirely concerned with Sri Lanka, and he has built up his knowledge of the subject at hand by means of three or four years of reading to a purpose as well as by undertaking a brief "pilgrimage to Hawai'i to check my version against that of scholars of Hawai'ian history and culture."

But since both scholars are relying on essentially the same limited corpus of primary materials—ships' logs, sailors' journals, written-down oral histories; missionary accounts, some drawings and engravings, some letters—this is not, in itself, a decisive difference. It is just one that puts more of a burden of proof on Obeyesekere—whose way with arguments tends to be rather relaxed methodologically—than he seems to appreciate. ("I find it awfully hard to accept," "one could as easily argue," "it . . . seems reasonable to assume," "it is hard to believe," "I find this account . . . extremely plausible," and other such appeals to the supposed obviousness of the very things that are in dispute punctuate his text from beginning to end.) If this were the college debate it sometimes sounds like, Sahlins, wittier, more focused, and better informed, would win hands down.

But it is not such a debate. Despite the scientistic rhetoric on both sides about the "search for truth," and the crafted and rather unnecessary scholarly insults (Obeyesekere says, apropos of nothing, that Sahlins lacks "deep ethical concern," while Sahlins says, apropos of that, that Obeyesekere is a literary "terrorist"), and the endless parading of fine detail that only a lawyer could love, the matters that divide them are not, at bottom, mere questions of fact. Even were they able to agree on how the Hawaiians regarded Cook, and he them—and they are not really so far apart on that as they pretend—they would still be in total opposition with respect to just about everything of importance in anthropology. What divides them, and a good part of the profession with them, is their understanding of cultural difference: what it is, what produces it, what maintains it, and how deeply it goes. For Sahlins, it is substance; for Obeyesekere, it is surface.

∞

Over the past twenty-five years or so, the post-everything era (postmodernism, structuralism, colonialism, positivism), the attempt to portray "how the 'natives' think" (or thought), or even what they are doing when they do what they do, has come in for a good deal of moral, political, and philosophical attack. The mere claim "to know better," which it would seem any anthropologist would have at least implicitly to make, seems at least faintly illegitimate. To say something about the forms of life of Hawaiians (or anybody else) that Hawaiians do not themselves say opens one to the charge that one is writing out other peoples' consciousness for them, scripting their souls. The days of simple "the Dangs believe, the Dangs don't believe" anthropology seem truly over.

The reactions to this state of affairs—what Sahlins in one of his most recent essays calls "Goodbye to *Tristes Tropes*"—have been various, worried, and more than a little disarranged.[3] Postmodernists have questioned whether ordered accounts of other ways of being in the world—accounts that offer monological, comprehensive, and all-too-coherent explanations—are credible at all, and whether we are not so imprisoned in our own modes of thought and perception as to be incapable of grasping, much less crediting, those of others. The politically driven scholars, intense and unhesitant, sure of their ground, have called for anthropological work that advances the fortunes of the peoples described, whatever those fortunes are taken to be, and for deliberate subversion of the power inequalities between "the West and the Rest." There have been demands for the "contextualization" of particular societies in the "modern ('capitalist,' 'bourgeois,' 'utilitarian') world system," as opposed to isolating them as, in another of Sahlins's punning titles, "islands of history." There have been demands for the restoration of a historical dimension to "primitive" or "simple" cultures, so often portrayed as "cold," unchanging, crystalline structures—human still-lifes. And there have been pleas for a reemphasis on homely, panhuman common characteristics (we all reason, we all suffer, we all live in a world indifferent to our hopes), as against sharp and incommensurable contrasts in logic and sensibility between one people and another.

All these themes run through the quarrel between Obeyesekere and Sahlins, appearing and reappearing in different form in different connections—in intense debates over whether nineteenth-century Hawaiian accounts of their customs and traditions are usable for reconstructing the historical past or are too infected by the Christianizing prejudices of the missionaries who recorded them to be trusted; over whether Cook and his associates had learned enough Hawaiian to understand what the Hawaiians were saying to them; and over whether the structuralist approach has to assume the beliefs of the Hawaiians to have been uniform throughout the entire population, whose members are stereotypically presented, Obeyesekere charges, "as if [the Hawaiians] were acting out a cultural schema without reflection." But in the end the arguments, opposed on every point, divide into a stark and simple, almost Manichaean, contrast.

For Obeyesekere, the Hawaiians are "pragmatic," "calculating," "strategizing" rationalists; rather like ourselves, indeed rather like everybody, save perhaps Sahlins, they "reflectively assess the implications of a problem in terms of practical criteria." For Sahlins, they are distinct others, existing within a distinctive "schema," a "total cultural system of human action," "another cosmology," thoroughly discontinuous with "modern, bourgeois rationality," governed by a logic "that [has] the quality of not seeming necessary for us yet being sufficient for them." "Different cultures," he says, "different rationalities."

Obeyesekere's "practical, rationality," says Sahlins (he also calls it "pidgin anthropology" and "pop nativism"), shows that the utilitarian, instrumentalist "philosophy of Hobbes, Locke, Helvétius & Co. is still too much with us." Sahlins's "structural theory of history," says Obeyesekere (he calls it "reified," "superorganic," "rigid," and "pseudohistorical"), shows that what is still too much with us is the irrationalist model of primitive mentality—Lévy-Bruhl, Lévi-Strauss, Tzvetan Todorov's group-think Aztecs, and the Freud of *Totem and Taboo,* who thought children, savages, and psychotics were of a piece.

What is at stake here is thus a question that has haunted anthropologists for over a hundred years and haunts us even more now that we work in a decolonized world: What are we to make of cultural practices that seem to us odd and illogical? How odd are they? How illogical? In what precisely does reason lie? This is a question to be asked not only about eighteenth-century Hawaiians, parading noisily about with birdskin images, taking a coconut tree ("a man with his head in the ground and his testicles in the air") to be the body of a god, and enfolding their lives in so elaborate a skein of sacrality and prohibition—the notorious tabu—that they sometimes can barely move. It is to be asked as well about eighteenth-century Englishmen, sailors and navigators, wandering womanless about the oceans in search of discoveries—arcadias, curiosities, anchorages, delicacies, and the Northwest Passage—and of the inquisitive, aggressive society, the knowledge-is-glory world that, hoping, ultimately, for a temporal salvation, sent the Englishmen there.[4]

The Hawaiians and the Enlightenment navigators are far away from us now in both time and space. At least that is true of the Hawaiians who lived in the Ku and Lono rhythm of existence. (Kamehameha II more or less ended that rhythm with his famous bonfire of the vanities in the nineteenth century, a real reversal of signs; and what he didn't finish off by eating with women and throwing icons into the sea, Christianity, sugar cane, and the steamship did.) And it is also true of the navigators who forced their way into that rhythm of existence, bold, unknowing, and hellbent upon improvement. We look back at these two "peoples," and at their legendary "first contact" encounter, through the haze of the modern order of life (or, now that the Euro-American empires and the "East-West" world divide have weakened or disappeared, that of the postmodern order). We look back on them, moreover, from our particular positions within that order. We make of them what we can, given who we are or have become. There is nothing fatal in this, either to truth or fairness. But it is inevitable, and foolish to pretend otherwise.

To their great credit, neither Obeyesekere nor Sahlins pretends otherwise. Both their personal positions and their professional agendas are upfront and visible. Obeyesekere argues that, as an authentic "native" (or "postnative"?), directly caught up in the current travails of an ex-colony wracked with induced violence, he is both immunized against Western self-deceptions and especially well-situated to see the eighteenth-century Pacific, both white and colored, as it really was. He dedicates his book to a murdered Sri Lankan taxi driver, who used to drive him about Colombo, as a memorial to "the thousands who have been killed all over the world . . . ordinary people, whose families haven't even been given a chance to mourn." He writes that "it is precisely out of [my] existential predicaments that my interest in Cook [and his 'ire' over Sahlins and his work] developed and flowered."

In response, Sahlins wonders, as well he might, how he and Cook have become "somehow responsible for the tragedy of Obeyesekere's friend," and whether the enlisting of such a tragedy in the service of a scholarly dispute is altogether appropriate. He says that, white and Western as he may be, he is rather less encumbered with ethnocentric prejudices than someone who, explicating "early Hawaiian concepts of White men by Sri Lankan beliefs and his own experience . . . gets farther and farther from the Hawaiian and closer and closer to the native Western folklore of divine vs. human, spiritual vs. material."

> The ultimate victims . . . are the Hawaiian people. Western empirical good sense replaces their own view of things, leaving them with a fictional history and a pidgin ethnography. . . . Traditional rituals are . . . dissolved; social cleavages on which Hawaiian history turned . . . are effaced. . . . Hawaiian people appear on stage as the dupes of European ideology. Deprived . . . of agency and culture, their history is reduced to

a classic meaninglessness: they lived and they suffered—and then they died.

It is this curious reversal—the offended and injured "native subject" as Enlightenment universalist and the removed and ironical "stranger observer" as relativizing historicist—that gives this debate its extraordinary pathos and, in the end, threatens to turn it from a search for an elusive past into a private quarrel. Even if, following Obeyesekere, one is conscious of the necessity of taking full account of the fact that what we know of "first contact" Hawaii comes to us sifted through the perspectives of those who have told us about it, and that no one anywhere has ever lived a world wholly removed from practical concerns, the reduction of that Hawaii to so much "European mythmaking" still seems more a product of unfocused resentment—ideological "ire"—than of evidence, reflection, and "common sense."

And even if, following Sahlins, one sees the danger of losing forever the deep particularities of vanished peoples in vanished times by turning them into generalized reasoners driven by practical concerns, and recognizes that there are more ways to silence others than are imagined in postcolonial revisionism, there are still problems. The enclosure of such particularities in sharp-edged forms fitted tightly together like pieces in a picture puzzle still risks the charge of ethnographical jiggery and excessive cleverness.

Full of certainties and accusations, thoroughly consumed with scoring points, Obeyesekere and Sahlins have, for all that, together managed to pose, in a way they could never have done separately, fundamental theoretical questions; and they have raised critical methodological issues with respect to the delicate business of "other-knowing." (Questions and issues on which I perhaps should at this point come clean and say that, for my part, I find Sahlins, the structuralist glitter surrounding his analyses aside, markedly the more persuasive. His descriptions are more circumstantial, his portrayal of both the Hawaiians and the British more deeply penetrating, and his grasp of the moral and political issues involved surer, less prey to the confusing noises of the confused present.)

Whether they have raised the level of anthropological disputation, in the long run a more important matter for a field in which there really are no answers to be found in the back of the book, depends on whether those who come after them—already a gathering company on each side—can sustain their intensity while containing their impulse to take offense and argue for victory; whether they can, amid nurtured rancor and piqued honor, keep the conversation going.

Deep Hanging Out

All the human sciences are promiscuous, inconstant, and ill-defined; but cultural anthropology abuses the privilege. Consider:

First, Pierre Clastres. A thirty-year-old graduate student in the *berceau* of Structuralism, Claude Lévi-Strauss's *laboratoire anthropologique*, he sets off from Paris in the early sixties for a remote corner of Paraguay. There, in a hardly inhabited region of strange forests and stranger animals—jaguars, coatis, vultures, peccaries, tree snakes, howler monkeys—he lives for a year with a hundred or so "savage" Indians (as, approvingly, indeed somewhat in awe, he calls them), who abandon their aged, paint their bodies in bowed stripes and bent rectangles, practice polyandry, eat their dead, and beat menarcheal girls with tapir penises so as to make them, like the long nosed tapir, insanely ardent.

The book he publishes upon his return he calls, with deliberate, almost anachronistic, premodern flatness, as though it were a recently discovered missionary diary from an eighteenth-century Jesuit, *Chronique des indiens Guayaki*.[5] Worshipfully translated by the American novelist Paul Auster ("It is, I believe, nearly impossible not to love this book")—and belatedly published in the United States a quarter-century later—the work is, in form at least, old-style ethnographical to a fault. It gives a life-cycle description of "the Guayaki," beginning with birth, proceeding through ritual initiation, marriage, hunting, and warfare, to illness, death, funerals, and, after the funerals, cannibalism. There are the classic sort of carefully posed, aesthetical photographs: near-naked natives staring blankly into cameras. There are the pen and pencil museum sketches—hand axes, baskets, fire drills, mosquito fans, feather holders—that one hardly sees in monographs anymore. And despite occasional *Tristes Tropiques* lyricisms about the sounds of the forest or the colors of the afternoon, the prose style is straightforward and concrete. This happened, and that. They believe this, they do that. Only the musing, threnodic first-person voice, breaking every now and again into moral rage, suggests that there may be more going on than mere reporting of distant oddities.

Second, James Clifford. Trained as an intellectual historian at Harvard in the early seventies, but self-converted, first to anthropology and then to cultural studies (he now teaches in the History of Consciousness Program at the University of California, Santa Cruz), he is, at fifty-two, rather more along toward the Middle of the Journey than Clastres was when he took off for Paraguay; but they are of the same academic generation—the one the counterculture made. Clifford wanders about in the nineties, diffident and inquisitive, not among castaway "natives," or indeed any "peoples" at all, but among what he calls "contact zones"—ethnological exhibitions, tourist sites, art-show seminars, museum consultancies, cultural studies conferences, travelers' hotels. He visits Freud's archaeologically enhanced London home. He passes through the hyped and hybridized Honolulu of professional conventions, Pro Bowl football fans, and sunken battleships on Chinese New Year, just as Desert Storm erupts in the Persian Gulf. He reminisces about his youth as a "white ethnic," son of a Columbia academic, ridin' the subways through folk-song New York. He meditates upon history, domination, and "global dynamics" before a Russian stockade from the 1820s, reconstructed as a multicultural heritage park in "'postmodern' California."

The book assembling these excursions and stop-ins into a fable for our times he calls *Routes*, with the pun on "roots" heavily intended, to which he adds the carefully contemporizing subtitle, *Travel and Translation in the Late Twentieth Century*.[6] Here, though the first person voice again appears throughout, rather more assertive and far more self-referring, there is no continuous, building narrative, ethnographic or any other. There is, instead, an unordered series of "personal explorations," designed to depict neither "natives, in villages " nor "pure traditions and discrete cultural differences," but rather "people going places," "hybrid environments," "travelling cultures."[7]

The prose is various and indirect. Sometimes it is "academic," that is, abstract and argumentative, sometimes it is "experimental," that is, inward and impressionistic; always, it is discursive, backing and filling, giving with one hand and taking away with the other, turning aside to pursue a notion, retracing steps to get back to the subject. The pieces run from three or four pages to forty or fifty. The photographs are either reproduced catalogue illustrations—illustrations of illustrations—or amateur, unfocused snapshots, taken on the fly by Clifford as he goes. There are no descriptions of anyone marrying, fighting, worshiping, declaiming, dying, or mourning; no accounts of how children are raised or demons placated. And where, save for a passage from Montaigne, Clastres has but a single citation in his whole book, and that a paraphrase summary of some pages in a clerical history of the conquest of Paraguay, Clifford has literally hundreds, sometimes a dozen a page, running from Mikhail Bakhtin, Stuart Hall, Walter Benjamin, Antonio Gramsci, and Fredric Jameson to Malinowski, Mead, Rushdie, Gauguin, Amitav Ghosh, Michel de Certeau, and Adrienne Rich—most of them more atmospheric than substantive. He calls all this—"written under the sign of ambivalence . . . *in medias res* . . . manifestly unfinished"—a collage.[8] Like Joseph Cornell's magical boxes, "enclosed beauty of chance encounters—a feather, ball bearings, Lauren Bacall," or like those *déclassé* Parisian hotels, "places of collection, juxtaposition, passionate encounter" from which the Surrealists launched their "strange and wonderful urban voyages," *Routes* "asserts a relationship among heterogeneous elements in a meaningful ensemble, . . . struggle[s] to sustain a certain hope, and a lucid uncertainty."[9]

In sum: (1) A romantical pilgrim on a self-testing Quest, confronting the Ultimate Other down deep in the jungle. ("I had really arrived among savages," Clastres writes. "The enormous gap . . . between us . . . made it seem impossible for us ever to understand one another.")[10] (2) A reserved, middle-distance spectator moving uneasily through a postmodern hall of mirrors. ("Night in the crowded streets: smoke from food stands, running young men and women from a martial-arts club, a dragon, University of Hawaii jazz ensemble, all-Asian saxophone section. . . . In slow motion [an Iraqi] building implodes.")[11] They hardly seem to belong to the same universe, much less to the same profession.

And yet, these two world-describers, world-imaginers, world-comparers, differently trained, differently committed, and hardly, if at all, aware of one another (Clastres died, at forty-three, in a 1977 car crash, two years before Clifford began publishing; Clifford, for all his interest in French anthropology, never so much as alludes to Clastres), manage, between them, to frame, in its starkest terms, the most critical issue facing cultural anthropology in these, postcolonial, postpositivist, post-everything times. This is the value, the feasibility, the legitimacy, and thus the future of localized, long term, close-in, vernacular field research—what Clifford at one point lightly calls "deep hanging out," and Clastres exalts on almost every page ("I had only to look about me at the daily life: even with a minimum of attention I could always discover something new").[12]

Without a master theory, without a set-apart subject matter, and, now that all the natives are citizens and the primitives minorities, without even a settled and undisputed professional niche, cultural anthropology is more dependent for its identity, its authority, and its claim to attention on a particular research practice than is virtually any other science, social or natural. If fieldwork goes, or anyway so it is feared on the one hand and hoped on the other, the discipline goes with it.

⌒

Clastres's remote, unreadable "savages," enclosed in a world of hunting, violence, ordeal, and demoniacal animals—"the forest's fatal metaphors"—are, as a matter of fact, a good deal less pristine than might at first appear.[13] They are actually refugees, displaced by the Paraguay government two and a half years earlier to a state-run trading post at the edge of the forest—dispirited, decultured, "pacified." Thrown together there with former enemies (with whom they conclude an almost parodic "peace pact"), still wandering now

and again into the forest to hunt, and casually overseen by a Para-
guayan "protector," who is rather more sympathetic to them than
most of his compatriots, who regard them as cattle, they are, by the
time Clastres arrives, clearly and precipitously dying out.

By the time he leaves, they are down from their original hundred plus to at best seventy-five. Five years later, though he never
goes back to visit them during a visit to Paraguay ("I have not had
the heart to. What could I possibly find there?"), they are fewer
than thirty.[14] By the time of his own death they are gone altogether—"eaten away by illness and tuberculosis, killed by lack of
proper care, by lack of everything." They were, he says, in a haunting image, like unclaimed objects, left luggage. "Hopelessly forced to
leave their prehistory, they had been thrown into a history that had
nothing to do with them except to destroy them."

> The whole (colonial) enterprise that began in the fifteenth
> century is now coming to an end; an entire continent will soon
> be rid of its first inhabitants, and this part of the globe will
> truly be able to proclaim itself a "New World." "So many cities
> razed, so many nations exterminated, so many peoples cut
> down by the sword, and the richest and most beautiful part of
> the world overthrown for the sake of pearls and pepper! Me-
> chanical victories." So Montaigne hailed the conquest of
> America by Western Civilization.[15]

On the basis of some offhand, and extremely dubious, as well as
extremely old-fashioned, physical anthropology, Clastres regards the
Guayaki as, in all probability, remnants of the earliest human inhabitants of the area, perhaps of the entire continent. Though their
skin color ranges from "the Indian's classical copper, though less
pronounced, to white—not the European's pinkish white, but a
dull, grayish white, like the gray skin of a sick person," he calls
them, as the Paraguayans do, and the Spaniards did before them,
"white Indians." And so they see themselves: when an unusually
dark, thus cursed, child is born, its grandmother is obliged to stran-
gle it.

Whatever their color, most of these "original" Guayaki were
either killed off or assimilated in the course of a war of conquest by
the later-arriving, intensely militaristic, "mongoloid" Tupi-Guarani,

still the main Indian group in the area. The few who escaped simple annihilation abandoned the cultivation they long had practiced and fled into the forests to become nomadic hunters—driven into impoverishment, exile, and cultural regression, not, as elsewhere on the continent, by Europeans, who only began to have at them in the seventeenth century, but by other Indians. Thus, the Guayaki, the first of the first inhabitants, are not just "savages." They are the savages' savages—fading traces of the socially elemental:

> [The Guarani] cannot accept differences; unable to suppress these differences they try to include them in a familiar code, in a reassuring set of symbols. For [the Guarani] the Guayaki do not belong to a different culture, *because there can be no such thing as differences between cultures*: they are outside the rules, beyond common sense and above the law—they are Savages. Even the gods are against them. Every civilization . . . has its pagans.[16]

It is, thus, "Savagery," that is, *la civilisation sauvage*, and its fate that most concerns Clastres, and in this he is a quite orthodox Structuralist, though he never uses the term or applies its contrived vocabulary. Like his mentor, whose heir he was supposed to have been, he contrasts those societies (Lévi-Strauss calls them "hot") caught up in a relentless, unending process of historical change and those (Lévi-Strauss calls them "cold") which have refused, adamantly and entirely, to become part of that process, resisted it, and sought, with at best the most temporary of successes, to keep their cultures static, free, communal, and undeformed.

> "There are no grownups," someone [actually, it was that paladin of *la civilisation civilisée*, André Malraux, as Clastres knows and assumes his readers will know] wrote recently. This is a strange remark to make in our civilization, which prides itself on being the epitome of adulthood. But for this very reason, it might well be true, at least for our world. For once we step outside our own boundaries, whatever is true for us in Europe no longer applies. We ourselves may never become adults, but that does not mean there are no grown-ups elsewhere. The question

is: Where is the visible frontier of our culture, at what stage along the road do we reach the limit of our domain, where do different things exist and new meanings begin? This is not a rhetorical question, for we are able to situate the answer in a definite time and place. . . . The answer came at the end of the fifteenth century, when Christopher Columbus discovered the people from beyond—the savages of America.

In the Islands, in Montezuma's Mexico, and on the shores of Brazil, the white men crossed the absolute limit of their world for the first time, a limit they immediately identified as the dividing line between civilization and barbarity. . . . The Indians represented all that was alien to the West. They were the Other, and the West did not hesitate to annihilate them. . . . They were all inhabitants of a world that was no longer meant for them: the Eskimos, the Bushmen, the Australians. It is probably too early to gauge the most important consequences of this meeting. It was fatal for the Indians; but by some strange twist of fate, it might also turn out to be the cause of the unexpected death of our own history, the history of the world in its present form.[17]

It is to record, in as fine and circumstantial a detail as possible (though it is sometimes unclear whether he is describing something he has seen, something he has only heard about, or something he thinks must be the case), the beliefs and practices that were Guayaki life—the jaguar myths and the life-stage ordeals, the inconclusive, undirected wars and the powerless, ephemeral nature of leadership—that Clastres writes his book. More exactly, he writes it to expose to us, who can never ourselves encounter these savage grownups as he has, the logic of that life and—cannibalism, infanticide, tapir penises, and all—its moral beauty:

For myself, I most of all want to remember the [Guayaki's] piety, the gravity of their presence in the world of things and the world of beings. To underscore their exemplary faithfulness to a very ancient knowledge that our own savage violence has squandered in a single instant. . . . Is it absurd to shoot arrows over the new moon when it slides among the trees? Not for the

[Guayaki]: they knew that the moon was alive and that its appearance in the sky would make the [women] bleed menstrual blood, which was . . . bad luck for the hunters. They took revenge, for the world is not inert, and you must defend yourself. . . . For many centuries [they] tenaciously maintained their furtive and timid life as nomads in the secret life of the forest. But this shelter was violated, and it was like a sacrilege.[18]

In any case, sacrilege, conquest, or the modern mania for change and progress, they had no choice. "There was nothing to be done. . . . There was death in their souls. . . . Everything was over."[19]

∞

Although Clifford shares Clastres's fierce hostility to (in Clifford's more fashionable, if less eloquent, phrasings) "globalism," "empires," "Western hegemony," "rampant neoliberalism," "commodification," "the ongoing power imbalances of contact relations," "caste and class hierarchies," and, of course, "racism," and shares, as well, his sympathy for the "dominated," the "exoticized," the "exploited," and the "marginalized," he most definitely does not share Clastres's belief in total immersion in the simple and the distant as the royal road to recovering *les formes élémentaires de la vie sociale*. Instead, he sees his mission to be one of "deliver[ing] a sharp critique of [the] classic quest—"exoticist, anthropological, orientalist"—for revelatory "cultural types, villagers, or natives," "condensed epitome[s] of social wholes." Which is, of course, precisely what Clastres was trying with such passion to do: to get to the bottom of things by examining a handful of battered and powerless, left-luggage Indians up close and personal.

Clifford, who is not much interested in the bottom of things, says he wants only to displace what he calls "the fieldwork habitus"—"an ungendered, unraced, sexually inactive subject [interacting] intensively (on hermeneutic/scientific levels at the very least) with its interlocuters"—from its position as the defining characteristic of "real anthropology" and "real anthropologists." He wants to undercut the "licensing function" of going into jungles, to deconstruct the "normative power" of living among people who shoot arrows at the moon. But he has, clearly, a rather larger, more radical aim in mind, than this familiar, tiresome sloganizing suggests. He's out to set anthropology free of its first-world parochialism, its compromised past, and its epistemological illusions—to propel it, and forcefully, "in postexoticist and postcolonial directions."

> Intensive fieldwork does not produce privileged or complete understandings. Nor does the cultural knowledge of indigenous authorities, of "insiders." We are differently situated as dwellers and travelers in our cleared "fields" of knowledge. Is this multiplicity of locations merely another symptom of postmodern fragmentation? Can it be collectively fashioned into something more substantial? Can anthropology be reinvented as a forum for variously routed fieldworks—a site where different contextual knowledges engage in critical dialogue and respectful polemic? Can anthropology foster a critique of cultural dominance which extends to its own protocols of research? The answer is unclear: powerful, newly flexible, centralizing forces remain.[20]

Clifford's wanderings through museums, exhibitions, tourist traps, heritage parks, and the like are less casual, and less innocent, than they look. They are designed to accelerate a rerouting, and "rerooting," of anthropological research: to turn it away from static, high-resolution, Clastres-like descriptions of this or that people, in this or that place, living in this or that way; to turn it toward loose-limbed, "decentered" accounts of peoples, ways of life, and cultural products in motion—traveling, mixing, improvising, colliding, struggling for expression and domination. Such spaces, events, sites, or settings are what he means, borrowing a term from Mary Louise Pratt's study of colonial travel writing, *Imperial Eyes*, by "contact zones."[21]

A contact zone is, in Pratt's words (which Clifford quotes), "the space in which peoples geographically and historically separated come into contact with each other and establish ongoing relations, usually involving conditions of coercion, radical inequality, and intractable conflict." It emphasizes, she says, "how subjects are constituted in their relations to each other"; stresses "copresence, interaction, interlocking understandings and practices . . . within radically asymmetrical relations of power."[22] To view the sort of institutions with which Clifford is concerned, places of cultural display and commemoration, from this perspective is to regard them as political arenas—"power-charged set(s) of exchanges, of push and pull." In such arenas, consequential collages, real-life magic boxes, Clifford's drifting, freestyle anthropology finds its "field."

Among the pieces assembled in *Routes*, most of which seem thoroughly ephemeral, this is perhaps best demonstrated in the one called "Four Northwest Coast Museums," a comparison not just of the museums as such, two national and majoritarian, two tribal and oppositional, but of their contrasting approaches to the collection and display of Indian artifacts, and, even more effectively, in the essay called "Fort Ross Meditation," a highly original, powerful, if somewhat serpentine, portrayal of the North Pacific—Siberia, Alaska, and the Pacific Coast—as "a regional contact zone." "Russian America was an extension of Siberia." "At Fort Ross . . . 'Western' history arrives from the wrong direction."[23]

But throughout, even in the least substantial, throwaway pieces, and despite his genteel, *noli me tangere* persona, the moral seriousness of Clifford's work, his personal concern for the human future and the place of the dispossessed within it, displays itself as intensely, as clearly, and as unremittingly as, in his more *mano a mano*, prophetical voice, Clastres's does:

> At Fort Ross, I hope to glimpse my own history in relation to others in a regional contact zone. . . . Located on the rim of the Pacific, my home of eighteen years, the fort's nineteenth century stories, seen from an uncertain fin-de-siècle, may provide just enough "depth" to make sense of a future, some possible futures. . . . History is thought from different places within an unfinished global dynamic. Where are we in this process? Is it too late to recognize "our" diverse paths into and through modernity? Or too early? . . . All at once, the millennium feels like a beginning.[24]

∞

So: drawing near versus hanging back, confident empiricism versus "lucid uncertainty," the immediacies of the local versus the refractions of the uncentered, insular (and doomed) stability versus global (and encouraging) commotion. These may be a bit crude as binaries; and in such matters there are no pure types. But, for adepts of the special, the singular, the different, and the concrete—that is, among others, anthropologists—they do rather capture the question here: How are we now to practice our trade?

The ready way of dealing with all this would be to see Clastres as the nostalgic voice of a disappeared, exhausted past, professional no less than actual—like Lévi-Strauss's famous characterization of the tropics, out of date—and to see Clifford as a man with the future in his bones, designing an anthropology for an oncoming age of global interconnection, movement, instability, hybridity, and dispersed, anti-hegemonical politics. But that will hardly do. The choice is not between regretting the past and embracing the future. Nor is it between the anthropologist as hero and as the very model of postmodern major general. It is between, on the one hand, sustaining a research tradition upon which a discipline, "soft" and half-formed perhaps but morally essential, has been built and, on the other, "displacing," "reworking," "renegotiating," "reimagining," or "reinventing" that tradition, in favor of a more "multiply centered," "pluralistic," "dialogical" approach, one which sees poking into the lives of people who are not in a position to poke into yours as something of a colonial relic.

There is very little in what the partisans of an anthropology in which fieldwork plays a much reduced or transformed role—an active and growing group of which Clifford is only one of the more prominent members—have so far done that would suggest they represent the wave of the future.[25] It is true that Clastres's Rousseauian primitivism, the view that "savages" are radically different from us, more authentic than us, morally superior to us, and need only to be protected, presumably by us, from our greed and cruelty, is, some New Age enthusiasts aside, not much in favor these days. (Clastres wrote another book before his death, *Society Against the State*, in which he developed some of the ideas set forth in the *Chronicle* in more explicit, not to say polemical, terms, but has not been much noticed.)[26] Even those working desperately to protect peoples like the Guayaki against Western exploitation are not trying to freeze their cultures in time or preserve their societies in aspic; they are trying to give them a voice in their own, surely untraditional, future. But whether the sort of middle-distance, walk-through research Clifford practices and recommends is an advance on the close-in, dogged-does-it sort Clastres carried out with such devotion is far from clear.

Routes, which Clifford says is an extension of his earlier, much praised and much pilloried, *The Predicament of Culture* (a stronger, less desultory, and better written book than *Routes*, as a matter of fact), seems to show a hesitant, stuttering quality (what can I say? how can I say it? with what right do I do so?) not wholly attributable to its exploratory, unfinished nature.[27] Clastres, whatever his orthodoxy and his straight ahead temperament, knew where he was going, and he got there. Clifford, whatever his originality and his openness to experiment, seems stalled, unsteady, fumbling for direction. It is, perhaps, rather too early to exchange roots for routes.

History and Anthropology

One hears a fair amount these days, some of it hopeful, much of it skeptical, and almost all of it nervous, about the supposed impact of Anthropology, the Science, upon History, the Discipline. Papers in learned journals survey the problem with a certain useless judiciousness: on the one hand, yes; on the other, no; you should sup with the devil with a long spoon. Articles in the public press dramatize it as the latest news from the academic front: "hot" departments and "cold"; are dates out of date? Outraged traditionalists (there seems to be no other kind) write books saying it means the end of political history as we have known it, and thus of reason, freedom, footnotes, and civilization. Symposia are convened, classes taught, talks given, to try to sort the matter out. There seems to be a quarrel going on. But a shouting in the street, it's rather hard to make out just what it is about.

One of the things it may be about is Space and Time. There seem to be some historians, their anthropological educations having ended with Malinowski or begun with Lévi-Strauss, who think that anthropologists, mindless of change or hostile to it, present static pictures of immobile societies scattered about in remote corners of the inhabited world, and some anthropologists, whose idea of history is roughly that of Barbara Tuchman, who think that what historians do is tell admonitory, and-then, and-then stories about one or another episode in Western Civilization: "true novels" (in Paul Veyne's phrase), designed to get us to face—or outface—facts.

Another thing the quarrel may be about is Big and Little. The penchant of historians for broad sweeps of thought and action, the Rise of Capitalism, the Decline of Rome, and of anthropologists for studies of small, well-bounded communities, the Tewa World (*which?*), the People of Alor (*who?*), leads to historians accusing anthropologists of nuancemanship, of wallowing in the details of the obscure and unimportant, and to anthropologists accusing historians of schematicism, of being out of touch with the immediacies and intricacies, "the feel," as they like to put it, considering themselves to have it, of actual life. Muralists and miniaturists, they have a certain difficulty seeing what the other sees in contained perfections or in grand designs.

Or perhaps it is about High and Low, Dead and Living, Written and Oral, Particular and General, Description and Explanation, or Art and Science. History is threatened (one hears it said) by the anthropological stress on the mundane, the ordinary, the everyday, which turns it away from the powers that really move the world—Kings, Thinkers, Ideologies, Prices, Classes, and Revolutions—and toward bottom-up obsessions with charivaris, dowries, cat massacres, cock fights, and millers' tales that move only readers, and them to relativism. The study of living societies, it is held, leads to presentism, snapshots of the past as ourselves when young ("The World We Have Lost," "The Fall of Public Man"), as well as to the illegitimate reading of contemporaries as ancestors (*kula* exchanges in Homeric Greece, ritual kingship in Versailles). Anthropologists complain that the historian's reliance on written documents leaves us prey to elitist accounts and literary conventionalisms. Historians complain that the anthropologist's reliance on oral testimony leaves us prey to invented tradition and the frailties of memory. Historians are supposed to be swept up in "the thrill of learning singular things," anthropologists in the delights of system building, the one swamping the acting individual in the onrush of surface events, the other dissolving individuality altogether in the deep structures of collective existence. Sociology, Veyne says, meaning by this any effort to discern constant principles in human life, is a science of which the first line has not been written and never will be. History, Lévi-Strauss says, meaning by this any attempt to understand such life sequentially, is an excellent career so long as one eventually gets out of it.

If this is what the argument is really about, this methodological thrashing around amid the grand dichotomies of Western metaphysics, Being and Becoming revisited, it is hardly worth pursuing. It has been quite some time now since the stereotypes of the historian as mankind's memorialist or the anthropologist as the explorer of the elementary forms of the elemental have had very much purchase. Examples of each doubtless remain; but in both fields the real action (and the real divide) is elsewhere. There is as much that separates, say, Michel Foucault and Lawrence Stone, Carl Schorske and Richard Cobb, as connects them; as much that connects, say, Keith Thomas and Mary Douglas, Fernand Braudel and Eric Wolf, as separates them.

The centrifugal movement—any time but now, any place but here—that still marks both enterprises, their concern with what has recently come to be called, with postmodern capital letters and post-structuralist shudder quotes, "The Other," assures a certain elective affinity between them. Trying to understand people quite differently placed than ourselves, encased in different material conditions, driven by different ambitions, possessed of different notions as to what life is all about, poses very similar problems, whether the conditions, ambitions, and notions be those of the Hanseatic League, the Solomon Islands, the Count-duke of Olivares, or the Children of Sanchez. Dealing with a world elsewhere comes to much the same thing when elsewhere is long ago as when it is far away.

Yet, as the irreversibility of the slogan that is commonly used to express this view, L. P. Hartley's "the past is another country" (another country is quite definitely *not* the past), shows, the question is rather more complex; the equivalence of cultural distance between, say, us and the Franks and us and the Nigerians is a good deal less than perfect, particularly as there may be, these days, a Nigerian living around the corner. Indeed, not even the "us," "the Self" that is seeking that comprehension of "the Other," is exactly the same thing here, and it is that, I think, which accounts both for the interest of historians and anthropologists in one another's work and for the misgivings that arise when that interest is pursued. "We" means something different, and so does "they," to those looking back than it does to those looking sideways, a problem hardly eased when, as is increasingly the case, one tries to do both.

The main difference is that when "we" look back, "the Other" appears to us as ancestral. It is what somehow led on, however vagrantly, to the way we live now. But when we look sideways that is not the case. China's bureaucracy, pragmatism, or science may remind us forcibly of our own; but it really is another country, in a way even Homeric Greece, with adulterous gods, personal wars, and declamatory deaths—which remind us mainly of how our minds have changed—is not. To the historical imagination, "we" is a juncture in a cultural genealogy, and "here" is heritage. To the anthropological imagination, "we" is an entry in a cultural gazetteer, and "here" is home.

These at least have been the professional ideals, and until fairly recently reasonable approximations of the actualities as well. What has progressively undermined them, both as ideals and as actualities, and stirred up all the anguish is not mere intellectual confusion, a weakening of disciplinary loyalty, or a decline of scholarship. Nor, for the most part, has "trendiness," that voluminous sin academic Tories attribute to anything that suggests to them that they might think thoughts other than those they have already thought, played much of a role. What has undermined them has been a change in the ecology of learning that has driven historians and anthropologists, like so many migrant geese, on to one another's territories: a collapse of the natural dispersion of feeding grounds that left France to the one and Samoa to the other.

This can be seen, these days, on all sides: in the greater attention by Western historians to non-Western history, and not only of Egypt, China, India, and Japan, but of the Congo, the Iroquois, and Madagascar, as autonomous developments, not mere episodes in the expansion of Europe; in anthropological concern with English villages, French markets, Russian collectives, or American high schools, and with minorities in all of them; in studies of the evolution of colonial architecture in India, Indonesia, or North Africa as representations of power; in analyses of the construction of a sense of the past (or senses of it) in the Caribbean, the Himalayas, Sri Lanka, or the Hawaiian Islands. American anthropologists write the history of Fijian wars, English historians write the ethnography of Roman emperor cults. Books called *The Historical Anthropology of Early Modern Italy* (by a historian) or *Islands of History* (by an anthropologist), *Europe and the People without History* (by an anthropologist) or *Primitive Rebels* (by a historian), seem quite normal. So does one called *Anthropologie der Erkenntnis*, whose subject is the intellectual evolution of Western science.[28] Everybody seems to be minding everybody else's business.

As usual, what such shifts in the direction of interest come to practically can be more securely grasped by looking at some work in fact going on—real geese, really feeding. In the human sciences, methodological discussions conducted in terms of general positions and abstracted principles are largely bootless. A few possible exceptions possibly apart (perhaps Durkheim, perhaps Collingwood), such discussions mainly lead to intramural bickering about the proper way to do things and the dreadful results ("relativism," "reductionism," "positivism," "nihilism") that ensue when, perversely or in ignorance, they aren't done that way. The significant methodological works in both history and anthropology—*The King's Two Bodies*, *The Making of the English Working Class*, or *The Structure of Scientific Revolutions*; *The Social Organization of the Western Pueblos*, *Trade and Markets in the Early Empires*, or *The Forest of Symbols*—tend at the same time to be significant empirical works, which is perhaps one of the deeper characteristics that, across whatever divides of aim and topic, most connects the two fields.[29]

I shall take as my cases in point, then, two moderately sized bodies of work. The first is that of a small, fairly definable clutch of social historians who, involving themselves with anthropological ideas and anthropological materials, have found themselves drawn more and more deeply into the darknesses that plague that discipline. The second is that of a rather larger number of historians and anthropologists, who, having discovered an interest in common they did not know they had, have produced a series of unstandard writings suffused with uncertain debate. The one, which I shall refer to as the Melbourne Group, mainly because its protagonists are from Melbourne and form a group, provides a nice progression of examples of the continuum between anthropologized history and historicized anthropology; the other, which I shall refer to as the Symbolic Construction of the State, because that is what its wranglers are wrangling about, provides a well-bounded instance of what happens when historians and anthropologists explicitly try to coordinate their efforts with respect to a topic traditional to them both. These are but samples, partial and quite arbitrary, and schematicized at that, of what is going on right now in looking backward/looking sideways sorts of study. But they do reveal something of the promise offered, the difficulties encountered, and the achievements already in place.

☙

The members of the Melbourne Group with whom I will be concerned (there are apparently some others, whose work I do not know) are Rhys Isaac, whose *The Transformation of Virginia* is a study of the vicissitudes of colonial culture on the way to the revolution; Inga Clendinnen, whose *Ambivalent Conquests* is an analysis of the encounter of Spanish and Indian forms of life in the Yucatan peninsula during the middle of the sixteenth century; and Greg Dening, whose *Islands and Beaches* seeks to trace the destruction of Marquesan society under the impact of Western intrusions into it after the 1770s.[30] Three places, three times, one problem: the disequilibration of established ways of being in the world.

This paradigm, if that is what it is, is most bluntly apparent in Isaac's book, because he divides his work into two more or less equal halves, one static, one dynamic. The first, called "Traditional Ways of Life," presents the outlines of planter-dominated culture up to around 1750 or 1760 in a synchronic, snapshot manner—a social order not without interior strains or endogenous directions of change, but essentially in balance. The second, called "Movements and Events," traces the disruption of this settled order by the appearance of elements—most especially evangelical Christianity and, toward 1776, American nationalism—that its simple hierarchies could not contain. An image, thus, of a social cosmos—Planter Life, and all that went with it (country houses, horse races, court day, patriarch slavery, formal dancing, and the muster field)—coming apart along the fissures induced in it by "stern faced [Northern] preachers," New Lights and others, exciting the populace and "factious [Southern] republicans," Patrick Henry and others, haranguing the elite: "[The] great men [set] up fine brick courthouses and churches as emblems of the rule they sought to exercise and of the divinity legitimizing that rule . . . Within half a century of its apparent consolidation the system [was] overturned."[31]

This picture of the ragged Forces of History shattering the crystal Patterns of Culture, consensus first, dissensus after, makes possible a quite straightforward approach toward sorting the gazetteer from the genealogy as frameworks for placing a distant society in relation to one's own. The first goes in the first part, constructing the image, the second goes in the second, accounting for its transience. Anthropology gets the tableau, History gets the drama; Anthropology the forms, History the causes.

At least partly out of the same impulse—the desire to distinguish the events that arise from differences in outlook from the differences in outlook that arise from events—Clendinnen, too, divides her book into more or less equal, dialectical halves. But in her case the division is not between what is moved and what moves it; it is between two peoples, one a cultural scouting party a long way from home, one a cultural fortress deeply *in situ*, locked in an encounter neither of them can really understand.

The two parts of her book are thus called simply "Spaniards" and "Indians," and the same sort of distribution, though rather less radical, of historical narrative to the one half and ethnographic portraiture to the other takes place. Here, however, the order is reversed; the drama comes before the tableau, the disruption before what was disrupted. In the first, "Spanish" section, the historical actors—"explorers," "conquerors," "settlers," "missionaries"—are set out and their exploits, and exploitations, chronicled, as are the conflicts among them, the crisis through which their enterprises passed, the mental world within which they operated, and the final outcome, the consolidation of Spanish power. In the second, "Indian" section, an image of Mayan society and the passions that animated it—stoicism, cosmography, human sacrifice—is delicately reconstructed out of what is admittedly a fragile and fragmentary native record.

The story the book has to tell (or the picture it has to present) is consequently not one of a consensual social order forced into disarray by the entrance onto its public stages of obstreperous men with contrarious ideas, but of a profound cultural discontinuity between intruder and intruded upon, a discontinuity that grows only more profound as their relations intensify. Familiarity breeds incomprehension: to the Spanish, possessed of "that extraordinary European conviction of their right to appropriate the world," the Maya appear less and less reachable the closer they come to them; to the Maya, "the objects and victims of Spanish world-making," the Spanish appear less and less assimilable the more they become entrenched. Everything ends in a terrible, and blood-drenched "hall of mirrors"—clerical floggings and folk crucifixions: "The product of the miserable confusion which besets men when they do not understand the speech of others, and find it easier to make of them familiar monsters than to acknowledge them to be different."[32] An Anthropological tragedy with a Historical plot.

Dening, too, divides his book in half, putting what historians would call the story in the one part and what anthropologists would call the analysis in the other. Only he does it, so to speak, lengthwise. To each substantive chapter on one or another phase in the 160-year European-Marquesan encounter ("Ships and Men," "Beachcombers," "Priests and Prophets," "Captains and Kings"), he appends a topically oriented interchapter called a "Reflection" ("On Model and Metaphor," "On Rites of Passage," "On Boundaries," "On Religious Change," "On Dominance," "On Civilizing"), which sets forth a more or less systematic array of ideas for interpreting what has just been related. The textual movement here is less between what was and what happened to it, as in Isaac, or between incommensurable sensibilities, as in Clendinnen, as between alternative styles of rendering such matters—cultural mutation and cultural misconnection—generally intelligible. Though he started as a historian and ended as one, Dening took a doctorate in anthropology along the way, and he is engaged in an enterprise somewhat eccentric to both fields: the writing, as he puts it, of a "discourse on a silent land."

It is silent because, unlike the Virginia Planters, echoes of whose outlook persist today, if only as social claims and ancestral fantasies, or the Mayan Indians, segments of whose civilization continue as folk tradition beneath the Hispanic personality of modern Mexico, the Marquesans, as Marquesans, simply are no more: "Death [carried them] off . . . before they had the time or the will to make any cultural adaptation to their changed environment."[33] There are people living in the Marquesas, of course, at least some of them physical descendants of those who lived here before the Captains, Priests, and Beachcombers arrived; but they are "dispossessed," their history ruptured, themselves turned into generalized, indefinite "Pacific Islanders":

> Everybody's past is dead, [the Europeans' and the Marquesans'] together. Events happen only once. Actions are gone with their doing. Only the history of the past has some permanence, in the ways consciousness gets preserved in writing or in memory or in the presumptions of every social act. But for [the Marquesans] even their history is dead. All the history that is left to them . . . binds them to those whose intrusion on their Land caused them to die. Events, actions, institutions, roles become history by being translated into words. In [the Marquesans'] case, these are [the Europeans'] words in their description of the Land. Even [the Marquesans'] own words about their lives, collected in legends or even in dictionaries, cannot escape this fundamental reality. There is not a legend or a genealogy that has survived that was not collected many years after [the Europeans'] intrusion. They belong to the time of their writing down.[34]

The behindhand collectors, the appropriating writers-down, were, these being "primitives," mainly anthropologists, though a few originals, like that expansive beachcomber Herman Melville, were also involved. The classic ethnographers of the place, those from whom we know most of whatever we know about Marquesan society in that *illo tempore*, "the ethnographic present"—Karl von Steinem, E.S.C. Handy, Ralph Linton—all came to the islands well after the Western mariners, traders, missionaries, and vagabonds had done their civilizing, or decivilizing, work. (Handy's *The Native Culture in the Marquesas*, upon which "virtually every model of [indigenous Marquesan society that] have been constructed" are founded, was published only in 1923.)[35] The result is that "Marquesan Culture" has become a Western reality, no longer a Marquesan one.

> [A]t one time [the Marquesans'] legends, their genealogies, the very continuity of their living culture kept them conscious of their past, told them the way their world should be. They were dispossessed even of these. Like their material artefacts, their customs and their ways were transformed into [European] cultural artefacts. Their living culture died and was resurrected as a curiosity and a problem about such things as cannibalism or polyandry. . . . All [their] words, [their] consciousness, [their] knowledge, were extracted from [the islands] and put in the service not of continuity or identity for the [Marquesans], but of entertainment, education and edification for the Outsiders. The [Marquesans'] lives ceased to be part of their discourse with themselves [which, unlike that of the Virginians and the Mayans was of course wholly unwritten] and became instead part of [European] discourse.[36]

We have moved (logically, not chronologically—Dening's book is the earliest of the three, Clendinnen's the most recent) from Anthropology as the state of affairs upon which History acts, through Anthropology as the jungle through which History stumbles, to Anthropology as the grave in which History is buried.

Taken together, these three works suggest that the conjoining of History and Anthropology is not a matter of fusing two academic fields into a new Something-or-Other, but of redefining them in terms of one another by managing their relations within the bounds of a particular study: textual tactics. That sorting things into what moves and what moves it, what victimizes and what is victimized, or what happened and what we can say about what happened, will not, in the end, really do, is hardly the point. In the end, nothing will really do, and believing otherwise will but bring forth monsters. It is in efforts such as these, and in others employing other rhythms and other distinctions, that what, beside polemic and mimicry, this kind of work has to offer (not least, I suspect, a critique of both fields) will be discovered.

∞

My second example of history-anthropology relations in action is of a rather different sort—not a deliberate tacking between variant modes of discourse, but an unintended, almost happenstance convergence of them upon a common concern: the enmeshment of meaning in power. Since at least the time Burckhardt called the Renaissance state "a work of art," Kantorowicz began to talk about "medieval political theology," or Bagehot noted that Britain was ruled by "an elderly widow and an unemployed youth," historians have become more and more interested in the role of symbolic forms in the development and operation—the construction, if you will—of the state. And since at least the time Frazer began to talk about royal immolation, Eliade about sacred centers, or Evans-Pritchard about divine kings on the upper Nile, anthropologists have become so as well. An odd reference now and then aside, the two interests developed more or less independently until rather recently, when they began, with some force, to break in upon one another. The results have been as one would expect: a burst of work, a bigger burst of questions.

The burst of work is apparent on both sides. A classical historian has written on the celebration of Roman emperors in the Greek towns of Asia Minor; a modern historian has written on Victoria's Diamond Jubilee. There have been studies on the meaning of Constantine's coronation, on imperial funerals in Rome, on "models of rulership in French royal ceremonial," on "rituals of the early modern popes," and someone has brought Kantorowicz forward to Elizabethan times in a work called *The Queen's Two Bodies*.[37]

On the other, the anthropological, hand, where I have myself been a witting, or half-witting, conspirator with my work on "the theatre state" in Java and Bali, there have been studies of the ritual royal bath in Madagascar, a book on *Le roi ivre, ou l'Origine de l'état,*[38] another on "the ritual context of [contemporary] British royalty," in which Princess Di, Elizabeth's handbag ("perhaps the most intriguing royal accessory"), fox hunting, and the Emir of Qatar all figure, as well as more standard ethnographies of the histrionics of sovereignty in Chad, Nepal, Malaysia, and Hawaii. Royal marriage, royal death, royal tombs, and royal succession have all come in for the sort of attention that used to be reserved for kinship terminology, as have regicide, deposition, and whatever the technical term may be for royal incest. A recent, quite partial, bibliographic review lists over fifty titles, from "The Queen Mother in Africa" to "The Stranger King, Dumézil among the Fijians" in the last ten years alone, and "symbolic domination" has become, even if no one is entirely certain just what it means, a standard term of art and invective.

It is from the interplay of the two lines of thought as they have discovered one another that the burst of questions has come. Most of this interplay remains citational in nature; historians of Renaissance Italy mentioning ethnographers of Central Africa, ethnographers of Southeast Asia mentioning historians of Renaissance France. But recently there have been some more intimate conjunctions in the form of symposia collections containing both sorts of study and setting them off against one another in the interests of some more general overview. In two of the best of these, *Rites of Power: Symbols, Ritual, and Politics since the Middle Ages,* emerging from the Davis Center for Historical Studies at Princeton a couple of years ago, and *Rituals of Royalty, Power and Ceremonial in Traditional Societies,* emerging from the Past and Present group in Britain last year, the problems that have arrived with the advances are as apparent as they are unresolved.[39]

The most vexed of these, and the most fundamental, is simply: How much does the symbolic apparatus through which state power forms and presents itself, what we are used to calling its trappings, as though it were so much gaud and decoration, really matter? To do this sort of work at all involves the abandonment of a "smoke and blue mirrors" view of the issue, and of the simpler forms of reductionism—military, economic, structural, biological—that go with it. The signs of power and the substance of it are not so easily pried apart. The Wizard of Oz or How Many Battalions has the Pope won't do, and neither will mutterings about swindles and mystifications. But the question nonetheless remains, and indeed grows more pointed, as to what precisely, and how important, the effects of these royal baths and lordly tooth-filings, majestic effigies and imperial progresses (or, for that matter, television summits and congressional impeachment hearings), are. How are they come by? How are they not? What sort of force does spectacle have?

Sean Wilentz, in the introduction to the Princeton volume, focuses the issue as having to do with "the limitations . . . of symbolic interpretation . . . the limits of *verstehen* in any scholarly enterprise":

If . . . all political orders are governed by master fictions [as anthropologists have claimed], is there any point in trying to find out where historical rhetoric and historical reality diverge? Can historians of the symbolic even speak of objective "reality" except as it was perceived by those being studied, and thereby transformed into yet another fiction? Once we respect political mystifications as both inevitable and worthy of study in their own right—once we abandon crude and arrogant explanations of the origins of "false consciousness" and vaunt the study of perception and experience—is there any convincing way to connect them to the social and material characteristics of any hierarchical order without lapsing into one form or another of mechanistic functionalism? Some historians [he cites E. P. Thompson, Eugene Genovese, and Felix Gilbert] insist that it is still possible—indeed imperative—to make these connections, and they warn of the rise of an "anthropologized" idealism, disrespectful of historical contexts, in which a new fetish of elegant presentation replaces the old fetish of sociological abstraction and cumbersome prose. Others [he cites Natalie Davis, Carlo Ginsburg, and Bernard Cohn] respond that such fears, although justified, need not block the historical study of perception and political culture in ways influenced by the anthropologists' insights.[40]

Cumbersome Prose and Elegant Presentation aside, dire crimes that they doubtless are, the general anxiety that if meaning is too much attended to, reality will tend to disappear (meaning by "meaning" mere ideas and by "reality" munitions and the lash), does haunt this sort of work. The anthropological desire to see how things fit together sits uneasily with the historical desire to see how they are brought about, and the old, nineteenth-century insults, "idealist!" "empiricist!" get trotted out for one more turn around the track. "A world wholly demystified is a world wholly depoliticised," an anthropologist contributor feels called upon to proclaim, as though it were some sort of revelation;[41] "power is, after all, something more than the manipulation of images,"[42] a historian contributor is moved to assure us, as though there were people around who thought otherwise.

This question—how can we bring the articulations of power and the conditions of it into some comprehensible relation?—continues to trouble the discussions, in some ways even more internally torn, in the Past and Present collection.

David Cannadine, who introduces the volume with an essay that seems to change direction with every paragraph, sees the problem as arising from the combination of a general recognition, on the part of both anthropologists and historians, that "the whole notion of power as a narrow, separate and discreet [sic] category [is] inappropriate . . . the idea that splendour and spectacle is but . . . window-dressing . . . ill-conceived," with the absence in either field of anything in the way of a more adequate conception. "If conventional notions of power seem to be unsatisfactory, what if anything may be better put in their place?" We need, he says, and his contributors for the most part follow him, to ask such questions as: "Why exactly is it that ceremonies impress?" "[W]hat are the building bricks from which [such ceremonies] are actually constructed? "[D]oes ceremonial convert systems of belief about celestial hierarchies into statements of fact about earthly hierarchies . . . [or]

does ceremonial convert statements of fact about power on earth into statements of belief about power in heaven?" "Why . . . do some societies seem to need more ceremonial than others?" "How does pomp appear to the alienated or the dispossessed?" "What is the connection between the overthrow of royalty and the overthrow of rituals?" "Why does some pageantry take root and 'work,' and some dwindle and die?"[43]

Except for the fact that the problem may lie less in a too narrow conception of power than in a too simple conception of meaning, a philosophical mistake not a definitional one, these are indeed the sort of questions this odd coupling of semiotical anthropologists and institutional historians has cast up. And if navigating in strange waters doesn't induce fears of going overboard so intense as to inhibit motion altogether, some of them may even come to be, in some degree, and however rephrased to make them less flat-footed, answered.

Certainly they seem likely to go on being asked. A recent book (by an anthropologist, but it could these days be as easily by a historian) on *Ritual, Politics, and Power* discusses, among other things, Ronald Reagan's visit to Bitburg, the funeral rites for Indira Gandhi, the arms control meetings between Soviet and American leaders, the cannibal rites of the Aztec state, the inauguration of American presidents, a parade of Ku Klux Klan members in the 1940s, the activities of contemporary terrorist groups, the "healing" ceremonies of seventeenth-century French and British kings, and May Day march-bys in Moscow.[44] What looked like a nice little problem now looks like a nice little mess—which is perhaps what one should expect when the two most multifarious enterprises in the human sciences, however opportunistically, however nervously, combine forces.

∞

The recent surge of anthropologists' interest not just in the past (we have always been interested in that), but in historians' ways of making present sense of it, and of historians' interest not just in cultural strangeness (Herodotus had that), but in anthropologists' ways of bringing it near, is no mere fashion; it will survive the enthusiasms it generates, the fears it induces, and the confusions it causes. What it will lead to, in surviving, is distinctly less clear.

Almost certainly, however, it won't lead much further than it already has either to the amalgamation of the two fields into some new third thing or to one of them swallowing up the other. That being the case, a good deal of the anxiety on either hand concerning the dissipation of proper scholarly character (usually referred to, limply, as "rigor"), and the defensive polemics it gives rise to, are, to say the least, misplaced. Most particularly, the concern on the History side (which seems the greater, perhaps because there are more Personages there) that trafficking with anthropologists will lead to soul loss is, given the enormous discrepancy in the size of the two fields, to say nothing of their cultural weight, ludicrous. Any conjunction, whether as a mixture of discourses or as a convergence of attention, is bound to be an elephant and rabbit stew ("take one elephant, one rabbit . . ."), about which the elephant need not unduly worry as to its savor coming through. As for the rabbit, it is used to such arrangements.

If work of the originality, force, and fine subversiveness as that I have reviewed, and an enormous lot, reaching out from all parts of both fields toward all parts of the other, that I have not, is to prosper (to get through a discussion like this without mentioning the *Annales*, structuralism, Marxism, *The Life and Death of the Senecas*, or Philippe Ariès is a bit of a tour de force in itself), a sharper sensitivity to the conditions—practical, cultural, political, institutional—under which it is taking place would seem to be necessary. The meeting, collusively or otherwise, of a scholarly tradition, vast, venerable, and culturally central, closely connected to the West's effort to construct its collective self, and a much smaller, much younger, culturally rather marginal one, closely connected to the West's effort to extend its reach, has a structure of its own. In the end, it may be in a deeper understanding of the "and" in the "History and Anthropology" *accouplement* that progress lies. Take care of the conjunctions and the nouns will take care of themselves.

"Local Knowledge" and Its Limits: Some Obiter Dicta

1. "Local" clearly is a "relative" term. In the Solar System, Earth is local (as has been brought home, in good anthropological manner, by leaving it at least temporarily to look back at it from the Moon

and other orbits); in the Galaxy, the Solar System is local (*Voyager* should help with that); and in the Universe, the Galaxy is local (a while to wait, perhaps, for this). To a high energy physicist, the particle world—or zoo—is, well, the world. It's the particle, a thread of vapor in a cloud of droplets, that's local.

2. Thus the opposition, if we must have one (and I am not persuaded an opposition—*another* opposition—is what we need or ought to want, rather than a shifting focus of particularity), is not one between "local" knowledge and "universal," but between one sort of local knowledge (say, neurology) and another (say, ethnography). As all politics, however consequential, is local, so, however ambitious, is all understanding. No one knows everything, because there is no everything to know.

3. The failure to see this shining truth by people otherwise apparently rational is the result, in part, of an endemic confusion in the social (or human) sciences (or scientists) among: (a) *universals* ("everybody has," to quote a false, or at least a highly misleading example, "the incest taboo"); (b) *generalizations*, which may be probabilistic, have exceptions or contradictions without fatality, or may be mere *ceteris paribus*, "as a rule" approximations that are instrumentally useful ("Horticultural societies are more peaceful than pastoral ones"—but consider the Maya, regard the Lapps); and (c) *laws*. (It is hard to produce an example—"group marriage to matriliny to patriliny"—in cultural anthropology, or indeed anywhere in the human sciences, that is not laughable or outmoded. Perhaps a proposal from a few years back that cultural traits diffuse—that is, migrate across the globe—on an average of plus or minus two miles a year conveys some of the comic effect involved.)

4. My own view, merely to give it, because in a short compass I can hardly defend it, is that either: (a) most (conceivably all) universals are so general as to be without intellectual force or interest, are large banalities lacking either circumstantiality or surprise, precision or revelation, and thus are of precious little use ("People everywhere have views about differences between the sexes"; "All societies have systems of social ranking"; "Powerlessness tends to corrupt, absolute powerlessness tends to corrupt absolutely"—this last, which is of course my transformation, exemplifies another char-

acteristic of many universals: like reversible raincoats, they can be worn either way); or (b) if universals do have some degree of non-triviality, circumstantiality, and originality, if they actually assert something interesting enough to be wrong (the ubiquity of the Oedipus complex, the functional necessity for psyches and societies of mourning customs, the solidarity-making force of the gift), they are ill-based. We are ethnographically acquainted with only a very small proportion of the societies that have existed; of those, only an even smaller proportion have been systematically studied, and those that have been systematically studied have not been studied evenly or comprehensively. We may or may not know something about Oedipus notions in the Trobriands or Sri Lanka; I don't know that anyone has even thought to look into the matter for the Havasupai—or, if perchance (I haven't checked) someone has, then the Montenegrins, the Incas, or the Kabyles. There is a tremendous unevenness, as well as a tremendous instability, in anthropological attention. Nothing gets studied everywhere or for very long. Until not long ago, there wasn't much of use on the kinship system of the Navajo, though kinship is one of our most obsessively investigated subjects and the Navajo are one of our most thoroughly researched groups.

This is not remediable—not by setting up Notes-and-Queries-type schedules, standardized research training programs, or what-ever. Nor should we, in my view, try thus to remedy it. The search for universals leads away from what in fact has proved genuinely productive, at least in ethnography (I don't think *only* in ethnography, but I will let others argue the other cases)—that is, particular "intellectual" obsessions (Malinowski's about exchange, Lévi-Strauss's about animal symbolism, Evans-Pritchard's about divina-tion)—toward a thin, implausible, and largely uninstructive com-prehensiveness. If you want a *good* rule-of-thumb generalization from anthropology, I would suggest the following: Any sentence that begins, "All societies have . . . " is either baseless or banal.

5. Generalities of the "not in the South" sort can, of course, be had and can, of course, be useful; but more as heuristic starting points for deeper-going local inquiries than as bankable conclusions fit for textbooks. ("Funeral rites are a good thing to look into if you are interested in a people's conceptions of the self." "In Southeast

Asia, status differentiation tends to be unusually important, gender contrast rather less so; in North Africa, contrariwise," "Child raising practices have a lot to do with adult personality.") Most of the more valuable of these are *conceptual* generalities of a proof-of-the-pudding sort: if they really get you somewhere, fine; if not, the hell with them. Linguistic ones, back in favor of late, in part as a result of the Chomskyan revolution (or, as I think, counterrevolution, but let that pass for the prejudice it is), tend to be like this: noun/verb distinctions, markedness regularities, etc. They do indeed seem to have broad applications, though claiming they are universally applicable is either dogmatical, tautological, or a regress to the vacuities I discussed just above. As surface signs of more deeply-lying matters, however, they are the shale (it is hoped) above the oil field.

All this is not the same as saying that the search for broad generalities is the obvious or best way to go, though there is admittedly something about anthropology—its up-from-the-ape, study-of-man sweep, perhaps—that seems to encourage it. To put the matter another way, even the generalizations of so-called cognitive anthropology—the ethnobotany work, Berlin and Kay's color work (often misread, perhaps even by its authors, in "universals" terms)—are surely to some degree cosmopolitan in nature, though how cosmopolitan is not always clear. Reading them into the world in a "realist" manner, as part of the very furniture of things, is another matter, one I also cannot get into here, save to say that I think it a dubious proposition. "Species" are "real," so far as they are, precisely in the way that (so far as it is) "power" is.

6. As for laws, I have already suggested that I can't think of any serious candidates in my field with which to contend. One of the most irritating things in my field is people who say you're not doing "real science" if you don't come up with laws, thereby suggesting that they themselves have done so, without actually telling you what these laws are. On the rare occasions they do tell you—two miles a year, cannibalism and protein shortage—the situation is worse. Scientism, and here I *will* talk of the human sciences overall, is mostly just bluff. It's one thing to call the spirits from the misty deep, quite another to make them come when you do call them. But it is not just imposture that's involved: the utopianism induced

by a misconceived view of pre-twentieth-century physics (the world before Maxwell) that was imported into the human sciences has led not to the gates of paradigm-land, but to a great deal of wasted motion and high proclamation.

7. So much for negatives. What are the virtues of a "local knowledge" sort of tack?

a. *Limits*. The title of this discussion seems to assume that the existence of limits is a counterargument to something. (Why isn't it called "'Universal Knowledge' and Its Limits"? Possibly because to do so would raise the possibility that, being universal, it hasn't got any, and therefore isn't knowledge.) To my limited mind, direct and open acknowledgment of limits—this observer, in this time, at that place—is one of the things that most recommends this whole style of doing research. Recognition of the fact that we are all what Renato Rosaldo has called "positioned (or situated) observers" is one of its most attractive, most empowering features. The renunciation of the authority that comes from "views from nowhere" ("I've seen reality and it's real") is not a loss, it's a gain, and the stance of "well, I, a middle-class, mid-twentieth-century American, more or less standard, male, went out to this place, talked to some people I could get to talk to me, and think things are sort of rather this way with them there" is not a retreat, it's an advance. It's unthrilling perhaps, but it has (something in short supply in the human sciences) a certain candor. (Views from nowhere can be imaginatively constructed, of course. If they are done well they can be, and in the natural sciences have been, immensely useful. But thus constructed, they are in fact a particular variety of view from somewhere—the philosopher's study, the theorist's computer.)

b. *Circumstantiality*. We can at least say something (not of course that we always do) with some concreteness to it. I have never been able to understand why such comments as "your conclusions, such as they are, only cover two million people [Bali], or fifteen million [Morocco], or sixty-five million [Java], and only over some years or centuries," are supposed to be criticisms. Of course, one can be wrong, and probably, as often as not, one is. But "just" or "merely" trying to figure out Japan, China, Zaire, or the Central Eskimo (or better, some aspect of their life along some chunk of their world line) is not chopped liver, even if it looks less impressive than explanations, theories, or whatnot which have as their object "History," "Society," "Man," "Woman," or some other grand and elusive upper-case entity.

c. Of course, comparison is both possible and necessary, and it is what I and others of my persuasion spend most of our time doing: seeing particular things against the background of other particular things, deepening thus the particularity of both. Because one has located, one hopes, some actual differences, one has something genuine to compare. Whatever similarities one might find, even if they take the form of contrasts . . . or incomparabilities . . . are also genuine, rather than abstract categories superimposed on passive "data," delivered to the mind by "God," "reality," or "nature." (Otherwise, Santayana's comment that people compare when they can't get to the root of the matter becomes all too true.) Theory, which is also both possible and necessary, grows out of particular circumstances and, however abstract, is validated by its power to order them in their full particularity, not by stripping that particularity away. God may not be in the details, but "the world"—"everything that is the case"—surely is.

8. But the critical issue involved in the local versus universal tension in the "human sciences" (and I have already indicated my discomfort with that way of putting things—"versus" should be left to prize fights, elections, wars, and the law courts) is: What do we want from those "sciences"? What does, or should, "science" mean here? There is not much point in arguing about whether to involve ourselves with matters inextricable from "this time or that place," or to look past such matters to ask how everything, everywhere, always is, unless we are clear about what we expect to gain by taking one tack or the other. The dispute, which seems to be about the worth of different paths to an agreed destination, is really about the worth of alternative destinations, however arrived at. We are divided less by method—one uses what avails—than by what we are up to.

The contrast here is familiar, but not less important for that: between those who believe that the task of the human sciences (though they are more likely to call them "behavioral") is to discover facts, set them into propositional structures, deduce laws, predict outcomes, and rationally manage social life, and those who believe that the aim of those sciences (though sometimes they will not agree to call them "sciences") is to clarify what on earth is going on among various people at various times and draw some conclusions about constraints, causes, hopes, and possibilities—the practicalities of life.

Whether the first view is, as some people have said, a bit like wanting to know where you will die so as never to go near the place, or the second, as others have said, is like blowing out the candle and cursing the darkness, is perhaps less important (though it is hardly unimportant) than which enterprise we in fact see ourselves as pursuing. If advances in the technical, fine-tuning control of social life (Bentham's dream, Foucault's nightmare) is what you are after, then universality talk is, I guess, the talk to talk. If you are after refinements in our ability to live lives that make some sense to us and of which we can on balance approve (Montaigne's skeptical hope, Weber's desperate one)—moral skills, not manipulative ones—then something less vaulting would seem to be called for.

Those of us who take the second view (a growing number, I think, now that the ideologies of disincarnate knowing have been somewhat shaken) have, of course, much to make clear and even more to make persuasive. But we are working on it and need not be unduly worried, except perhaps politically, about measuring up to standards emerging from the first one, fishing for other fish, perhaps inedible, in other seas, perhaps unpopulated. What Stephen Toulmin has called "the recovery of practical philosophy" has its own agenda and its own ideas about how to advance it. What he lists as "the return to the oral" (he really means to rhetoric, utterances, speech acts, discourse, narrative, conversation, and language games—not the literally oral, but the linguistically so), to "the particular," to "the local," and to "the timely," is a movement not a doctrine and, like any movement, needs achievement not *dicta* to sustain it. What we need (to give a dictum) are not contemporary reenactments of old debates nomothetic and ideographic, *erklären* and *verstehen*, but demonstrations, on the one side or the other, of either an effective technology for controlling the overall directions of modern social life or the development and inculcation of more delicate skills for navigating our way through it, whatever directions it takes. And when it comes to that, I am reasonably confident both as to which is the more desirable and the more likely actually to occur.

Who knows the river better (to adopt an image I saw in a review of some books on Heidegger the other day), the hydrologist or the swimmer? Put that way, it clearly depends on what you mean by "knows," and, as I have already said, what it is you hope to accomplish. Put as which sort of knowledge we most need, want, and might to some degree conceivably get, in the human sciences anyway, the local variety—the sort the swimmer has, or, swimming, might develop—can at the very least hold its own against the general variety—the sort the hydrologist has, or claims method will one day soon provide. It is not, again, a matter of the shape of our thought, but of its vocation.

I don't know if this is an adequate "response to the critical claims of universality and authority" against work which emerges from "historical point(s) in time or . . . geographical point(s) in space" (as the charge to this discussion puts it), or even what would count as "adequate" here. But, like all "local knowledge," it is substantive, somebody's, and will do for the moment.

Notes

1. Gananath Obeyesekere, *The Apotheosis of Captain Cook: European Mythmaking*, Princeton: Princeton University Press, 1992; Marshall Sahlins, *How "Natives" Think, About Captain Cook, for Example*, Chicago: University of Chicago Press, 1995.

2. The simplest and most accessible of Sahlins's many statements of his views is probably *Historical Metaphors and Mythical Realities: Structure in the Early History of the Sandwich Islands Kingdom*, Ann Arbor: University of Michigan Press, 1981, later expanded in a chapter of his *Islands of History*, Chicago: University of Chicago Press, 1985. For Obeyesekere's more general views, see his *The Work of Culture: Symbolic Transformation in Psychoanalysis and Anthropology*, Chicago: University of Chicago Press, 1990.

3. "Goodbye to *Tristes Tropes*: Ethnography in the Context of Modern World History," *The Journal of Modern History* 65 (1993): 1–25.

4. Neither author has very much to say about this, though Obeyesekere promises us a psychoanalytic biography of Cook, relating Cook's conception of

himself as a Prospero "domesticating a savage land" when he is actually a Kurtz who "becomes the very savage he despises" to his "complex sexuality," where perhaps more will be offered. For an extensive examination of the cultural environment (Wordsworth's Cambridge) from which one explorer-discoverer emerged, a young astronomer killed in a manner rather similar to Cook, but on Oahu and thirteen years later, see Greg Dening, *The Death of William Gooch: A History's Anthropology*, Honolulu: University of Hawaii Press, 1995.

5. P. Clastres, *Chronicle of the Guayaki Indians*, tr. Paul Auster, New York: Zone Books, 1998. (Originally published as *Chroniques des indiens Guayaki*, Paris: Plon, 1972.)

6. J. Clifford, *Routes: Travel and Translation in the Late Twentieth Century*, Cambridge: Harvard University Press, 1997.

7. *Ibid.*, pp. 21, 5, 2 17.

8. *Ibid.*, pp. 10, 12.

9. *Ibid.*, pp. 18, 12.

10. Clastres, *Chronicle*, pp. 91–92.

11. Clifford, *Routes*, p. 241.

12. *Ibid.*, p. 56 and note 2; Clastres, *Chronicle*, p. 315.

13. Clastres, *Chronicle*, p. 276.

14. *Ibid.*, p. 345.

15. *Ibid.*, pp. 345–346.

16. *Ibid.*, p. 15, italics in original.

17. *Ibid.*, pp. 141–142.

18. *Ibid.*, p. 348.

19. *Ibid.*, p. 346.

20. Clifford, *Routes*, p. 91.

21. M. L. Pratt, *Imperial Eyes: Travel Writing and Transculturation*, London: Routledge, 1992.

22. *Ibid.*, pp. 6–7.

23. Clifford, *Routes*, pp. 302, 304, 303.

24. *Ibid.*, pp. 343–344.

25. For a general view of this school of thought, see Clifford and Marcus, eds., *Writing Culture: The Poetics and Politics of Ethnography*, Berkeley: University of California Press, 1986. The emerging field of "cultural studies," with which Clifford has become increasingly involved, provides even clearer examples of this sort of nonimmersive, hit-and-run ethnography.

26. Clastres, *Society Against the State: The Leader as Servant and the Human Uses of Power among the Indians of the Americas*, New York: Urizen Books, 1977.

27. J. Clifford, *The Predicament of Culture*, Cambridge: Harvard University Press, 1988.

28. P. Burke, *The Historical Anthropology of Early Modern Italy*, Cambridge: Cambridge University Press, 1987; E. R. Wolf, *Europe and the People*

without History, Berkeley: University of California Press; E. J. Hobsbawm, *Primitive Rebels: Studies in Archaic Forms of Social Movement in the Nineteenth and Twentieth Centuries*, New York: Praeger, 1963; Y. Elkana, *Anthropologie der Erkenntnis*, Frankfurt-am-Main: Shrkamp, 1988.

29. E. H. Kantorowicz, *The King's Two Bodies*, Princeton: Princeton University Press, 1957; E. P. Thompson, *The Making of the English Working Class*, New York: Vintage, 1963; T. S. Kuhn, *The Structure of Scientific Revolutions*, Chicago: University of Chicago Press, 1962; F. Eggan, *The Social Organization of the Western Pueblos*, Chicago: University of Chicago Press, 1962; K. Polanyi et al., eds., *Trade and Markets in the Early Empires*, Glencoe, Ill.: Free Press; V. Turner, *The Forest of Symbols*, Ithaca: Cornell University Press, 1967.

30. R. Isaac, *The Transformation of Virginia, 1740–1790*, Chapel Hill: University of North Carolina Press, 1982; I. Clendinnen, *Ambivalent Conquests: Maya and Spaniard in Yucatan, 1517–1570*, Cambridge: Cambridge University Press, 1987; G. Dening, *Islands and Beaches, Discourses on a Silent Land: Marquesas 1774–1880*, Melbourne: Melbourne University Press, 1980.

31. Isaac, *The Transformation of Virginia*, p. ix.

32. Clendinnen, *Ambivalent Conquests*, pp. xi, 128, 188.

33. Dening, *Islands and Beaches*, p. 287.

34. *Ibid.*, p. 273.

35. See E. S. C. Handy, *The Native Culture in the Marquesas*, Honolulu: University of Hawaii Press, 1923. The quote is from Dening, *Islands and Beaches*, p. 279.

36. Dening, *Islands and Beaches*, p. 329.

37. M. Axton, *The Queen's Two Bodies: Drama and the Elizabethan Succession*, London: Royal Historical Society, 1977.

38. L. de Heusch, *The Drunken King, or, The Origin of the State*, Bloomington: Indiana University Press, 1988.

39. S. Wilentz, ed., *Rites of Power: Symbols, Ritual and Politics since the Middle Ages*, Philadelphia: University of Pennsylvania Press, 1985; Cannadine and S. Price, eds., *Rituals of Royalty, Power and Ceremonial in Traditional Societies*, Cambridge: Cambridge University Press, 1987.

40. S. Wilentz, "Introduction," in Wilentz, ed., *Rites of Power*, pp. 7–8.

41. C. Geertz, "Centers, Kings, and Charisma: Reflections on the Symbolics of Power," in *ibid.*, p. 30.

42. J. H. Elliott, "Power and Progaganda in the Spain of Philip IV" in *ibid.*, p. 147.

43. D. Cannadine, "Introduction," in Cannadine and Price, eds., *Rituals of Royalty*, p. 15.

44. D. I. Kertzer, *Rituals, Politics, and Power*, New Haven: Yale University Press, 1988.

$\mathcal{V}I$ ∞

The Strange Estrangement: Charles Taylor and the Natural Sciences

In the opening paragraphs of the introduction of his *Philosophical Papers*, Charles Taylor confesses himself to be in the grip of an obsession.[1] He is, he says, a hedgehog, a monomaniac endlessly polemicizing against a single idea—"the ambition to model the study of man on the natural sciences." He calls this idea many things, most often "naturalism" or "the naturalistic world view," and he sees it virtually everywhere in the human sciences. The invasion of those sciences by alien and inappropriate modes of thought has conduced toward the destruction of their distinctiveness, their autonomy, their effectiveness, and their relevance. Driven on by the enormous (and "understandable") prestige of the natural sciences in our culture, we have continually been led into a false conception of what it is to explain human behavior.

The purpose of this polemic, aside from the desire to rid the human sciences of some "terribly implausible," "sterile," "blind," "half-baked" and "disastrous," enterprises[2]—Skinnerian behaviorism, computer-engine psychology, truth-conditional semantics, and primacy-of-right political theory—is to clear a space in those sciences for "hermeneutic" or "interpretivist" approaches to explanation. Interpretation, the "attempt to make sense of an object of study" in some way "confused, incomplete, cloudy . . . contradictory . . . unclear,"[3] is an irremovable part of any would-be science of human affairs. And it is precisely that which "the natural science model," with its passion for *Wertfreiheit*, predictability, and brute facts—defensible enough in its proper domain—effectively blocks.

Those who, like myself, find the argument that the human sciences are most usefully conceived as efforts to render various matters on their face strange and puzzling (religious beliefs, political practices, self-definitions) "no longer so, accounted for,"[4] to be altogether persuasive, and Taylor's development of it magisterial, may nonetheless find themselves disturbed to notice after a while that the "opposing ideal"[5] to which this view is being so resolutely contrasted, "natural science," is so schematically imagined. We are confronted not with an articulated description of a living institution, one with a great deal of history, a vast amount of internal diversity, and an open future, but with a stereotype and a scarecrow—a Gorgon's head that turns agency, significance, and mind to stone.

Taylor's references to "natural science," though extremely numerous, appearing in almost every essay in *Philosophical Papers*, are, both there and elsewhere in his work, marked by two characteristics: they are virtually never circumstantial, in the sense of describing actual examples of work in physics, chemistry, physiology, or whatever in a more than glancing fashion, and they are virtually all to the opening stages of the scientific revolution—Galileo, Bacon, Descartes, Newton, Boyle—not to anything in any way remotely contemporary. Like so many of the "Others" that we construct these days to haunt us with their sheer alterity, The Japanese, The Muslims, or *L'age classique*, his countercase to the interpretively oriented human sciences is generically characterized and temporally frozen. A foil for all seasons.

One can see the reasons for this. The conception of what it is to be "truly scientific" in the human sciences has indeed normally been both rigid and anachronistic, as well as deeply uninformed about the realities of the "real sciences" whose virtues are to be imported into these "softer," "weaker," "less mature" enterprises. Taylor is not wrong to think that the Skinnerian version of behaviorism or the Fodorian version of cognitivism are less extensions of a proven approach to explanation into new fields than parodies of it. Nor is he wrong to think that the rejection of such parodies, and others like them, does not condemn the human sciences to a the-world-is-what-I-say-it-is "Humpty Dumpty subjectivism,"[6] incapable of either framing an honest hypothesis or confronting one with genuine evidence. Yet, it may be that the creation of an out-and-out, fixed and uncrossable gulf between the natural and human sciences is both too high and unnecessary a price to pay to keep such muddlements at bay. It is obstructive at once of either's progress.

The notion of such a gulf, a dichotomy as opposed to a mere difference (which latter no one clothed and in their right mind would want to deny), traces, of course, back to the *Geisteswissenschaften* versus *Naturwissenschaften*, *verstehen* versus *erklären* conceptualization under which, with Dilthey, modern hermeneutics got definitively under way, and which, with Heidegger and Gadamer, Ricoeur and Habermas, "is very strong in the later twentieth century."[7] And there can be little doubt (at least, I don't have any) that this to-each-its-own view of things did yeoman service in defending the integrity and vitality of the human sciences—sociology, history, anthropology, political science, less so psychology, less so yet economics—under the enormous pressures exerted upon them in the heyday of positivism, logical or otherwise. Without it, Taylor's worst nightmares might well have come true and we would all be sociobiologists, rational-choice theorists, or covering-law axiomatizers. The issue is whether so radically phrased a distinction is any longer a good idea, now that the point has been made, and made again, that the human sciences, being about humans, pose particular problems and demand particular solutions, and that the idea of a "social physics" seems a quaint fantasy of times gone by. Are either the human or the natural sciences well served by it? Is the conversation across the *corpus callosum* of our culture inhibited, or prevented, by this sort of commissural surgery? Is such surgery to the disadvantage of both, reductive to half-brained reasoning? Is an eternal methodological civil war, the Hermeneuts versus the Naturalists, in anyone's interest?

The questions are, of course, rhetorical—not to say, tendentious. The homogenization of natural science, both over time and across fields, as a constant other, an "opposing ideal" permanently set off from other forms of thought, as Richard Rorty has put it, "by a special method [and] a special relation to reality," is extremely difficult to defend when one looks at either its history or its internal variety with any degree of circumstantiality.[8] The danger of taking objectivist reductionism as the inevitable outcome of looking to the natural sciences for stimulation in constructing explanations of human behavior is very great without a richer and more differentiated picture of what they are (and the plural is essential here), have been, and seem on their way toward becoming than Taylor has so far recognized. So also is the possibly even greater danger of isolating those sciences themselves in such an outmoded sense of their aim and essence (as well as an exaggerated sense of their own worth), beyond the reach of hermeneutic self-awareness. The tendency toward oversimplification Taylor so rightly deplores seems to thrive, in both the human and the natural sciences, precisely to the degree that the intellectual traffic between them is obstructed by artificial notions of primordial separateness.

∽

Both sorts of schematization of the natural sciences, that which sees them as being without a history, or anyway as having a history consisting only in the development to greater and greater levels of complexity of an epistemological paradigm laid down in the seventeenth century, and that which sees them as an only pragmatically differentiated mass basically defined by their adherence to that paradigm, are essential to the notion that they form a closed off world, sufficient unto itself. Without either, and certainly without both, such a notion seems distinctly less obvious.

The view that the history of natural science consists in the mere development from a once-and-for-all foundational act ("[The] great shift in cosmology which occurred in the seventeenth century, from a picture of a world-order based on the ideas to one of the universe as mechanism, was the founding objectification, the source and inspiration for the continuing development of a disengaged modern consciousness"[9]) not only neglects both historiographical works, of which Thomas Kuhn's is probably the most famous, stressing ruptures, wanderings, and discontinuities in the advance of those sciences and the complications that have been forced on the idea of "disengaged consciousness" by quantum-level theorizations—Heisenberg, Copenhagen, and Schrödinger's cat.[10] It more importantly leaves out a fact which Gyorgy Markus, speaking of "a second scientific revolution" which occurred during the second half of the nineteenth century, has pointed out: the characteristic features of the natural sciences, which Taylor takes to be so destructive when imported into psychology and politics, are not a direct-line projection into our times of Renaissance and Enlightenment ideas but a much more recent, and quite radical, transformation of them. "Natural science as the cultural genre which *we* know . . . is the product of a nineteenth-century development in which [its] cognitive structure, institutional organization, cultural forms of objectivity and . . . global social function have changed together."[11] The world before Maxwell is, in fact, not a very good model of "naturalism" as now understood. It was a stage in a project (or, more accurately, an assemblage of projects) still going on.

And as it is still going on, and not, so it looks from the outside, becoming all that consensual in its self-understandings, it may transform itself again; unless history really is over, it almost certainly will do so. There are, in fact, more than a few signs that it is already in the process of doing so. The emergence of biology (not just genetics and microbiology, but embryology, immunology, and neurophysiology) to the point where it threatens the status of physics as the archetype of scientific enquiry; the epistemological and ontological problems besetting physics itself ("don't ask how it can be that way, it can't be that way"); the increasing difficulty of "big," that is expensive, science in isolating itself from public scrutiny, as well as the increasing tenuousness of practical spin-off arguments for funding much of it; the return of cosmology as a general cultural concern, the appearance of experimental mathematics, the growth of computer-mediated "sciences of complexity" (negative entropy, fractals, and strange attractors)—all these matters, and others, suggest that the withdrawal of the natural sciences over the last 120 years or so from connections with any discourse but their own is not the permanent condition of things.[12]

It may not be the permanent condition of things (to my mind, it almost certainly is not) because, alongside the enormous gains in cognitive power that have accomplished it, there have been considerable costs as well, costs by now severe enough to imperil the gains. The most serious of these is, as Markus points out, precisely the extreme narrowing of the cultural significance of the natural sciences that Taylor, anxious to keep them away from interfering with our conceptualization of human affairs, seems so determined to reinforce:

> Seventeenth-to-eighteenth century "natural philosophy" still had a markedly multifunctional character and was in general successfully communicated to socially and culturally divergent groups of addressees. Even those works which represented the most formidable difficulties of understanding, like Newton's *Principia*, quickly became not only objects of widely read "popularizations," but also exercised a deep influence upon . . . other, already culturally . . . separated forms of discourse: theological, properly philosophical and even literary ones. In their turn, these discussions occurring in "alien" genres seriously influenced that more narrowly scientific impact of the works concerned, and were usually regarded as having a direct bearing upon the question of their truth. . . . It is only with the deep transformation of the whole organizational framework of natural scientific activities . . . that the audience's specialization and professionalization became established during the nineteenth century . . . simultaneously with the professionalization of the scientist-author's role itself. It is in this process that the *république des savants* of the eighteenth century, still loosely uniting scientists, philosophers, publicists and cultivated amateurs, has been transformed into a multitude of separated *research communities* comprising the professional specialists in the given area and now posited as the sole public for the relevant scientific objectifications.

This historical process in which the monofunctional character of the contemporary natural sciences has first been formed, at the same time meant a progressive *narrowing of their cultural significance*. . . . When the cultural closure of natural scientific discourse upon itself becomes a fact . . . the divorce of natural scientific inquiry from general culture and cultivation is also inevitable. . . . [It] is now posited as having no significance whatsoever for orienting men's conduct in the world they live in, or their understanding of this lived world itself. Tenbruck aptly formulated it: the view of nature provided by the sciences is no more a world-view.[13]

This is perhaps a bit overstated, even for the nineteenth century, when the "world view" transactions between the sciences technically defined and the general movement of "culture and cultivation" were not altogether attenuated, as witness the "ringing grooves of change" anxieties of a Tennyson or the heat death of the universe resonations of a Kelvin. And, in any case, this image of disconnection again applies rather more to the physical sciences than it does to the biological; the role that Newton, and Newtonianism, played in the eighteenth century, Darwin, and Darwinism, played in the nineteenth. But the general drift is clear enough. The same historical movement that dissolved "the *république des savants*" into "a multitude of separated research communities" produced as well the cultural disengagement of the natural sciences, the cultural entrenchment of the human ones which Taylor opposes to it, and the increasing awkwardness of the relations between them.

If the awkwardness is to be relieved (relieved only, hardly removed) and the natural sciences reinvolved in the self-reflective conversation of humankind, it cannot be by reversing history. The days of the *république des savants*, to the extent they ever existed, are over and unrecoverable. The unavailability of the technical interior of particle physics, neurophysiology, statistical mechanics, or the mathematics of turbulence (and of whatever succeeds them) to anyone beyond the research communities professionally involved with the matters they address is by now but a fact of life. The whole issue needs to be approached in some other way, one which rather than polarizing the intellectual world into a grand disjunction seeks to trace out its obscured dependencies.

∞

The beginning of such a reframing would seem to involve taking seriously the image (and the reality) of a loose assemblage of differently focused, rather self-involved, and variably overlapping research communities in *both* the human and the natural sciences—economics, embryology, astronomy, anthropology—and the abandonment therewith of the Taylor-Dilthey conception of two continental enterprises, one driven by the ideal of a disengaged consciousness looking out with cognitive assurance upon an absolute world of ascertainable fact, the other driven by that of an engaged self struggling uncertainly with signs and expressions to make readable sense of intentional action. What one has, it seems, is rather more an archipelago, among the islands of which, large, small and in between, the relations are complex and ramified, the possible orderings very near to endless. Such questions as (to quote Rorty again) "'what method is common to paleontology and particle physics?' or 'what relation to reality is shared by topology and entomology?'" are hardly more useful than (my inventions, not Rorty's), "is sociology closer to physics than to literary criticism?" or "is political science more hermeneutic than microbiology, chemistry more explanatory than psychology"[14] We need to set ourselves free to make such connections and disconnections between fields of enquiry as seem appropriate and productive, not to prejudge what may be learned from what, what may traffic with what, or what must always and everywhere inevitably come—"reductive naturalism"—from attempts to breach supposedly unbreachable methodological lines.

There is indeed some evidence from within the natural sciences themselves that the continental image of them as an undivided bloc, united in their commitment to Galilean procedures, disengaged consciousness and the view from nowhere, is coming under a certain amount of pressure. In a chapter of his *Bright Air, Brilliant Fire: On the Matter of Mind* called "Putting the Mind Back into Nature," the neurophysiologist and immunologist Gerald Edelman sounds almost like Taylor in his hedgehog resistance to the domination of such presumptions and preconceptions in his own field of enquiry, the development and evolution of the human brain:

> [As] Whitehead duly noted, the mind was put back into nature [from which physics had removed it] with the rise of physiology and physiological psychology in the latter part of the nineteenth century. We have had an embarrassing time knowing what to do with it ever since. Just as there is something special about relativity and quantum mechanics, there is something special about the problems raised by these physiological developments. Are observers themselves "things" like the rest of the objects in their world? How do we account for the curious ability of observers . . . to refer to things of the world when things themselves can never so refer? When we ourselves observe observers, this property of intentionality is unavoidable. Keeping in line with physics, should we declare an embargo on all the psychological traits we talk about in everyday life: consciousness, thought, beliefs, desires? Should we adopt the elaborate sanitary regimes of behaviourism? . . . Either we deny the existence of what we experience before we "become scientists" (for example, our own awareness), or we declare that science (read "physical science") cannot deal with such matters.[15]

Nor is it only vis-à-vis "behaviorism" that Edelman, the natural scientist, sounds like Taylor, the human scientist, railing against sterile, blind and disastrous models of analysis drawn from celebrated but inappropriate places, but with respect to computer-analogy cognitive psychology—AI and all that—as well. He even uses the same term of abuse for it:

> The term "objectivism" has been used to characterize a view of the world that appears at first sight to be both scientifically and commonsensically unexceptionable. . . . Objectivism assumes . . . that the world has a definite structure made of entities, properties, and their interrelationships. . . . The world is arranged in such a way that it can be completely modelled by . . . set-theoretical models. . . .

Because of the singular and well-defined correspondence between set-theoretical symbols and things as defined by classical categorisation, one can, in this view, assume that logical relations between things in the world exist *objectively*. Thus, this system of symbols is supposed to represent reality, and mental representations must either be true or false insofar as they mirror reality correctly or incorrectly. . . .

The . . . development of the computer . . . reinforced the ideas of efficiency and rigor and the deductive flavor that . . . already characterised much of physical science. The "neat" deductive formal background of computers, the link with mathematical physics, and the success of the hard sciences looked endlessly extensible. . . .

The computational or representationalist view is a God's-eye view of nature. It is imposing and it *appears* to permit a lovely-looking map between the mind and nature. Such a map is only lovely, however, as long as one looks away from the issue of how the mind actually reveals itself in human beings with bodies. When applied to the mind *in situ* [that is, in the brain], this [objectivist] view becomes untenable.[16]

It is, no doubt, easier to see the inadequacies of a sheerly oppositionalist "great divide" formulation of the relations between the "human" and the "natural" sciences in work like Edelman's, concerned with the development and functioning of our nervous system, and indeed perhaps in biology, generally, than in work on, say, phase transitions or angular momentum, where God's-eye views would seem less problematical and representationalist mirrorings more in order. But, even if they are (something that itself becomes at least questionable as "things" like wave functions and nonlocality find their way into physical theory), the loss of detail such an overly contrastive view produces obscures other ways of mapping out the landscape of knowledge, other ways of tying together, or separating out, the disciplinary islands of empirical enquiry. "If you don't know Russian," the mathematical physicist David Ruelle has written, "all books in that language will look very much the same to you."

Similarly, unless you have the appropriate training, you will notice little difference between the various fields of theoretical physics: in all cases what you see are abstruse texts with pompous Greek words, interspersed with formulas and technical symbols. Yet different areas of physics have very different flavors. Take for instance special relativity. It is a beautiful subject, but it no longer has mystery for us; we feel that we know about it all we ever wanted to know. Statistical mechanics, by contrast, retains its awesome secrets: everything points to the fact that we understand only a small part of what there is to understand.[17]

Leaving aside the particular judgment here (which I am, of course, incompetent to assess, as I am the strengths or weaknesses of Edelman's neurology), the disaggregation of "the natural sciences" would indeed seem essential to the sort of non-Taylorian, but also nonreductive non-"naturalistic" vision another mathematical physicist, Richard Feynman, in a passage Edelman uses as an epigraph to his book, has of the general project of human understanding:

Which end is nearer to God; if I may use a religious metaphor. Beauty and hope, or the fundamental laws? I think that . . . we have to look at . . . the whole structural interconnection of the thing; and that all the sciences, and not just the sciences but all the efforts of intellectual kinds are an endeavour to see the connections of the hierarchies, to connect beauty to history, to connect history to man's psychology, man's psychology to the working of the brain, the brain to the neural impulse, the neural impulse to the chemistry, and so forth, up and down, both ways. . . . And I do not think either end is nearer to God.[18]

∞

But it is not just from the natural science side, indeed it is not even mainly from that side, that the challenges to strongly binary images of "the whole structural interconnection of the thing" are coming, but precisely from the hermeneutic, intentionalist, agent-centered, language-entranced side that Taylor is, as I am also, so determined to defend against runaway objectivism. The historical, social, cultural, and psychological investigation of the sciences as such—what has come to be known in summary as "science studies"—has not only grown extremely rapidly in the past twenty years or so but has begun to redraw the lines among Markus' "multitude of separated research communities" in a more various, changeful, and particularized way. Looking at "science" from an interpretivist perspective has in itself begun to displace, or at the very least complicate, the Diltheyan picture that has so long held us captive.[19]

Of all the sorts of work that go on under the general rubric of the human sciences, those that devote themselves to clarifying the forms of life lived out (to take some real examples) in connection with linear accelerators, neuroendocrinological labs, the demonstration rooms of the Royal Society, astronomical observations, marine biology field stations, or the planning committees of NASA, are the least likely to conceive their task as limited to making out the intersubjective worlds of persons. Machines, objects, tools, artifacts, instruments are too close at hand to be taken as external to what is going on; so much apparatus, free of meaning. These mere "things" have to be incorporated into the story, and when they are the story takes on a heteroclite form—human agents and nonhuman ones bound together in interpretivist narratives.

The construction of such narratives, ones which enfold the supposedly immiscible worlds of culture and nature, human action and physical process, intentionality and mechanism, has been slow in coming, even in science studies, where they would seem unavoidable. ("Où sont les Mounier des machines, les Lévinas des Bêtes, les Ricoeur des faits?" cries perhaps the most strenuous advocate of such enfolding, the anthropologist of science, Bruno Latour.)[20] These issues were avoided, or, more accurately, never arrived at, by the initial sorties in science studies, then called the sociology of science and associated most prominently with the name of Robert Merton, which confined themselves to "externalist" issues, such as the social setting of science, the reward system driving it, and most especially the cultural norms governing it. "Internalist" issues, those having to do with the content and practice of science as such, were left beyond the range of enquiry. Later work, more influenced by the sociology of knowledge, attempted to address the operations of science more directly, studying such matters as the evolution of theoretical disputes

and the replication of experiments, but in no less objectivist terms—
"standing on social things" (usually summed up rather vaguely as "interests") "in order to explain natural things." It is only quite recently
that an interpretivist tack, one that attempts to see science as the
consilient interplay of thought and things, has begun to take hold.[21]

As they are quite recent, such interpretivist approaches are both
ill formed and variable, uncertain opening probes in an apparently
endless and, at least for the moment, ill-marked enquiry. There are
analyses of the rhetoric of scientific discourse, oral and written:
there are descriptions of human and nonhuman agents as coactive
nodes in ramifying networks of meaning and power; there are ethnographic, and ethnomethodological, studies of "fact construction"
and "accounting procedures"; there are investigations of research
planning, instrument construction, and laboratory practice. But,
however undeveloped, they all approach science not as opaque social precipitate but as meaningful social action: "We have never
been interested in giving a social explanation of anything . . . we
want to explain society, of which . . . things, facts and artefacts, are
major components."[22] This hardly seems the objectivist, agentless
"naturalism" of which Taylor is so rightly wary. Different as they are,
the natural sciences and the human may not be so radically other,
their intellectual congress not so inevitably barren.

⬤

Sciences, physical, biological, human, or whatever, change not only
in their content or their social impact (though they do, of course,
do that, and massively), but in their character as a form of life, a
way of being in the world, a meaningful system of human action, a
particular story about how things stand. Like all such ways, forms,
systems, stories—still life, say, or criminal law—they are constructed in time (and, despite their reach for universality, to an important degree in space as well), and thus any image of them that
remains stable over their entire course and across their whole range
of activities and concerns is bound to turn into an obscuring myth.
Such a myth indeed exists, and, as Taylor has demonstrated, has had
destructive effects upon attempts by those who have bought into it

to explain politics, language, selfhood and mind. But it has also had, as he seems not very clearly to realize, no less baneful effects on, to borrow Woolgar's borrowing of Davidson's slogan, the very idea of science itself.[23]

Taylor's resistance to the intrusion of "the natural science model" into the human sciences seems in fact to accept his opponents' view that there is such a model, unitary, well-defined, and historically immobile, governing contemporary enquiries into things and materialities in the first place; the problem is, merely, to confine it to its proper sphere, stars, rocks, kidneys, and wavicles, and keep it well away from matters where "mattering" matters.[24] This division of the realm, which reminds one of nothing so much as the way some nineteenth-century divines (and some pious physicists) attempted to "solve" the religion versus science issue—"you can have the mechanisms, we will keep the meanings"—is supposed to ensure that ideas will not trespass where they don't belong. What it in fact ensures is symmetrical complacency and the deflation of issues.

There are, as virtually everyone is at least dimly aware, massive transformations now in motion in the studies conventionally grouped under the rather baggy category (does mathematics belong? does psychopharmacology?) of the natural sciences, transformations social, technical, and epistemological at once, which make not only the seventeenth-century image of them, but the late nineteenth and early twentieth ones as well, clumsy, thin, and inexact. The price of keeping the human sciences radically separated from such studies is keeping such studies radically separated from the human sciences—left to the mercy of their own devices.

Such devices are not enough. The outcome of this artificial and unnecessary estrangement is, at once, the perpetuation within the various natural sciences of outmoded self-conceptions, global stories that falsify their actual practice, the "sterile," "half-baked," and "implausible" imitations that those outmoded conceptions and false stories induce in human scientists ignorant of what in fact, physics, chemistry, physiology, and the like come to as meaningful action, and, perhaps worst of all, the production of various sorts of New Age irrationalisms—Zen physics, Maharishi cosmology, parapsychology—supposed to unify everything and anything at some higher, or deeper or wider level.[25]

Fighting off the "naturalization" of the human sciences is a necessary enterprise, to which Taylor has powerfully contributed; and we must be grateful to him for the dauntlessness of his efforts in that regard, and for their precision. Possessed himself of some dusty formulas, he has, to our general loss, not so contributed to the no less necessary enterprise of reconnecting the natural sciences to their human roots, and thus of fighting off *their* naturalization. It is an enormous pity that some of the most consequential developments of contemporary culture are taking place beyond the attention of one of that culture's profoundest students.

Notes

1. The "Introduction" is repeated, with slightly different pagination, in volume 2. The themes in Taylor's work I discuss here run throughout the whole of it, from *Explanation of Behavior*, London: Routledge and Kegan Paul, 1964, to *Sources of the Self*, Cambridge: Harvard University Press, 1989, but for simplicity I shall confine direct citations to *Philosophical Papers*, Cambridge: Cambridge University Press, 1985, 2 vols.

2. Taylor, *Philosophical Papers*, 1: 1, 2: 21, 1: 187, 1: 247, and 2: 92.

3. *Ibid.*, 2: 15.

4. *Ibid.*, 2: 17.

5. *Ibid.*, 2: 117.

6. *Ibid.*, 1: 11.

7. *Ibid.*, 1: 45, 2: 15. As Taylor recognizes, the genealogy of this notion is both deep and wide in Western thought and in its modern version is perhaps as often dated from Vico as Dilthey, its defining exemplar as often seen to be Weber as Gadamer. For a subtle and detailed tracing of the contrast as it has worked itself out from the ancient world forward, sometimes as a difference, sometimes as a dichotomy, sometimes as a mere unclarity, under the original Greek distinction (they seem to have invented *this* too) of *nomos* and *physis*, see Donald Kelley's important study, *The Human Measure, Social Thought in the Western Legal Tradition*, Cambridge: Harvard University Press, 1990.

8. Richard Rorty, "Is Natural Science a Natural Kind?," in his *Philosophical Papers*, Cambridge: Cambridge University Press, 1991, 1: 46. Rorty is, of course, as I am, questioning such a view.

9. Taylor, *Philosophical Papers*, 1: 5.

10. Thomas Kuhn, *The Structure of Scientific Revolutions*, 2nd ed., Chicago: University of Chicago Press, 1977. For an accessible discussion of "quantum weirdness," see Heinz Pagels, *The Cosmic Code: Quantum Physics as the Language of Nature*, New York: Bantum, 1983. The absence from Taylor's major study of "the making of the modern identity," *Sources of the Self*, of any signifi-

cant discussion of developments in physical theory as such is, given this tracing of "modern consciousness" to the mechanical world view, at the very least,
odd. Like the Deist's god, "Science"—Descartes and Bacon, Newton and
Boyle—got the enterprise going, but doesn't seem to have had much of a hand
in it since.

11. Gyorgy Markus, "Why Is There No Hermeneutics of Natural Sciences? Some Preliminary Theses," *Sciences in Context* 1 (1987): 5–51; quotations at 42, 43 (emphasis in original).

12. The "don't ask" quotation has been attributed to Richard Feynman,
but I have no citation for it. For discussions of some of the matters mentioned,
see, again, Heinz Pagels, *The Cosmic Code*; see also *The Dreams of Reason: The
Computer and the Rise of the Sciences of Complexity*, New York: Simon and
Schuster, 1988, and *Perfect Symmetry: The Search for the Beginning of Time*, New
York: Bantam, 1986.

13. Markus, "Why Is There No Hermeneutics of Natural Sciences?," pp.
26, 27, 28, 29; references omitted, reparagraphed, emphases original.

14. Rorty, "Is Natural Science a Natural Kind?," p. 47.

15. Gerald M. Edelman, *Bright Air, Brilliant Fire: On the Matter of the
Mind*, New York: Basic Books, 1992, p. 11.

16. *Ibid.*, pp. 230, 231, 232; emphasis original. For Taylor's very similar
animadversions against "machine modelled explanations of human performance," see his essay, "Cognitive Psychology," *Philosophical Papers*, 1: 187–212;
on "objectivism," "Theories of Meaning," 1: 248–292. For a related attack on
"objectivism" in neurology, there called "diagram making," see Israel Rosen-
feld, *The Strange, Familiar and Forgotten: An Anatomy of Consciousness*, New
York: Knopf, 1992.

17. David Ruelle, *Chance and Chaos*, Princeton: Princeton University
Press, 1991, p. 122. The notion of "appropriate training" necessary to appreciate the differences Ruelle, in a book designed after all for an audience that
doesn't have it, wishes us to appreciate rather more raises a question, and in a
guild-protective form, than answers it. Translation exists, and commentary too
(Ruelle's being a fine example): I don't know Russian, and thus miss much; but
Dostoevsky does not look the same to me as Tolstoy.

18. Cited in Edelman, *Bright Air, Brilliant Fire*, p. vii. The last line suggests that "hierarchy" may not be the best figure, either, for tracing out such a
meshwork of connections.

19. For a brief general review, see Steve Woolgar, *Science, the Very Idea*,
Chichester: Ellis Horwood, 1988; for a current collection of debates and positions in this creatively disorganized, usefully combative field, see Andrew Pickering, ed., *Science as Practice and Culture*, Chicago: University of Chicago Press,
1992; for a sustained study, crossing the human-natural division with something of a vengeance, see Steven Shapin and Simon Schaffer, *Leviathan and the
Air Pump: Hobbes, Boyle, and the Experimental Life*, Princeton: Princeton University Press, 1985.

20. Bruno Latour, *Nous n'avons jamais été modernes: Essai d'anthropologie symétrique*, Paris: La Découverte, 1991, p. 186. This is Latour's most general, and most provocative, statement of position; for more detailed discussion, see his *Science in Action: How to Follow Scientists and Engineers through Society*, Cambridge: Harvard University Press, 1987; for a specific application, *The Pasteurization of France*, Cambridge: Harvard University Press, 1988.

21. The quotation is from H. M. Collins and Steven Yearley, "Journey into Space," a polemic against Latour, in Pickering, ed., *Science as Practice and Culture*, p. 384. For the Merton approach, see his *The Sociology of Science: Theoretical and Empirical Investigations*, Chicago: University of Chicago Press, 1973. For the sociology of (scientific) knowledge approach (SSK), sometimes referred to as "the strong program," see Barry Barnes, *Interests and the Growth of Knowledge*, London: Routledge and Kegan Paul, 1977. I borrow the limpid, if antique, term "consilient" (which seems to me an improvement over, or anyway a useful supplement to, the aesthetical "coherent" as applied to texts, the formalistic "consistent" as applied to beliefs, the functionalist "integrated" as applied to institutions, or the psychologistic "attuned" as applied to persons) from Ian Hacking, "The Self-Vindication of the Laboratory Sciences," in Pickering, ed., *Science as Practice and Culture*, pp. 29–64, a searching examination of the course it celebrates. For an extended discussion, cf. his *Representing and Intervening*, Cambridge: Cambridge University Press, 1985. (Since this note was written, the sociobiologist E. O. Wilson has introduced the word in a quite different sense, totally opposed to mine. See E. O. Wilson, *Consilience: the Unity of Knowledge*, New York: Alfred Knopf, 1998. The term is originally due to William Whewell, whose use comports with my and Hacking's sense, not with Wilson's.)

22. Michel Callon and Bruno Latour, in Pickering, ed., *Science as Practice and Culture*, p. 348. They continue: "Our general . . . principle is . . . not to alternate between natural realism and social realism but to obtain nature and society as twin results of another activity, one that is more interesting for us. We call it network building, or collective things, or quasi-objects, or trials of force; and others call it skill, forms of life, material practice" (references eliminated).

23. Woolgar, *Science*. Cf. Donald Davidson, "On the Very Idea of a Conceptual Scheme," *Proceedings and Addresses of the American Philosophical Association* 47 (1973–74): 5–20.

24. Taylor, *Philosophical Papers*, 1: 197.

25. For some interesting comments on this latter, see Jeremy Bernstein, *Quantum Profiles*, Princeton: Princeton University Press, 1991, esp. pp. vii–viii, 77–84.

$\mathcal{VII}$ ∞

The Legacy of Thomas Kuhn:
The Right Text
at the Right Time

The death of Thomas Kuhn—"Tom" to all who knew him, and considering his principled refusal to play the role of the intellectual celebrity he clearly was, an extraordinary number of people did— seems, like his professional life in general, on the way to being seen, in these days of pomos and culture wars, as but another appendix, footnote, or afterthought to his *The Structure of Scientific Revolutions*, written in the fifties and published in 1962.[1] Despite the fact that he produced a number of other important works, including the at least as original and rather more careful *The Essential Tension* (1977) and the meticulously researched *Black-body Theory and the Quantum Discontinuity, 1894–1912* (1978),[2] whose tepid reception by the physics community, jealous as always of its origin myths, much pained him, it was *Structure*, as he himself always referred to it, that defined him both in the world's eyes and, reactively, in his own. He lived, anguished and passionate, in its shadow for nearly thirty-five years. His obituaries, which were numerous, concentrated almost exclusively on it, including a peculiarly unpleasant one, obtuse and disingenuous, in the London *Economist*, which ended with a taste-less witticism about his undergoing a paradigm shift. And as, in the very last days of his battle with lung cancer, he finally brought his long-awaited, oft-previewed, second pass at its subject, how the sciences change, near enough to completion to be released for publication, his reputation will be fueled by it for many years ahead.

The question then arises: why has *Structure* had such an enormous impact? Why has everyone, from particle physicists and philosophers to sociologists, historians, literary critics, and political theorists, not to speak of publicists, popularizers, and counterculture know-nothings, found in it something either to turn excitedly toward their own ends or to react, equally excitedly, against? It can't just be that the book is bold, innovative, incisive, and marvelously well written. It is all that, and in addition scholarly and deeply felt. But there are other books, within the history of science and outside of it, with such virtues. Excellence and significance, however real, assure neither fame nor consequence—how many people, after all, have attended to Suzanne Langer's *Feeling and Form*? In some mysterious and uncertain way, mysterious and uncertain even to Kuhn, who never ceased to be amazed, puzzled, and seriously troubled about his book's reception, *Structure* was the right text at the right time.

From about the 1920s (and especially after Karl Mannheim's *Ideologie und Utopie* was published in 1929), what came to be called "the Sociology of Knowledge" was applied to one field of intellectual activity after another. Religion, history, philosophy, economics, art, literature, law, political thought, even sociology itself, were subjected to a form of analysis that sought to expose their connections to the social context within which they existed, that saw them as human constructions, historically evolved, culturally located, and collectively produced. Some of this was crude and deterministic, Marxist reductionism or Hegelian historicism. Some of it was subtle and hesitant, a circumstantial tracing of local developments, a qualified suggestion of specific relationships. But, crude or subtle, headlong or tentative, it was, a few exceptions that remained exceptions aside, not applied to what had become the most prestigious, the most forbidding, and, by midcentury, the most consequential intellectual activity of all—the natural sciences.

Set apart in a self-propelled world of thought, physics, chemistry, the earth sciences, even biology, remained unsoiled with sociology, or anyway with the sociology of knowledge. What history there was was mostly practitioner history, monumental and whiggish to a fault; a story of landmark achievements leading, one on to the next, toward truth, explanation, and the present condition of things. What sociology there was, Max Weber's or Robert Merton's, remained largely "externalist," concerned with the social effects of science, the institutional norms which govern it, or the social origin of scientists. So-called internalist matters—why and how the theories and practices of scientists take the forms they do, excite the interest they do, and develop the sway they do—were beyond its reach, explicable, if at all, by the energies of reason, the mysteries of genius, or the simple nature of things impressing themselves on the qualified mind.

It was this apparently unquestionable, supposedly uncrossable line separating science as a form of intellectual activity, a way of knowing, from science as a social phenomenon, a way of acting, that Kuhn in *Structure* first questioned and then crossed. He was, of course, not the only one to do so. Such diverse figures as Norwood Russell Hanson, Michael Polanyi, Paul Feyerabend, Mary Hesse, Imre Lakatos, and later on Michel Foucault and Ian Hacking, some of them critics of some of Kuhn's particular arguments, some of them rivals, some of them simply on trajectories of their own, crossed it as well from the fifties on. But, more than any of these, Kuhn, and *Structure*, cleared the path and, because it is not always either prudent or comfortable to be out in front in a raiding party, drew the fire of the Old Believers. Because the book, originally designed as a maverick entry in Neurath, Carnap, and Morris's positivist-inspired *International Encyclopedia of Unified Science*, was so schematic, sweeping, confident, and uncompromising, it set, by itself, the terms of debate. It became the very image of the study of science as a worldly enterprise; became, to coin a phrase, its dominant paradigm, ripe for imitation, extension, disdain, or overthrow.

It is unnecessary here, and anyway impossible, to review again the hundreds of arguments, for and against, the theses that *Structure* advanced: that scientific change is discontinuous, alternating between long periods of "normal" stability and short bursts of "revolutionary" upheaval; that "normal" scientific research is governed by established exemplars, the famous paradigms, that present models to the relevant community for puzzle-solving; that such paradigms are "incommensurable," and that scientists operating under different paradigms grasp one another's views but partially at best; that "theory choice," the movement from one paradigm to another, is better described as a matter of a gestalt-shift intellectual "conversion" than as a gradual, point-by-point confrontation of the abandoned view with the embraced one; and that the degree to which paradigms have crystallized in a science is a measure of its maturity, its "hardness" or "softness," as well as its distance and difference from nonscientific enterprises. Some of these formulations Kuhn himself modified in a series of appendices, restatements, replies, and "second thoughts." Many he thought were distorted and misunderstood, indeed misused, by his critics and his supporters alike. A few, most especially the claim that scientific change does not consist in a relentless approach to a waiting truth but in the rollings and pitchings of disciplinary communities, he maintained against all attacks from all quarters.

It was, in fact, this last and most far-reaching of its propositions, that made *Structure* itself revolutionary—a call to arms for those who saw science as the last bastion of epistemic privilege or a sin against reason for those who saw it as the royal road to the really real. Whether or not theoretical discontinuities are as prominent in other fields as they supposedly are in physics; whether or not gestalt shifts and incommensurability are the norm in theory change or are ever thoroughgoing; whether theory and generalized statement, conceptual schemes and world views, are really the heart of the matter in the first place—all these can be left to be fought out in the very sort of study *Structure* instances and calls for. What remains as Kuhn's legacy, what enrages his most intransigent opponents and befuddles his most uncritical followers, is his passionate insistence that the history of science is the history of the growth and replacement of self-recruiting, normatively defined, variously directed, and often sharply competitive scientific communities. Or, to quote *Structure* at last, rather than merely alluding to it: "Both normal science and revolutions are . . . community-based activities. To discover and analyze them, one must first unravel the changing community structure of the sciences over time. A paradigm governs . . . not a subject matter but rather a group of practitioners. Any study of paradigm-directed or of paradigm-shattering research must begin by locating the responsible group or groups."[3]

With this firm emplacement of "the sciences" in the world where agendas are pursued and careers made, where alliances are formed and doctrines developed, the world of group efforts, group clashes, and group commitments—the world, in short, we all of us live in—*Structure* opened the door to the eruption of the sociology of knowledge into the study of those sciences about as wide as it could be opened. As the sociology of knowledge was, in the nature of the case, itself ridden with debate, division, and variety of view (as well as, in some of its more exuberant practitioners, a contrarian tone designed to set establishment teeth on edge), its engagement with the sciences was, and remains, more fraught than it had been with literature, history, or political thought, reminiscent, in fact, of its scuffles, prolonged and venomous, with religion. Once launched, however, this application of the categories, reasonings, procedures, and purposes characteristic of the human sciences to the practices of the sciences tendentiously called "real," cannot now be reversed by even the most desperate of countermeasures. Despite cries of "subjectivism," "irrationalism," "mob psychology," and, of course, the favored execration of the entrenched these days, "relativism," all of which have been repeatedly launched against *Structure* (and against "Kuhn," who has been accused, by people from whom one would expect a rather higher level of argument, of disbelieving in the existence of an external world), its agenda, whatever the fate of its particular assertions, is here to stay. The subjection of the sciences to the attentions, sustained and superficial, informed and ignorant, of historians, sociologists, anthropologists, economists, even of science writers and English professors, unwilling to stop at the borders of disciplinary authority or to cower before the solemnities of Nobel laureates, grows apace. This particular genie, once out of the bottle, can't be stuffed back in, however frightening or ill-behaved he (she?) may be—or to whom.

That Kuhn was imperfectly aware of how unruly the genie would turn out to be, and how large, when he published *Structure* is plain enough. The great outburst of sociohistorical science studies, Edinburgh, Paris, Bielefeld, Boston, Jerusalem, San Diego, and so on, as well as the great outburst of jeremiads against them, largely postdated what Kuhn himself characterized in its opening pages as but a reflective essay about some things that had been bothering him since his drifting days in graduate school and in the Harvard Society of Fellows. The causes of all this critique and countercritique, which soon spread to non- (or would-be) scientific fields as well, are various, ill-understood, and much discussed. The changing place of the sciences (and scientists) in contemporary culture, the moral concerns arising from their military applications, and their increasing distance from general intelligibility have all been advanced. So have the growing skepticism about the possibility of value-neutral inquiry, the deepening ambivalence toward rapid technological change, and the university explosions of the late sixties. For others, the end of modernity, New Age mysticism, feminism, deconstruction, the decline of Western hegemony, the politics of research funding, or some combination of these, is the culprit.

Though Kuhn was cognizant of most of these issues, he was not himself so much concerned with them as he was with understanding how science got from Aristotle to Newton, from Newton to Maxwell, and from Maxwell to Einstein, and, given the world's contingencies, what the reasons for its improbable success in doing so might be. "The Bomb" debate aside, to which, so far as I know, he never publicly addressed himself, those reasons were hardly prominent, much less central, in the worried but still composed world of the late fifties and early sixties. They became so independently after the appearance of *Structure*, and were then polemically attached to it by its unexpected, and unintended, mass audience—positively, as a demystification of scientific authority, its re-enclosure in time and society; negatively, as a revolt against it, a repudiation of objectivity, detachment, logic, and truth. He had prayed for rain and got a flood.

Whatever his attitude toward the works, meta-works, and meta-meta works that collected around *Structure* after the late sixties—and it was decidedly mixed—Kuhn found himself in the position of having to state his views over and over again in various sorts of forms and forums. Not that those views were unclear or anything less than direct and straightforward in their first expression. If anything, they may have been a bit too clear. But they had to make their way in a very different intellectual environment from the one in which they were originally formed. Having begun as a "normal" physicist and become a "normal" historian (his case-centered historiography, learned apparently from James Bryant Conant, was as conventional as his arguments were heterodox), Kuhn was far from comfortable with doctrines that questioned either the possibility of genuine knowledge or the reality of genuine advances in it. Nor, for all his emphasis on sociological considerations in understanding theory change, was he ever anything less than scornful of the notion that such considerations affect the truth value of theories of how light propagates or planets move.

Kuhn is not the first person to have accomplished, early on in a career, something which upset a lot of apple carts and who had then to come to terms with its far-reaching implications, some more than a bit unpalatable, as it became in its turn common wisdom. That is surely true of Gödel, who seems rather to have wished his proof had come out the other way and spent a fair part of the rest of his life trying to establish the integrity of reason by other means. And it may have been true of Einstein as well, disturbed by the cleavage in physical theory introduced by his quantal conception of light, and seeking thereafter somehow to close it up again. Living through the aftershocks of an earthquake one has played a major role in bringing about can be as difficult, and as consequential, as producing the original tremor. One needs both serene conviction and settled self-irony to be able to do it. The revolution that Kuhn (who had an embroidered motto hanging in his house which said "God Save This Paradigm") put in motion will be disturbing our certitudes, as it disturbed his, for a very long time to come.

Notes

1. T. S. Kuhn, *The Structure of Scientific Revolutions*, Chicago: University of Chicago Press, 1962.

2. T. S. Kuhn, *The Essential Tension*, Chicago: University of Chicago Press, 1977; Kuhn, *Black-body Theory and the Quantum Discontinuity, 1894–1912*, Chicago: University of Chicago Press, 1978.

3. *The Structure of Scientific Revolutions*, pp. 179–180.

VIII ∞

The Pinch of Destiny:
Religion as Experience,
Meaning, Identity, Power

When, in the last chapter of *The Varieties of Religious Experience*—the one he uneasily calls "Conclusions" and immediately affixes with a corrective postscript which he then promptly disavows—William James comes to look back at what he has been doing for nearly five hundred close-set pages, he confesses himself somewhat taken aback about how soulful it all has been. "In rereading my manuscript, I am almost appalled at the amount of emotionality which I find in it. . . . We have been literally bathed in sentiment."[1] It has all been a matter, he says, of "secret selves" and "palpitating documents"—fragment autobiographies, recounting one or another shaking and evanescent inward episode. "I do not know how long this state lasted, nor when I fell asleep," reads one such, "but when I woke up in the morning *I was well.*"[2] "Everything I did, and wherever I went," reads a second, "I was still in a storm."[3] "[It] seemed to come over me in waves," reads yet a third, "to fan me like immense wings."[4] And so on and so forth, page after confessional page. Religion, James says, with that proverblike concision he uses to rescue himself from the abundance of his own prose, is "the individual pinch of destiny" as the individual feels it. "[The] recesses of feeling, the darker, blinder strata of character," he writes, "are the only places in the world in which we catch real fact in the making . . . directly perceive how events happen . . . how work is done."[5] The rest is notation: it stands to the reality of the thing as a menu does to a meal, a painting of a hurtling locomotive does to its energy and speed, or perhaps, though he doesn't quite bring himself all the way to saying this, as science does to life.

This way of marking out "religion" and "the religious"—the radical individualism ("If an Emerson were forced to be a Wesley, or a Moody forced to be a Whitman, the total human consciousness of the divine would suffer"[6]); the attraction to the wilder shores of sentiment ("I took these extremer examples as yielding the profounder information"[7]); and, above all, the distrust of schemes and schemas (James calls them, his own included, "pallid," "poverty-stricken," "bodiless," and "dead")—gives to *Varieties*, when we look back at it from wherever it is we are now, a curiously double aspect. It seems at once almost ultra-contemporaneous, as though it had been written yesterday about New Age and Postmodern excitements of one sort or another, and quaintly remote, suffused with period atmosphere, like *The Bostonians*, "Self-Reliance," or *Science and Health*.

The sense of contemporaneity is largely an illusion—the derangements of the last fin de siècle are quite different from those of this, and so also are our ways of coping. But the perception that James's great book is, in a nonpejorative sense, if there is a nonpejorative sense, dated, has rather more substance. We see religion in other terms than James did, not because we know more about it than he did (we don't), or because what he discovered no longer interests us or seems important (it does), or even because it itself has changed (it has and it hasn't). We see it in other terms because the ground has shifted under our feet; we have other extremes to examine, other fates to forestall. The pinch is still there, sharp and nagging. But it feels, for some reason, somehow different. Less private, perhaps, or harder to locate, more difficult exactly to put one's finger on; not so surely a reliable indicator or a revelatory sign, not so surely a metaphysical ache.

For what seems most to distance us from James, to separate our spirituality, if that word can be made to mean anything anymore, save moral pretension, from his, is the word I carefully left out of his glittering motto in adopting it for my title: "individual"; "the *individual* pinch of destiny." "Religion," or "religiousness," in his pages, and in his world—transcendentalist New England at the end of its run—is a radically personal matter, a private, subjective, deep-experience "faith-state" (as he calls it), adamantly resistant to the growing claims of the public, the social, and the everyday "to be the sole and ultimate dictators of what we may believe."[8] Growing in James's day, as the United States began not just to be powerful but to feel itself so, such claims have, in ours, become altogether overwhelming. Cordoning off a space for "religion" in a realm called "experience"—"the darker, blinder strata of character"—seems, somehow, no longer so reasonable and natural a thing to try to do. There is just too much one wants to call "religious," almost everything it sometimes seems, going on outside the self.

When the phrase "religious struggle" appears, as it does so often these days, in the media, in scholarly writing, even in churchly harangues and homilies, it tends not to refer to private wrestlings with inner demons. Dispatches from the battlements of the soul are largely left to talk shows and the autobiographies of recovering celebrities. Nor does it refer very often any longer to the effort, so prominent at the last century's turn, when the churches seemed deplete and shriveling and Mammon on the march, to protect the waning authority of religious conviction by removing it to an autonomous realm beyond the reach of the bitch-goddess seductions of secular life, Auden's place of making where executives would never want to tamper. These days, "religious struggle" mostly refers to quite outdoor occurrences, *plein air* proceedings in the public square—alleyway encounters, high court holdings. Yugoslavia, Algeria, India, Ireland. Immigration policies, minority problems, school curricula, sabbath observations, head scarves, abortion debates. Riots, terrorism, fatwas, Aum Supreme Truth, Kach, Waco, Santeria, the storming of the Golden Temple. Political monks in Sri Lanka, born-again power-brokers in the United States, warrior saints in Afghanistan. Anglican Nobelist, Desmond Tutu, works to get South Africans to confront their past; Roman Nobelist, Carlos Ximenes Belo, works to encourage East Timorese to resist their present. The Dalai Lama haunts the world's capitals to keep the Tibetan cause alive. Nothing particularly private—covert perhaps, or surreptitious, but hardly private—about all that.

∞

In James's time it seemed that religion was becoming more and more subjectivized; that it was, in the very nature of the case, weakening as a social force to become a matter wholly of the heart's affections. Secularists welcomed this supposed fact as the sign of progress, modernity, and liberty of conscience; believers were resigned to it as the necessary price of those things. (James, characteristically, was of both minds.) To both, religion seemed to be gravitating to its appropriate place, removed from the play of temporal concerns. But that is not how things have in the event turned out. The developments of the century since James gave his lectures— two world wars, genocide, decolonization, the spread of populism, and the technological integration of the world—have done less to drive faith inward toward the commotions of the soul than they have to drive it outward toward those of the polity, the state, and that complex argument we call culture.

"Experience," however ineradicable it may be from any discourse on faith that is responsive to its regenerative claims (a point I shall return to in the end, when I try to recuperate James from my own critique), no longer seems adequate to frame by itself our understanding of the passions and actions we want, under some description or other, to call religious. Firmer, more determinate, more transpersonal, extravert terms—"Meaning," say, or "Identity," or "Power"—must be deployed to catch the tonalities of devotion in our time. When, as I write, a Roman Catholic could conceivably become the prime minister of India if the present Hinduist government falls, Islam is, de facto anyway, the second religion of France, biblical literalists seek to undermine the legitimacy of the president of the United States, Buddhist mystagogues blow up Buddhist politicians in Colombo, liberation priests stir Mayan peasants to social revolt, an Egyptian mullah runs a world-reforming sect from an American prison, and South African witch finders dispense justice in neighborhood shabeens, to talk of religion as (quoting James's own italicized "Circumscription of the Topic") "*the feelings, acts, and experiences of individual men in their solitude, so far as they apprehend themselves to stand in relation to whatever they may consider the divine,*" would seem to pass over a very great deal of what is going on in the hearts and minds of the pious nowadays.[9]

Nor is this merely a vocational matter, the voice of the psychologist fascinated with emotional depths against that of the anthropologist dazzled by social surfaces. James was not an individualist because he was a psychologist; he was a psychologist because he was an individualist. It is this last, the notion that we believe, if we do believe (or disbelieve, if we disbelieve) in solitude, standing alone in relation to our destiny, our own private pinch, that needs perhaps a certain reconsideration given the warrings and disorders which surround us now.

∞

"Meaning" in the upmarket sense of "the Meaning of Life" or "the Meaning of Existence"—the "Meaning" of Suffering, or Evil, or Chance, or Order—has been a staple of scholarly discussion of religion since anyway the eighteenth century when such discussion began to be phrased in empirical rather than apologetical terms. But it was only with Max Weber's attempt, the boldness of which still astonishes, to demonstrate that religious ideals and practical activities tumble forward together as they move through history, forming in fact an impartible process, that "Meaning" began to be seen as something more, or something other, than a set gloss applied to a settled reality.

When, with this recognition behind us, we look out now at our media-ready world to try to see what is, by some reasonable understanding of the term, "religious" about what is going on there, we do not see, as James did with his absorbed converts, ecstatic solitaries, and sick souls, a bright line between eternal concerns and those of the day; we don't see much of a line at all. Arnold's long, withdrawing roar of the sea of faith from the blanch'd shores of ordinary life is, apparently, for the moment pretty well stilled; the tide is in, and flooding. Meaning (assuming it ever was really away, outside of southern England) is back. The only problem is that it is very hard to figure out what that means.

Most everywhere (Singapore perhaps is still excluded, though, even there, there are evangelist stirrings), we see religiously charged conceptions of what everything, everywhere is always all about propelling themselves to the center of cultural attention. From northern and western Africa, through the Middle East and Central Asia, to South and Southeast Asia, a vast, motley collection of ideologies, movements, parties, programs, visions, personalities, and conspiracies announcing themselves as authentically Islamic have entered the competition for societal hegemony—or, in some cases (Iran, Afghanistan, perhaps Sudan), more or less ended it. On the Indian subcontinent, the place for which the word "myriad" could have been invented, religious nationalisms, subnationalisms, and sub-subnationalisms jockey in a "million mutinies now" scramble for sway, domination, and the right to prescribe the public morality. Yugoslavs, alike in everything but their memories, seize upon religious differences previously unstressed in order to justify their opaque hatreds. The papacy globalizes, reaching out to shape secular society in Africa, Eastern Europe, and Hispanic America. Orthodoxy revives to return Russia to Russianness; prophetic scripturalism revives to return America to Americanness. There are, of course, places where religious views, received or renovated, seem to play little role in public affairs (China, perhaps, or Rwanda-Burundi, also perhaps). But there are more than enough where they play a prominent one to take that fact as a sign of our times.

Reading this sign, unpacking its meaning, or otherwise accounting for it, determining why it is so and how it has become so, what it tells us about how things stand with us these days, is, of course, a different thing altogether. Given the long and honored tradition in the social sciences, one that even Weber was apparently not powerful enough to break, of looking everywhere for the explication of religious developments but to those developments themselves, there has been over the last two or three decades a great outpouring (the Iranian revolution, in 1979, probably marks the return of religion to an important place on our professional agenda, though such matters as Partition, the Kuala Lumpur riots, Vatican II, Martin Luther King, and the recrudescence of the Irish troubles should have alerted us earlier) of theories and explanations invoking political and economic, sociological and historical, in some cases even mass psychological, "madding crowd," circumstances as the underlying forces pushing, determining, causing, shaping, driving, stimulating—all those things "forces" do—religious developments. "Religion" is everybody's favorite dependent variable.

There is nothing in itself so very wrong with this. Despite the encouragement it gives to the besetting sin of sociological study, favorite-cause analysis ("it all comes down to" . . . the personalities of leaders, the strains of modernization, historical memory, mass poverty, the breakup of tradition, inequality, geopolitics, Western imperialism . . .), it has led to suggestive intrepretations both of particular cases and, less often, of the phenomenon in general. There is little doubt that the Milosevics, Karadzics, Tudjmans, and Izetbegovics, to say nothing of the homeboy subcontractors who killed in their names, were, and are, manipulative personalities, driven a good deal more by the vanities of earthly glory, ambition, calculation, jealousy, and self-infatuation than they are by religious, or even ethno-religious, enthusiasms. Equally, it is altogether clear that "Political Islam," as it has come, misleadingly, to be called, whether in the form of Algerian radicalism, Egyptian clericalism, Pakistani militarism, Malaysian traditionalism, or the harassed and scattered progressivist movements that somehow manage to persist just about everywhere, feeds on stagnation and poverty and represents an effort on the part of Muslims finally to engage the demands and energies of the modern world. And the rising tide of communal conflict in India, Nigeria, Sri Lanka, and Indonesia is, in significant part, surely a response to attempts to build strong, centralized, national states in those polyglot, polycultural, polyreligious countries.

All that is well and good. But at the same time Karadzic would not have been able to stir up fears of what he called, with blithe anachronism, "The Turk" in Sarajevo or Tudjman to stir up Croats against the large Serbian minority in Zagreb by plastering the town with "God Protects Croatia" posters, if there wasn't something already there to be stirred up, even in those (then) cosmopolitan, relaxed, and generally secular places. Without a widely diffused sense among the Cairene or Karachi masses of Islam abused and neglected, the Prophecy unheeded and the Prophet demeaned, movements to restore and purify it, and confound its enemies, would have little attraction. And without worries in all sorts of groups, of all sorts of sizes, and all sorts of faith—an anthology of devotions—about politically enforced spiritual exclusion, repression, marginalization, even elimination, state building would seem unlikely, just by itself, to bring on communal riot. To leave religion out of all this, save as a symptom or index of "underlying," "real" dynamics, is not so much to stage the play without the prince as without the plot. The world does not run on believings alone. But it hardly runs without them.

There is, however, a problem in invoking, as I have just been doing to catch your attention, examples in which mass violence is involved—James's "extremer cases . . . yielding the profounder information" (an uncertain principle, in my view). Reliance on such notorious instances obscures the generality and pervasiveness, the mere normalcy, of what is going on by confusing religious contention, which is marked, widespread, and intense enough, with religious fury, which is focused, generally sporadic, and often enough the child of accident. Not every place is Algeria or Sri Lanka, Beirut or Vukovar, Kashmir or Ulster. Twenty million Muslims migrating to the European Union over the course of several decades have caused considerable tension but, so far at least, only scattered brutality. Christians, Hindus, and Muslims have existed in arm's-length peace in Indonesia for fifty years (they have murdered one another for other reasons), though that may now at length be ending. Ethiopia, since the end of, first the emperor, and then the Dergue, seems, more recently, to have managed its religious variety at least reasonably well. The concentration on violence—riots, assassinations. uprisings, and civil war—valuable in itself for understanding how such things happen and what might be done to hinder them from happening, as well as for showing to what red hells our sightless souls may stray, gives a misleading picture of religious conflict by representing it in its most pathological forms. There are profounder matters at work than mere unreason, to which, after all, all human enterprises are subject, not just those concerned with the Meaning of Everything.

Among such profounder matters is surely what has come to called "the search for identity." As "identity politics," "identity crises," "identity loss," "identity construction," the term "identity" has doubtless of late been much abused, pressed into the service of one cause or another, one theory or another, one excuse or another. But that in itself attests to the fact that, for all the jargonizing and slogan mongering, and for all the *partis pris*, something important is afoot. Something, something rather general, is happening to the ways in which people think about who they are, who others are, how they wish to be portrayed, named, understood, and placed by the world at large. "The presentation of self in everyday life," to invoke Erving Goffman's famous phrase, has also become less of an individual matter; less a personal project, more a collective, even a political, one. There are, just about everywhere now, organized efforts, sustained and assiduous, sometimes a good deal more than that, to advance the worldly fortunes of one or another variety of public selfhood. What we have here is a contest of kinds.

Again, not all these kinds are "religious," even under the most extended sense of the term. When someone is asked "who," or more precisely "what," he or she "is," the answer is as likely to be ethnic ("a Serb"), national ("an Australian"), supernational ("an African"), linguistic ("a Francophone"), or even racial ("a White"), or tribal ("a Navajo"), and all sorts of combinations of these ("a Luo-speaking Black Kenyan") as it is religious—"a Baptist," "a Sikh," "a Lubavitcher," "a Bahai," "a Mormon," "a Buddhist," or "a Rastafarian." But, also again, not only are religious self- (and other-) identifications increasingly prominent in public square, "secular" discourse, but some extraordinarily powerful ones, "Hindu," for example, or "Shi'i," have taken on an aggressive world-political currency only rather recently.

The question is, why have religious kinds, and the tensions between religious kinds, come to such prominence? Why have communities of faith become, in so many instances, the axes around which the struggle for power—local power, national power, even to some extent international power—swirls? There is, of course, no single answer to this question, none that will fit the United States, Turkey, Israel, Malaysia, Peru, Lebanon, and South Africa equally well, and the scramble of the so-called New (that is, post-Meiji) Religions in Japan is a phenomenon in itself. But some tentative suggestions and observations may be offered in the way of a preface to exacter and more comprehensive discussions still to be developed of what one can only call the religious refiguration of power politics.

The first such observation is that, as just noted, it is not only religious identities, but ethnic, linguistic, racial, and diffusely cultural ones, that have grown in political salience in the years since decolonization shattered the *outre-mer* empires, and most especially in the decade or so since the fall of the Wall, the collapse of the Soviet Union, and the end of the Cold War shattered the great power relationships in place since Teheran and Potsdam. The strongly binary, not to say Manichaean, East-West alignment of international power balances and the overmastering side-effects that alignment had everywhere from Zaire and Somalia to Chile and Cuba, and within states as well as between them (think of the Philippines, think of Angola, think, alas, of Korea and Vietnam), has largely dissolved, leaving just about everyone uncertain about what now goes with what and what does not—where the critical demarcations lie and what it is that makes them critical. This disassembly of the post-Wall world, its scatteration into parts and remainders, has brought more particular, and more particularistic, forms of collective self-representation to the fore—and not just in Yugoslavia or Czechoslovakia, for example, where the effect is clear and direct, but generally. A proliferation of autonomous political entities, as unlike in their temper as they are in their scale, "a world in pieces," as I call it below in chapter XI, encourages circumscribed, intensely specific, intensely felt, public identities, at the same time as such identities fracture in their turn the received forms of political order that attempt to contain them, most notably these days the nation-state. The projection of religiously defined groupings and loyalties onto all aspects of collective life from the family and neighborhood outward is, thus, part of a general movement very much larger than itself: the replacement of a world tiled with a few very large, ill-fitting, analogous blocks by one tiled, no more evenly and no less completely, with many smaller, more diversified, more irregular ones.

That, of course, is nowhere near the whole of it. Not only are there counterforces at play (economic globalization is ritually invoked as one such, though the recent disarray on the Asian Rim, the accelerating problems in Latin America, and the fumblings of the European Union may begin to make clear that interdependency is very much not the same thing as integration), but there is much more going on than a mere hunkering down within castellated identities. There is increased mobility: Turks in Bavaria, Filipinos in Kuwait, Russians in Brighton Beach. It is not easy any longer to avoid encountering people with other sorts of beliefs than those one grew up with—not even in the American Midwest, where your doctor may well be a Hindu, or in *la France profonde*, where your garbage man is almost certain to be a Muslim.

Thus, religious distinctions not only become, in many places, more fraught; they have also become more immediate. In a footloose world—what good are roots, as Gertrude Stein once said, if you can't take them with you?—simple, to-each-his-own physical separation no longer works very well. We have a great deal of difficulty these days staying out of one another's way: witness British confoundment in the Rushdie affair, witness American court cases about child betrothal, animal sacrifice, municipal crèches, or ritual clitorodectomy. Differences of belief, sometimes quite radical ones, are more and more often directly visible, directly encountered: ready-to-hand for suspicion, worry, repugnance, and dispute. Or, I suppose, for tolerance and reconciliation, even for attraction and conversion. Though that, right now, is not exactly common.

As I say, one could go on this way, listing possible contributing factors to the prominence of religious identities in the dispersed, semiordered, political structure that has, for the moment anyway, replaced the magnificent simplicities of the Cold War. There is the "everything else hasn't worked" argument: successive disillusion with the ideological master narratives—liberalism, socialism, nationalism—as frameworks for collective identity, especially in the newer states, has left only religion as, so the slogan goes, "something which hasn't failed yet." There is the "evils of modernization" argument: the spread of the media, the ravages of development, commerce, and consumerism, and, in general, the moral confusion of contemporary life have turned peoples toward more familiar, more deeply rooted, closer-to-home ideas and values.

And so on. But, the validity of these and similar notions aside (and they remain for the most part unresearched suggestions), there is a more fundamental issue to be addressed if we are to get a handle on what is happening to spiritual life at the end of what some have called, not without evidence, the worst century yet. And this returns us, as I suppose was inevitable, to James's concern, if not necessarily to his way of formulating it: What is going on, to quote him again, in the "recesses of feeling, the darker, blinder strata of character" of those caught up in religiously conceived and religiously expressed struggles for meaning, for identity, and for power? What has become of "the pinch of destiny," now that it seems so much in the world? "Experience," pushed out the door as a radically subjective, individualized "faith state," returns through the window as the communal sensibilty of a religiously assertive social actor.

∞

Communal, yet personal. Religion without interiority, without some "bathed in sentiment" sense that belief matters, and matters terribly, that faith sustains, cures, comforts, redresses wrongs, improves fortune, secures rewards, explains, obligates, blesses, clarifies, reconciles, regenerates, redeems, or saves, is hardly worthy of the name. There is, of course, a great deal of sheer conventionalism about. Hypocrisy, sanctimony, imposture, and self-serving—to say nothing of swindle and simple nuttiness—we have always with us. And there remains, I suppose, the haunting question whether any faith, however profound, is anywhere near adequate to its ends. But the view, which seems to underlie so many analyses of religious expression in these neo-Nietzschean, will-to-power days, that our driving passions are purely and simply political, or politico-economic, and that religion is but mask and mystification, an ideological cover-up for thoroughly secular, more or less selfish ambitions, is just not plausible. People do not burn a Mughal mosque they take to be sited on Lord Rama's birthplace, seek to revive pre-Columbian rituals in Mayan pueblos, oppose the teaching of evolution in Texas and Kansas, or wear headscarves in *l'école primaire* simply on the way to some pragmatical and exterior material end. To rework, and perhaps misuse, Stanley Cavell's celebrated Wittgensteinian title, they mean what they say.

The problem, however, is that if the communal dimensions of religious change, the ones you can (sometimes) read about in the newspapers are underresearched, the personal ones, those you have (usually) to talk to living people in order to encounter, are barely researched at all. We simply don't know very much about what is going on right now in James's shadow world of immense wings and unfleeable storms. And as a result the Weberian interworking of religious convictions and practical actions, the impartibility of belief and behavior, tends to be lost sight of: the two get separated out again, as "factors," "variables," "determinants," or whatnot. The whole vast variety of personal experience, or, more carefully, representations of personal experience, that James, on the one hand, so exquisitely explored, and, on the other, so resolutely walled off from those "dictators of what we may believe," the public, the social, and the everyday, is not only isolated once more from the convolutions of history—it goes unremarked altogether.

Or almost. As an example, a small and preliminary example I can recount only schematically here, of the sort of work that remains to be done in this area and the sort of understandings that can be gained from it, I want to turn, to a recent study by a young anthropologist, Suzanne Brenner, of the reactions some, also young, Javanese women displayed after they suddenly adopted an emphatic form of "Islamic" dress, called after the Arabic for traditional women's clothing, *jilbab*.[10]

Indonesia in general, and Java in particular, have long been religiously variegated to an extraordinary degree. After nearly a millennium of Indic influence, especially on Java, where large and powerful Hindu, Buddhist, and Hindu-Buddhist states arose from the fourth century, it experienced, after 1300 or so, also mainly via South Asia, a strong incursion of Islamic piety, Sufistic in the first instance, and, as time passed and Middle Eastern connections developed via the pilgrimage and otherwise, orthodox Sunni. Finally, or at least finally so far (who knows what is coming next?), after the seventeenth century, when the Dutch arrived, it was subjected to Christian missionizing, both by Catholics and by the various sorts of Protestants that the Netherlands has always been so fertile in producing. The result, by the time of Independence in 1950, was, again most particularly on Java, where 70 percent of the population lives, the copresence of all these faiths, plus a scattering of indigenous ones, differentially distributed through a complex social structure. Eighty or 90 percent nominally Muslim—or, as the Javanese ironically say, *muslim statistik*—the island was, in fact, a forest of beliefs.

In the late seventies, and growing in force through the eighties (the present situation, like so much in Indonesia right now, is not entirely clear), an intensified seriousness, amounting to a new rigorism, began to appear among some of the more self-consciously Muslim Javanese—"an Islamic resurgence," as it has come to be called—stimulated to some degree by the so-called return of Islam generally across the world, but for the most part home-grown, internally driven, and locally focused. There have been a number of expressions of this heightened seriousness—the proliferation of new devotional organizations, the expansion of religious education, the publication of books, journals, magazines, and newspapers and the appearance of a class of, often foreign-educated, Islamic-minded artists, intellectuals, and politicians associated with them, the critical reevaluation and reinterpretation of local traditions from a Quranic point of view, and so on. But one of the most striking, and most controversial, of such expressions has been the adoption by a growing number of young women, most especially educated young women, of Middle Eastern–style clothing: a long, loose-fitting, monochrome gown, reaching to the ankles, designed to conceal the shape of the body, and a long, winding scarf, usually white, designed to conceal the hair and neck.

Such dress (the aforementioned *jilbab*) was occasionally found previously, especially among older, pious women, especially in the countryside. But the adoption of it by younger, urban women—a sharp contrast to the form fitting, low-cut blouse, tightly wrapped sarong, and carefully arranged hair the vast majority of Javanese women traditionally affect—stirred opposition, suspicion, puzzlement, and anger. Intended as a statement, it was taken as one. The women found themselves criticized as "fanatics" or "fundamentalists," often by their own families and their closest friends, some of whom tried strenuously to dissuade them from making the change. ("Why didn't you bring your camel, too?" one girl's enraged father asked her.) They were gossiped about as self-righteous, hypocritical, magically malignant. They were sometimes discriminated against in the job market, and Suharto's "New Order" state instituted dress code regulations (or tried to, in the face of angry demonstrations) designed to discourage them. Occasionally they were even physically attacked, stones thrown at them, their shawls torn from their heads. The decision to wear the *jilbab*, Brenner says, was not one to be made lightly:

> The remarks that women made about the psychological and practical obstacles to [adopting the *jilbab*] that they encountered indicated that it was a decision that required much soul-searching, determination, and even stubborness on their part. [Wearing the *jilbab*] marks a woman as "different" in Java, where norms of behavior are very strong and where defying convention has immediate repercussions for an individual's relationships with others. Donning *jilbab* often leads to a marked change in a young woman's social and personal identity as well as to a potential disruption of the social ties on which she has hitherto relied.[11]

Brenner interviewed twenty women who had made what she calls the "conversion" to *jilbab*. Most were university students or recent graduates in their twenties. All resided in the large central Javanese court cities, Yogyakarta and Surakarta, where religious diversity, even syncretism, has always been particularly marked. Most came from middle- or lower-middle-class backgrounds. Many grew up in religiously undutiful households. All were active in organizations and devotional groups connected with "the Islamic Resurgence."

"The women who spoke to me," Brenner writes,

> were intelligent, strong-minded people who consciously and intellectually struggled with the contradictions of everyday life

and who had their own, highly personal reasons for choosing the routes they had chosen. Most women chose [to wear *jilbab*] partly out of religious conviction, insisting that [it] was a requirement . . . of Islam. Beyond this, however, their narratives exhibited certain themes that showed that adherence to religious doctrine was not the sole impetus. . . . Their motivations . . . were simultaneously personal, religious, and political. . . . [Even] the most personal and emotionally laden stories of conversion to *jilbab* contained within them elements of a larger story that encompasses the contemporary Indonesian Islamic movement.[12]

Brenner has much to say about the connection of all this to Indonesian political developments, to modernization, to the broader movement to reinvigorate Islam, to the revision of gender definitions and expectations, and to the search for personal and collective identity in a rapidly changing world. But for us, what is most to the point is the sort of answers she got when she started asking these young women James-like questions about what becoming a *jilbab* wearer amounted to personally, what it felt like, as something lived through, undergone, "experienced." Intensified self-awareness, the fear of death, the panoptic surveillance of God, a sense of rebirth, a regaining of self-mastery, all the familiar inflections of the pinch of destiny—who am I? what am I supposed to do? what is to become of me? where does finality lie?—appeared, as if on cue.

"Each of the women . . . indicated that changing her clothing in this way" Brenner writes, "changed her feelings about herself and her actions."

For several women the decision . . . had been precipitated by a profound anxiety; that anxiety had then given way to a feeling of relative calm and a sense of renewal after they had begun to wear *jilbab*. The immediate cause of the anxiety . . . had been an overwhelming fear of dying and . . . what death might mean for them if they had failed to fulfill the requirements of Islam. The new awareness of sin they had acquired had led them to a deep distress about how they might suffer in the afterlife as a consequence of their own sinning. . . . They experienced deep confusion, self-doubt, and a sense of being out of control. Donning *jilbab* . . . alleviated their anxieties about death and [gave] them a new feeling of control over their futures in this life and the next.[13]

And she quotes, from a popular magazine, the inspirational words of a young film actress, about to give birth: "I was terrified. I was really afraid I was going to die. Because if I were to die, what would be the price for all my sins?" Images of her past, of being drunk, of wandering about at night, of frequenting discotheques, of appearing nude on the screen, came before her eyes. It was, she said, "as if [she] heard 'the whisper of heaven' at that moment."[14]

This may be more than a little formulaic, as indeed many, if not most, of James's accounts of spiritual renewal are, for we are again dealing here not with experience *simpliciter*, whatever that might be, but with representations of it offered to the self and others, to tales about it.[15] And, as with James's accounts, the tales recur and recur:

One day Naniek [one of Brenner's informants who resisted pressures from friends to wear *jilbab*] was suddenly overcome with the fear that she would die even though she was not ill. She realized that there were teachings of Islam that she had not yet observed, including the requirement to wear *jilbab*. . . . She woke up in the night in terror, thinking, "What can I do? I don't have any [Islamic] clothes."

She confides in her brother, who buys the material for her, and a few days later (she recalled the exact date) she began to wear *jilbab*. As soon as she accepted it, wearing Islamic clothing became easy for her, and "the clothes just came by themselves," even though she had little money. Her fears of death subsided.[16]

And, yet another commentator, writing in an Indonesian-language mass market book called *Muslim Women Toward the Year 2000*, designed apparently to instruct such women in what to feel, invokes the rebirth imagery explicitly:

The most important . . . question for a woman who is aware in this day and age is "who am I?" With that question, she tries to understand with full awareness that she cannot remain the way she is now. . . . She wants to be self-determining. . . . She wants to develop herself. She always aims to be reborn. In that rebirth, she wants to be her own midwife.[17]

Brenner has other testimony of the emotional correlates of this change of clothing which is a change of the way of being in the world: worries about living up to the demands of the new dress, intensified concerns about minor transgressions, and the feeling of being constantly under exacting moral surveillance, not just by God and conscience but by everyone around, searching avidly for failings and lapses. But perhaps enough has been said to make the point: in what we are pleased to call the real world, "meaning," "identity," "power," and "experience" are hopelessly entangled, mutually implicative, and "religion" can no more be founded upon or reduced to the last, that is, "experience," than it can to any of the others. It is not in solitude that faith is made.

∞

Other beasts, of course, other mores. The responses Brenner elicited from these Javanese young women seeking to become more Muslim are hardly what one would get from Indian Hindus, Burmese Buddhists, French Catholics, or even other sorts of Muslims. In Morocco, where I also worked, the Indonesian responses would be seen as unscriptural, sentimental, antinomian, or worse. Men rather than women, the aged rather than the young, uneducated peasants rather than educated urbanites, Africans, East Asians, Americans, Latins, or Europeans rather than Southeast Asians would surely produce quite different pictures—quite different because quite differently constructed, in quite different situations, out of quite different materials. The movement of religious identities and religious issues toward the center of social, political, and even economic life may be widespread and growing, in both scale and significance. But it is not a unitary phenomenon to be uniformly described. There are as many varieties of "religious experience," or, again, expressions of religious experience, as there ever were. Perhaps more.

This returns us to the question of James's usefulness to us now, to the double sense, I remarked in beginning, that the *Varieties* seems at once dated and exemplary, suffused with a period atmosphere and a model of the sort of work that, like Brenner's, seems cutting-edge, the next necessary thing. It is a cliché, but like many clichés nonetheless true, that major thinkers, like major artists, are both completely engulfed in their time—deeply situated, as we now would say—and transcendent of those times, vividly alive in other times, and that these two facts are internally connected. Certainly this is true of James. The radically individualistic, subjectivistic, "brute perception" concept of religion and religiousness, which his location as heir to New England intuitionism and his own encounters with the pinch of destiny led him into, was complemented by the intense, marvelously observant, almost pathologically sensitive attention to the shades and subtleties of thought and emotion they also led him into.

It is this last, circumstantial accounts of the personal inflections of religious engagement that reach far beyond the personal into the conflicts and dilemmas of our age, that we need now. And for that we need James, however other his age or his temper now may seem. Or at least we need the sort of inquiry he pioneered, the sort of talents he possessed, and the sort of openness to the foreign and unfamiliar, the particular and the incidental, yes, even the extreme and the brainsick, he displayed.

We have had massive, continental shifts in religious sensibility before whose impact on human life, we now see, was, despite their raggedness, radical and profound, a vast remaking of judgment and passion. It would be something of a pity were we to be living in the midst of such a seismic event and not even know that it was going on.

Notes

1. William James, *The Varieties of Religious Experience, A Study in Human Nature*, New York: Modern Library, 1929 [originally 1902], p. 476.
2. *Ibid*, p. 119; emphasis in original.
3. *Ibid.*, p. 171.
4. *Ibid.*, p. 250.
5. *Ibid.*, p. 492.
6. *Ibid.*, p. 477.
7. *Ibid.*, p. 476.
8. *Ibid.*, p. 418.

9. *Ibid.*, p. 31; italics in original.

10. S. Brenner, "Reconstructing Self and Society: Javanese Muslim Women and 'The Veil,'" *American Ethnologist* (1996): 673–697. As the internal quotation marks around "veil" suggest, what is involved is not the familiar Middle Eastern veil (*hijab*) but the headscarf and long gown (*jilbab*, "garment," "woman's dress")—a fact which Brenner makes clear in her initial footnote. As this is, for reasons I need not go into here, a matter I think of some consequence, I shall silently replace "veil" by *jilbab* when quoting from Brenner. As I myself worked from the early 1950s to the late 1980s on Java, and most especially on Javanese religious practices, views, and feelings, Brenner's work seems to me at once a continuation of mine and a substantial advance beyond it. See, *inter alia*, Geertz, *The Religion of Java*, Glencoe, Ill.: The Free Press, 1960, and Geertz, *Islam Observed: Religious Development in Morocco and Indonesia*, New Haven: Yale University Press, 1968. For more recent observations, Geertz, *After the Fact: Two Countries, Four Decades, One Anthropologist*, Cambridge: Harvard University Press, 1995. Cf. S. Brenner, *The Domestication of Desire: Women, Wealth, and Modernity in Java*, Princeton: Princeton University Press, 1998.

11. Brenner, "Reconstructing Self and Society."

12. *Ibid.*

13. *Ibid.*

14. *Ibid.*

15. For an extensive discussion and critique of the idea of "experience" as an "irreducible" ground of meaning and identity, a "reliable [source] of knowledge that comes from access to the real," in historical analysis ("Experience is . . . not the origin of our explanation, but that which we want to explain"), see J. Scott, "The Evidence of Experience," in J. Chandler et al., *Questions of Evidence: Proof, Practice, and Persuasion across the Disciplines*, Chicago: University of Chicago Press, 1991, pp. 363–387.

16. Brenner, "Reconstructing Self and Society."

17. Quoted in *ibid.*

IX ∞

Imbalancing Act: Jerome
Bruner's Cultural Psychology

What does one say when one says "psychology": James, Wundt, Binet, or Pavlov? Freud, Lashley, Skinner, or Vygotsky? Kohler, Lewin, Lévy-Bruhl, Bateson? Chomsky or Piaget? Daniel Dennett or Oliver Sacks? Herbert Simon? Since it got truly launched as a discipline and a profession in the last half of the nineteenth century, mainly by Germans, the self-proclaimed "science of the mind" has not just been troubled with a proliferation of theories, methods, arguments, and techniques. That was only to be expected. It has also been driven in wildly different directions by wildly different notions as to what it is, as we say, "about"—what sort of knowledge, of what sort of reality, to what sort of end it is supposed to produce. From the outside, at least, it does not look like a single field, divided into schools and specialties in the usual way. It looks like an assortment of disparate and disconnected inquiries classed together because they all make reference in some way or other to something or other called "mental functioning." Dozens of characters in search of a play.

From inside it doubtless looks a bit more ordered, if only because of the byzantine academic structure that has grown up around it (the American Psychological Association has forty-nine divisions), but surely no less miscellaneous. The wide swings between behaviorist, psychometric, cognitivist, depth psychological, topological, developmentalist, neurological, evolutionist, and culturalist conceptions of the subject have made being a psychologist an unsettled occupation, subject not only to fashion, as are all the human sciences, but to sudden and frequent reversals of course. Paradigms, wholly new ways of going about things, come along not by the century, but by the decade; sometimes, it almost seems, by the month. It takes either a preternaturally focused, dogmatical individual, who can shut out any ideas but his or her own, or a mercurial, hopelessly inquisitive one, who can keep dozens of them in play at once, to remain upright amidst this tumble of programs, promises, and proclamations.

There are, in psychology, a great many more of the resolved and implacable, *esprit de système* types (Pavlov, Freud, Skinner, Piaget, Chomsky) than there are of the agile and adaptable, *esprit de finesse* ones (James, Bateson, Sacks). But it is among the latter that Jerome Bruner, author or coauthor of more than twenty books, and god knows how many articles, on almost as many subjects, clearly belongs. In a breathless, lurching, yet somehow deeply consecutive career spanning nearly sixty years, Bruner has brushed against almost every line of thought in psychology and transformed a number of them.

That career began at Harvard in the forties, during the heyday of behaviorism, rat-running, the repetition of nonsense syllables, the discrimination of sensory differences, and the measurement of galvanic responses. But, dissatisfied with the piling up of experimental "findings" on peripheral matters (his first professional study involved conditioning "helplessness" in a rat imprisoned on an electrified grill), he quickly joined the growing band of equally restless colleagues, within psychology and without, to become one of the leaders of the so-called Cognitive Revolution.

By the late fifties, this revolution was under way, and "bringing the mind back in" became the battle cry for a whole generation of psychologists, linguists, brain modelers, ethnologists, and computer scientists, as well as a few empirically minded philosophers. For them, the primary objects of study were not stimulus strengths and response patterns; they were mental actions—attending, thinking, understanding, imagining, remembering, feeling, knowing. With a like-minded colleague, Bruner launched a famous series of "New Look" perception experiments to demonstrate the power of mental selectivity in seeing, hearing, and recognizing something. Poorer children see the same coin as larger than richer ones do; college students are either very much slower ("defensive") or very much quicker ("vigilant") to recognize threatening words than they are to recognize unthreatening ones. With two of his students, he carried out a landmark study of abstract reasoning. How do people, in fact, rather than in logic, test their hypotheses? How do they decide what is relevant to explanation and what is not? And in 1960, he and the psycholinguist George Miller, another restless soul, founded Harvard's interdisciplinary Center for Cognitive Studies, through which virtually all of the leading figures in the field, established or in the making, passed at one time or another and which set off an explosion of similar centers and similar work both here and abroad. "We certainly generated a point of view, even a fad or two," Bruner wrote of his and his colleagues' work during this period in his (as it turns out, premature) 1983 autobiography, *In Search of Mind.* "About ideas, how can one tell?"[1]

After awhile, Bruner himself became disenchanted with the Cognitive Revolution, or at least with what it had become. "That revolution," he wrote at the beginning of his 1990 *Acts of Meaning,* a "goodbye to all that" proclamation of a new direction,

> was intended to bring "mind" back into the human sciences after a long cold winter of objectivism. . . . [But it] has now been diverted into issues that are marginal to the impulse that brought it into being. Indeed, it has been technicalized in a manner that even undermines that original impulse. This is not to say that it has failed: far from it, for cognitive science must surely be among the leading growth shares on the academic bourse. It may rather be that it has become diverted by success, a success whose technological virtuosity has cost dear. Some critics . . . even argue that the new cognitive science, the child of the revolution, has gained its technical successes at the price

of dehumanizing the very concept of mind it had sought to reestablish in psychology, and that it has thereby estranged much of psychology from the other human sciences and the humanities.[2]

In saving the Cognitive Revolution from itself, distancing it from high-tech reductionism (the brain is hardware, mind is software, thinking is the software processing digitalized information on the hardware), Bruner has raised, over the last decade or so, yet another banner heralding yet another dispensation: "Cultural Psychology." What now comes to the center of attention is the individual's engagement with established systems of shared meaning, with the beliefs, the values, and the understandings of those already in place in society as he or she is thrown in among them. For Bruner, the critical "test frame" for this point of view, is education—the field of practices within which such engagement is, in the first instance, effected. Rather than a psychology that sees the mind as a programmable mechanism, we need one that sees it as a social achievement. Education "is not simply a technical business of well-managed information processing, nor even simply a matter of applying 'learning theories' to the classroom or using the results of subject-centered 'achievement testing.' It is a complex pursuit of fitting a culture to the needs of its members and their ways of knowing to the needs of the culture."[3]

⌒⌒

Bruner's concern with education and educational policy dates from the studies of mental development in infants and very young children that, in his growing resistance to machine cognitivism, he began to carry out in the mid-sixties, just—such are the workings of the *Zeitgeist*—as the Head Start program was coming, with Great Society fanfare, grandly into being. These studies led him to an "outside-in" view of such development, one which concerns itself with "the kind of world needed to make it possible to use mind (or heart!) effectively—what kinds of symbol systems, what kinds of accounts of the past, what arts and sciences."[4] The unfolding of the critical features of human thinking, joint attention with others to objects and actions, attribution of beliefs, desires, and emotions to others, grasping the general significance of situations, a sense of self-hood—what Bruner calls "the entry into meaning"—begins very early in the development process, prior not just to formal schooling but to walking and the acquisition of language. "Infants, it turned out, were much smarter, more cognitively proactive rather than re-active, more attentive to the immediate social world around them, than had been previously suspected. They emphatically did *not* in-habit a world of 'buzzing, blooming confusion': they seemed in search of predictive stability from the very start."[5]

The Head Start program began with a rather different, in some ways complementary, in others contrastive, view of early develop-ment based on a rather different set of scientific investigations: those showing that laboratory animals raised in "impoverished envi-ronments," ones with few challenges and reduced stimulation, did less well than "normals" on such standard learning and problem-solving tasks as maze running and food finding. Transferred, more metaphorically than experimentally, to schooling and to school-children, this led to the so-called cultural deprivation hypothesis. Children raised in an "impoverished" cultural environment, in the ghetto or wherever, would, for that reason, do less well in school. Hence the need for corrective action to enrich their environment early on, before the damage was done. Hence Head Start.

Aside from the fact that the idea of correcting for "cultural de-privation" depends on knowing what such deprivation consists in (what it has most often been taken to consist in is departure from the standards of an idealized, middle-class, "Ozzie and Harriet" American culture), such an approach seems to assume that "cultural enrichment" is a good to be provided to the deprived child by the wider society, like a hot lunch or a smallpox injection. The child is seen to be lacking something, not to be seeking something; regarded as receiving culture from elsewhere, not as constructing it *in situ* out of the materials and interactions immediately to hand. Bruner was a sometime advisor to Head Start, and he is still a defender of its very real successes and its possibilities for extension and reform (it is, after all, an "outside-in" program). But he argues that the results of his sort of research into the mental development of children—grown by now into a field in itself, turning up more and more evidence of the conceptual powers of children—renders the "deprivation" approach obsolete. Seeing even the infant and the preschooler as active agents bent on mastery of a particular form of life, on developing a workable way of being in the world, demands a rethinking of the entire educational process. It is not so much a matter of providing something the child hasn't got as enabling something the child already has: the desire to make sense of self and others, the drive to understand what the devil is going on.

For Bruner, the critical enabling factor, the thing that brings the mind to focus, is culture—"the way of life and thought that we construct, negotiate, institutionalize, and finally (after it is all settled) end up calling 'reality' to comfort ourselves."[6] Any theory of education that hopes to reform it, and there hardly is any other kind, needs to train its attention on the social production of meaning. The terms upon which society and child—the "reality" already there and the scuttling intellect thrust bodily into it—engage one another are in good part worked out in the classroom, at least they are in our school-conscious society. It is there that mentality is most deliberately fashioned, subjectivity most systematically produced, and intersubjectivity—the ability to "read other minds"—most carefully nurtured. At least in the favorable case, not perhaps entirely common, the child, "seen as an epistemologist as well as a learner," moves into an ongoing community of discoursing adults and chattering children where "she . . . gradually comes to appreciate that she is acting not directly on 'the world' but on beliefs she holds about that world."[7]

This turn toward concern with the ways in which the understandings abroad in the larger society are used by the schoolchild to find his feet, to build up an inner sense of who he is, what others are up to, what is likely to happen, what can be done about things, opens Bruner's "cultural psychology" to a host of issues normally addressed by other disciplines—history, literature, law, philosophy, linguistics, and most especially that other hopelessly miscellaneous and inconstant science, anthropology. Such a psychology, rather like anthropology, has an eclectic perspective and a vast ambition built directly into it. It seems to take all experience for its object, to draw on all scholarship for its means. With so many doors to open, and so many keys with which to open them, it would be folly to try to open all of them at once. That way lies knowing less and less about more and more. The door Bruner, sensitive as always to the practicalities of research, wants to open, not altogether surprisingly, given recent developments in "discourse theory," "speech-act analysis," "the interpretation of cultures," and "the hermeneutics of everyday life," is narrative.

Telling stories, about ourselves and about others, to ourselves and to others, is "the most natural and the earliest way in which we organize our experience and our knowledge."[8] But you would hardly know it from standard educational theory, trained as it is upon tests and recipes:

> It has been the convention of most schools to treat the art of narrative—song, drama, fiction, theater, whatever—as more "decoration" than necessity, as something with which to grace leisure, sometimes even as something morally exemplary. Despite that, we frame the accounts of our cultural origins and our most cherished beliefs in story form, and it is not just the "content" of these stories that grip us, but their narrative artifice. Our immediate experience, what happened yesterday or the day before, is framed in the same storied way. Even more striking, we represent our lives (to ourselves as well as to others) in the form of narrative. It is not surprising that psychoanalysts now recognize that personhood implicates narrative, "neurosis" being a reflection of either an insufficient, incomplete, or inappropriate story about oneself. Recall that when Peter Pan asks Wendy to return to Never Never Land with him, he gives as his reason that she could teach the Lost Boys there how to tell stories. If they knew how to tell them, the Lost Boys might be able to grow up.[9]

Growing up among narratives, one's own, those of teachers, schoolmates, parents, janitors, and various other sorts of what Saul Bellow once mordantly referred to as "reality instructors," is the essential scene of education—"we live in a sea of stories."[10] Learning how to swim in such a sea, how to construct stories, understand stories, classify stories, check out stories, see through stories, and use stories to find out how things work or what they come to, is what the school, and beyond the school the whole "culture of education," is, at base, all about. The heart of the matter, what the learner learns whatever the teacher teaches, is "that human beings make sense of the world by telling stories about it—by using the narrative mode for construing reality."[11] Tales are tools, "instrument[s] of mind on behalf of meaning making."[12]

∞

Bruner's most recent work is, then, dedicated to tracing out the implications of this view of narrative as "both a mode of thought and an expression of a culture's world view."[13] He has launched inquiries into the teaching of science, into "folk pedagogy," into the collaborative nature of learning, and into the child's construction of "a theory of mind" to explain and understand other minds. Autism as the inability to develop such a theory, the formal features of narrative, culture as praxis, and the approaches to education of Vygotsky, Piaget, and Pierre Bourdieu, related to Bruner's but in some tension with it, have all beem discussed, at least in passing. So have recent developments in primatology, cross-cultural studies of education, IQ testing, "metacognition" ("thinking about one's thinking"), relativism, and the uses of neurology. It is all rather on the wing; a wondrous lot goes by wondrously fast.

This is not that serious a fault, if it is a fault at all, in what is still a series of forays designed to open up a territory rather than to chart and settle it. But it does leave even the sympathetic critic at a bit of a loss as to where it all is going, what "cultural psychology" amounts to as a field among fields, a continuing enterprise with a budget of issues and an agenda for confronting them. One can, of course, get something of a sense of this by looking up Bruner's dozens upon dozens of technical investigations or by hunting down his even more numerous citations to studies by colleagues on everything from "the child's understanding of number" and "oral versions of personal experience," to "benefit-cost analysis of pre-school education" and "impaired recognition of emotion in facial expression following bilateral damage to the human amygdala."

But since most of this "literature," wrapped in statistics and enfolded in protocols, is scattered through professional journals and disciplinary symposia, few besides specialists are likely to find the patience for such a task. Genuine treatises, more summary, and thus more accessible, synthesizing works, authored by students, coworkers, and followers of Bruner, are beginning to appear in increasing numbers, from which one can get a somewhat clearer picture of where the whole enterprise is at the moment and what progress it is making.[14] And in the final section of his most recent book, a section called, with uncertain surety, "Psychology's Next Chapter," Bruner himself undertakes to lay out the directions in which cultural psychology should move and to describe how it should relate itself to other approaches to "the study of mind."

As usual, his attitude is conciliatory, eclectic, energetic, up-beat:

> Can a cultural psychology . . . simply stand apart from the kind of biologically rooted, individually oriented, laboratory dominated psychology that we have known in the past? Must the more situated study of mind-in-culture, more interpretively anthropological in spirit, jettison all that we have learned before? Some writers . . . propose that our past was a mistake, a misunderstanding of what psychology is about. . . . [But] I would like to urge an end to [an] "either-or" approach to the question of what psychology should be in the future, whether it should be entirely biological, exclusively computational, or monopolistically cultural.

He wants to show how

> psychology can, by devoting its attention to certain critical topics . . . illustrate the interaction of biological, evolutionary, individual psychological, and cultural insights in helping us grasp the nature of human mental functioning. [The] "next chapter" in psychology [will be] about "intersubjectivity"—how people come to know what others have in mind and how they adjust accordingly . . . a set of topics . . . central to any viable conception of a cultural psychology. But it cannot be understood without reference to primate evolution, to neural functioning, and to the processing capacities of minds.[15]

This is all very well, the sort of balanced and reasonable approach that softens contrasts, disarms enemies, skirts difficulties, and finesses hard decisions. But there remains the sense that Bruner is underestimating the explosiveness of his own ideas. To argue that culture is socially and historically constructed, that narrative is a primary, in humans perhaps the primary, mode of knowing, that we assemble the selves we live in out of materials lying about in the society around us and develop "a theory of mind" to comprehend the selves of others, that we act not directly on the world but on beliefs we hold about the world, that from birth on we are all active, impassioned "meaning makers" in search of plausible stories, and that "mind cannot in any sense be regarded as 'natural' or naked, with culture thought of as an add-on"—such a view amounts to rather more than a midcourse correction.[16] Taken all in all, it amounts to adopting a position that can fairly be called radical, not to say subversive. It seems very doubtful that such views, and others connected with them—perspectivism, instrumentalism, contextualism, antireductionism—can be absorbed into the ongoing traditions of psychological research (or indeed into the human sciences generally) without causing a fair amount of noise and upheaval. If "cultural psychology" does gain ascendancy, or even serious market share, it will disturb a lot more than pedagogy.

For it is in fact the case that not only is cultural psychology evolving rapidly, gathering force, and amassing evidence, but so as well are its two most important rivals, or anyway alternatives—information processing cognitivism and neurobiological reductionism. The introduction into cognitivism of distributive parallel processing (which Bruner dismisses at one point as but a "veiled version" of behaviorist associationism) and computer-mediated experimentalism has given it something of a second wind. A technology-driven spurt in brain research, the extension of evolutionary theory to everything from morality to consciousness, the emergence of a whole range of post-Cartesian philosophies of mind, and perhaps most important the dawning of the age of the absolute gene, have done the same for biologism. In the face of all this, and of the moral and practical issues at stake, courteous, to-each-his-own dividing up of the territory does not look to be in the cards.

"Psychology's next chapter" is more likely to be tumultuous than irenic as computational, biological, and cultural approaches grow in power and sophistication sufficient enough to assure that they will have transformative impacts upon one another. The simple assertion that biology provides "constraints" upon culture, as it does, and that computationally based cognitive science is incompetent to deal with "the messiness of meaning making," as it is, will hardly suffice to resolve the deep-going issues that, by its very presence, cultural psychology is going to make unavoidable. Bringing so large and misshapen a camel as anthropology into psychology's tent is going to do more to toss things around than to arrange them in order. At the climax of what is surely one of the most extraordinary and productive careers in the human sciences, a career of continuous originality and tireless exploration, Bruner seems to be in the midst of producing a more revolutionary revolution than even he altogether appreciates.

∞

Within anthropology, the clarity, the relevance, the analytic power, even the moral status of the concept of culture have been much discussed in recent years, to no very certain conclusion save that if it is not to be discarded as an imperialist relic, an ideological maneuver, or a popular catchword, as its various critics variously suggest, it must be seriously rethought. Giving it a central role in "psychology's next chapter," as Bruner suggests, should do much to encourage such rethinking, as well as to extend similar questionings to the no less embattled concept of mind he wishes to conjoin with it. But it will hardly simplify things. To the abiding puzzles afflicting psychology—nature and nurture, top down and bottom up, reason and passion, conscious and unconscious, competence and performance, privacy and intersubjectivity, experience and behavior, learning and forgetting—will be added a host of new ones: meaning and action, social causality and personal intention, relativism and universalism, and, perhaps most fundamentally, difference and commonality. If anthropology is obsessed with anything, it is with how much difference difference makes.

There is no simple answer to this question so far as cultural differences are concerned (though simple answers are often enough given, usually extreme). In anthropology, there is merely the question itself, asked and reasked in every instance. To throw so singularizing a science in among such determinedly generalizing ones as genetics, information processing, developmental psychology, generative grammar, neurology, decision theory, and neo-Darwinism is to court terminal confusion in a realm—the study of mental activity—already well-enough obscured by imperial programs, inimical world views, and a proliferation of procedures. What, in the days of Sartre, we would have called Bruner's "project" implies a good deal more than adding "culture" (or "meaning," or "narrative") to the mix—another variable heard from. It implies, as he himself has said, confronting the world as a field of differences, "adjudicating the different construals of reality that are inevitable in any diverse society."[17]

Or in any genuine inquiry. Trying to bring together, or perhaps more carefully, to relate in a productive manner, everything from "psychic universals" and "story telling" to "neural models" and "enculturated chimpanzees," from Vygotsky, Goodman, and Bartlett to Edelman, Simon, and Premack (not to speak of Geertz and Lévi-Strauss!) obviously involves as much mobilizing differences as it does dissolving them, "adjudicating" contrasts (not, perhaps, altogether the best word), rather than overriding them or forcing them into some pallid, feel-good ecumenical whole. It may just be that it is not the reconciliation of diverse approaches to the study of mind that is most immediately needed, a calming eclecticism, but the effective playing of them off against one another. If that miraculous cabbage, the brain itself, now appears to be more adequately understood in terms of separated processes simultaneously active, then the same may be true of the mind with which biologizers so often confuse it. History, culture, the body, and the workings of the physical world indeed fix the character of anyone's mental life—shape it, stabilize it, fill it with content. But they do so independently, partitively, concurrently, and differentially. They do not just disappear into a resultant like so many component vectors, or come together in some nicely equilibrated frictionless concord.

Such a view, that a useful understanding of how we manage to think must be one in which symbolic forms, historical traditions, cultural artifacts, neural codes, environmental pressures, genetic inscriptions, and the like operate coactively, often enough even agonistically, seems to be struggling toward exacter expression in recent work, at least in part stimulated by Bruner's own. Andy Clark's *Being There* is dedicated to nothing less than "putting brain, body and world together again." William Frawley's *Vygotsky and Cognitive Science* seeks "to show that the human mind is both a social construct and a computational device as opposed to one or the other."[18] So far as culture ("the symbolic systems that individuals [use] in constructing meaning") is concerned, what Clark calls "the image of mind as inextricably interwoven with body, world and action," and Frawley, "the mind in the world [and] the world . . . in the mind," makes it impossible to regard it any longer as external and supplementary to the resident powers of the human intellect, a tool or a prosthesis. It is ingredient in those powers.[19]

The course of our understanding of mind does not consist in a determined march toward an omega point where everything finally falls happily together; it consists in the repeated deployment of distinct inquiries in such a way that, again and again, apparently without end, they force deep-going reconsiderations upon one another. Constructing a powerful "cultural psychology" (or a powerful psychological anthropology—not altogether the same thing) is less a matter of hybridizing disciplines, putting hyphens between them, than it is of reciprocally disequilibrating them. At a time when monomanic, theory-of-everything conceptions of mental functioning, stimulated by local developments in neurology, genetics, primatology, literary theory, semiotics, systems theory, robotics, or whatever have come increasingly into fashion, what seems to be needed is the development of strategies for enabling Bruner's "different construals of [mental] reality" to confront, discompose, energize, and deprovincialize one another, and thus drive the enterprise erratically onward. Everything that rises need not converge: it has only to make the most of its incorrigible diversity.

The ways of doing this, of making disparate, even conflicting, views of what the mind is, how it works, and how it is most profitably studied into useful correctives to one another's assurances, are, of course, themselves multiple—extremely difficult to devise, extremely difficult to put in place once they are devised, extremely susceptible, once they are put in place, to bringing on an academic version of Hobbsean war. Again, so far as anthropology is concerned, what most positions it to contribute to such a task, and to avoiding its pathological outcomes, is not its particular findings about African witchcraft or Melanesian exchange, and certainly not any theories it may have developed about universal necessities and the ingenerate logic of social life, but its long and intimate engagement with cultural difference and with the concrete workings of such difference in social life. Surveying contrasts, tracing their implications, and enabling them somehow to speak to general issues is, after all, its metier.

Managing difference, or if that sounds too manipulative, navigating it, is the heart of the matter. As with all such enterprises, there are a good many more ways of getting it wrong than there are of getting it right, and one of the most common ways of getting it wrong is through convincing ourselves that we have gotten it right—consciousness explained, how the mind works, the engine of reason, the last word. Whitehead once remarked that we must build our systems and keep them open; but, given his own passion for completeness, certainty, and wholistic synthesis, he neglected to add that the former is a great deal easier to accomplish than the latter. The hedgehog's disease and the fox's—premature closure and the obsessive fear of it, tying it all up and letting it all dangle—may be equally obstructive of movement in the human sciences. But, "in nature," as the positivists used to say, the one is encountered far more frequently than the other, especially in these days of high-tech tunnel vision.

One thing that is certain, if anything is certain when one comes to talk of such things as meaning, consciousness, thought, and feeling, is that both psychology's "next chapter" and anthropology's are not going to be orderly, well-formed sorts of discourse, beginnings and middles neatly connected to ends. Neither isolating rival approaches to understanding mind and culture in fenced communities ("evolutionary psychology," "symbolic anthropology") nor fusing them into an inclusive whole ("cognitive science," "semiotics") is in the long run, or even the medium, really workable—the one because it reifies difference and exalts it, the other because it underestimates its ubiquity, its ineradicability, and its force.

The reason that the legalism "adjudication" may not be the best term to signal the alternative to these ways of avoiding issues is that it suggests an "adjudicator," something (or someone) that sorts things out, that reconciles approaches, ranks them, or chooses among them. But whatever order emerges in either mind or culture, it is not produced by some regnant central process or directive structure; it is produced by the play of . . . well, whatever it is that is, in the case, in play. The future of cultural psychology depends on the ability of its practitioners to capitalize on so turbulent and inelegant a situation—a situation in which the openness, responsiveness, adaptability, inventiveness, and intellectual restlessness, to say nothing of the optimism, that have characterized Bruner's work since its beginnings are peculiarly well-suited. His outlook and his example seem likely to flourish, whoever it is who continues the narrative, and whatever it is that it turns out to say.

Notes

1. J. Bruner, *In Search of Mind, Essays in Autobiography*, New York: Harper and Row, 1983, p. 126.

2. J. Bruner, *Acts of Meaning*, Cambridge: Harvard University Press, 1990, p. 1.

3. J. Bruner, *The Culture of Education*, Cambridge: Harvard University Press, 1996, p. 43.

4. *Ibid.*, p. 9.

5. *Ibid.*, pp. 71–72.

6. *Ibid.*, p. 87.

7. *Ibid.*, pp. 57, 49.

8. *Ibid.*, p. 121.

9. *Ibid.*, p. 40.

10. *Ibid.*, p. 147.

11. *Ibid.*, p. 130.

12. *Ibid.*, p. 41.

13. *Ibid.*, p. xiv.

14. Two such works have just now emerged: M. Cole, *Cultural Psychology, A Once and Future Discipline*, Cambridge: Harvard University Press, 1996, and B. Shore, *Culture in Mind, Cognition, Culture, and the Problem of Meaning*, Oxford: Oxford University Press, 1996. Cole, a developmental psychologist moving toward social anthropology, traces the history of cross-cultural research in psychology, in which he has himself played a major role, and develops a conceptual framework for the integration of anthropological and psychological

inquiry based on "the romantic science" ("the dream of a novelist and a scientist combined") of the Russian psychologists Alexei Leontiev, Alexander Luria, and Lev Vygotsky. Shore, a social anthropologist moving toward cognitive psychology, reviews some classical ethnographic studies, including his own on Samoa, as well as various contemporary cultural forms—baseball, interior decorating, air travel—in an effort to relate what he calls "personal" (that is, "cognitive") and "conventional" (that is, "cultural") mental models to one another and thus break down the long and unfortunate separation of anthropology and psychology.

Both these books bite off a good deal more than they can chew and do not come together very well; but they offer valuable accounts of the present state of play. For other such summary works, equally useful for getting a hands-on sense of the field and its prospects, see R. A. Shweder, *Thinking through Cultures, Expeditions in Cultural Psychology*, Cambridge: Harvard University Press, 1991; J. Stigler, R. A. Shweder, and G. Herdt, eds., *Cultural Psychology: The Chicago Symposia on Culture and Development*, Cambridge: Cambridge University Press, 1989; and R. A Shweder and R. A. Levine, eds., *Culture Theory: Essays on Mind, Self and Emotion*, Cambridge: University Press, 1984.

15. Bruner, *The Culture of Education*, p. 160.

16. *Ibid.*, p. 171.

17. Bruner, *Acts of Meaning*, p. 95.

18. A. Clark, *Being There: Putting Brain, Body, and World Together Again*, Cambridge: MIT Press, 1997; W. Frawley, *Vygotsky and Cognitive Science: Language and the Unification of the Social and Computational Mind*, Cambridge: Harvard University Press, 1997. For acknowledgments of the stimulus of Bruner's work, see, eg., Clark, p. 25; Frawley, p. 223.

19. Bruner, *Acts of Meaning*, p. 11; Clark, *Being There*, p. xvii; Frawley, *Vygotsky and Cognitive Science*, p. 295. For a constitutive as opposed to an add-on view of the role of culture in human evolution, see Clifford Geertz, "The Impact of the Concept of Culture on the Concept of Man" and "The Growth of Culture and the Evolution of Mind," in *The Interpretation of Cultures*, New York: Basic Books, 1973, pp. 33–54, 55–83.

X ∽

Culture, Mind, Brain/Brain, Mind, Culture

Between them, anthropology and psychology have chosen two of the more improbable objects around which to try to build a positive science: Culture and Mind, *Kultur und Geist, Culture et Esprit.* Both are inheritances of defunct philosophies, both have checkered histories of ideological inflation and rhetorical abuse, both have broad and multiple everyday usages that interfere with any effort to stabilize their meaning or turn them into natural kinds. They have been repeatedly condemned as mystical or metaphysical, repeatedly banished from the disciplined precincts of serious inquiry, repeatedly refused to go away.

When they are coupled, the difficulties do not merely add, they explode. Either more or less complicated, equally implausible reductions of the one to the other or the other to the one are proposed and elaborated, or some theoretically intricate system of interaction between them is described that leaves their separability unquestioned and their weight indeterminate. More recently, as the cognitive sciences have developed, there has been a tendency to finesse the terms more or less entirely, and talk instead of neural circuits and computational processing, programmable systems artifactually instructed—a tactic which renders both the question of the social habitation of thought and that of the personal foundations of significance untouched and untouchable.

So far as anthropology is concerned, these ill-framed or elided doubled questions, the mental nature of culture, the cultural nature of mind, have haunted it since its inception. From Tylor's ruminations on the cognitive insufficiencies of primitive religion in the 1870s, through Lévy-Bruhl's on sympathetic participations and pre-logical thought in the 1920s, to those of Lévi-Strauss on *bricolage*, mythemes, and *la pensée sauvage* in the 1960s, the issue of "primitive mentality"—the degree to which so-called natives think otherwise than the (also, so-called) civilized, advanced, rational, and scientific do—has divided and scrambled ethnographical theory. Boas in *The Mind of Primitive Man*, Malinowski in *Magic, Science, and Religion*, and Douglas in *Purity and Danger* have all wrestled with the same angel: bringing, as they and their followers variously put it, inner and outer, private and public, personal and social, psychological and historical, experiential and behavioral into intelligible relationship.

But it is, perhaps, precisely this presumption—that what is at issue and needs to be determined is some sort of bridging connection between the world within the skull and the world outside of it—which brings on the problem in the first place. Since Wittgenstein's demolition of the very idea of a private language and the consequent socialization of speech and meaning, the location of mind in the head and culture outside of it no longer seems to be but so much obvious and incontrovertible common sense. What is inside the head is the brain, and some other biological stuff. What is outside is cabbages, kings, and a number of things. The cognitive philosopher Andy Clark's subversive question, "Where does mind stop and the rest of the world begin?," is no more answerable than its equally unnerving correlate, "Where does culture stop and the rest of the self begin?"[1]

Much of the recent work in what has come to be known as "cultural psychology" has consisted of attempts, some rather impressive, some rather less so, all of them fumbling confusedly with the materials of several disciplines, to navigate around this double dilemma by reconceiving mentality and meaning in less border-drawing, this is this, that is that, terms. The very titles of the studies in this emerging genre—*Culture in Mind, Actual Minds, Possible Worlds, Thinking through Cultures, The Discursive Mind, The Inner*

Life: The Outer Mind, How Institutions Think, Steps Toward an Ecol-
ogy of Mind, Ways of Worldmaking—suggest both its expansive reach
and its uncertain grasp.[2] "Putting," to quote Clark again, this time
from *his* title, "brain, body, and world together again" is a bit of task,
diffuse and ambitious. But it is one which is, at length, now genuinely begun. Or, as the title of Michael Cole's recent survey of this
motley subject, *Cultural Psychology: The Once and Future Science*,
suggests, rebegun.[3]

As is so often the case with necessary departures from familiar
procedures, the first step in this effort to relate what inside-focused
psychologists have learned about how humans reason, feel, remember, imagine, and decide, to what outside-focused anthropologists
have learned about how meaning is constructed, learned, enacted,
and transformed, has been obvious for some time, but curiously difficult for either sort of inquirer to face up to. This is the abandonment of the notion that the homo sapiens brain is capable of autonomous functioning, that it can operate effectively, or indeed can
operate at all, as an endogenously driven, context-independent system. At least since the circumstantial description of the incipient,
prelinguistic stages of hominization (small skulls, erect stature, pur-
posed implements) began about a half century ago with the discovery of prepithecanthropine fossils and early Pleistocene sites, the
fact that brain and culture coevolved, mutually dependent the one
upon the other for their very realization, has made the conception
of human mental functioning as an intrinsically determined intra-
cerebral process, ornamented and extended, but hardly engendered
by cultural devices—language, rite, technology, teaching, and the
incest tabu—unsustainable. Our brains are not in a vat, but in our
bodies. Our minds are not in our bodies, but in the world. And as
for the world, it is not in our brains, our bodies, or our minds: they
are, along with gods, verbs, rocks, and politics, in it.

All this—the coevolution of body and culture, the functionally
incomplete character of the human nervous system, the ingredience
of meaning in thought and of thought in practice—suggests that
the way toward an improved understanding of the biological, the
psychological, and the sociocultural is not through arranging them
into some sort of chain-of-being hierarchy stretching from the phys-

ical and biological to the social and semiotic, each level emergent from and dependent upon (and, with luck, reducible to) the one beneath it. Nor is it through treating them as discontinuous, sovereign realities, enclosed, stand-alone domains externally connected ("interfaced," as the jargon has it) to one another by vague and adventitious forces, factors, quantities, and causes. Constitutive of one another, reciprocally constructive, they must be treated as such—as complements, not levels; aspects, not entities; landscapes, not realms.

That much perhaps is arguable. Certainly, it is much argued. What seems less arguable is that as our understanding of the brain, of information processing, of individual development, of social communication and collective behavior, of perception, emotion, fantasy, memory, and concept formation, and of reference, sense, representation, and discourse severally advance in some sort of wary and sidelong, corner-of-the-eye awareness of one another, the possibility of reducing all of them to one of them, sorting them into sealed compartments, or bringing them into a comprehensive, theory-of-everything synthesis, grows steadily more remote. We are not, apparently, proceeding toward some appointed end where it all comes together, Babel is undone, and Self lies down with Society.

On the contrary, we are witnessing an increasingly rapid proliferation, an onslaught, actually, of what Thomas Kuhn called disciplinary matrices—loose assemblages of techniques, vocabularies, assumptions, instruments, and exemplary achievements that, despite their specificities and originalities, or even their grand incommensurabilities, bear with intensifying force and evolving precision upon the speed, the direction, and the fine detail of one another's development. We have, and for the foreseeable future will continue to have, a more and more differentiated field of semi-independent, semi-interactive disciplines, or disciplinary matrices (and of research communities, sustaining, celebrating, critiquing, and extending them), devoted to one or another approach to the study of how we think and what we think with. And it is within such a field, dispersed, disparate, and continuously changing, that we must severally learn to pursue not a common project—Sigmund Freud and Noam Chomsky, Marshall Sahlins and E. O. Wilson, Gerald Edelman and

Patricia Churchland, Charles Taylor and Daniel Dennett, will never come close enough to one another to permit that to happen—but a half-ordered, polycentric collection of mutually conditioned ones.

That in turn suggests that someone who is, as I am here, attempting, not to report particular findings or evaluate particular proposals, but to describe the general state of play, is well advised to try to look synoptically at the overall field, straggling, irregular, and resistant to summary as it is. We have in recent years become increasingly used to dealing with distributive, partially connected, self-organizing, systems, especially in engineering and biology, and in computer simulations of everything from ant hills and neuron assemblies to embryonic development and object perception. But we are still not used to looking at disciplinary matrices, or the interplay of disciplinary matrices, in such a way. A field, once or future, like "cultural psychology," concerned with precisely such an interplay between dissimilar, impassioned, even jealous and uncongenial, approaches to "how we natives think," and between the ardent partisans driving them competitively forward, would seem well advised to become accustomed to doing so. It is not tightened coordination or negligent, to-each-his-own difference-splitting that we are going to find here. What we are going to find, and are finding, is exacting, sharpening, deepening argument. And if you think things are turbulent now, just wait.

To make all this a bit more concrete, rather than merely programmatic and hortatory, let me take, in way of brief example, some recent discussions in anthropology, in psychology, and in neurology of that most elusive and miscellaneous particularity of our immediate life, the one Hume thought reason was and ought to be everywhere the slave of, namely, "passion"—"emotion," "feeling," "affect," "attitude," "mood," "desire," "temper," "sentiment."

These words, too, define a space, not an entity. They overlap, differ, contrast, hang together only in oblique, family-resemblance terms—polythetically, as the phrasing goes; the problem is less to fix their referents (something that is notoriously hard to do—where is "envy"? what, "homesickness"?) than to outline their reach and application. I will start with anthropology, not only because I know the material more exactly, but because I have myself been somewhat implicated in the matter—accused, in fact, of having "helped to secure permission for cultural-symbolic anthropologists to develop an anthropology of self and feeling," apparently an unfortunate thing.[4] It is not my own work, however, which has been more advisory in this regard than authorizing, a word in the ear, not some sort of benediction or license to practice, that I want to discuss here, but that of the so-called culturalist, or symbolic-action, theorists of passion and sentiment.

Such theorists (and, as they all are, and primarily, field researchers), of whom Michelle Rosaldo, Catherine Lutz, Jean Briggs, Richard Shweder, Robert Levy, and Anna Wierzbicka are, *inter alia* and diversely, representative examples, take an essentially semiotic approach to emotions—one which sees them in terms of the signific instruments and constructional practices through which they are given shape, sense, and public currency.[5] Words, images, gestures, body-marks, and terminologies, stories, rites, customs, harangues, melodies, and conversations, are not mere vehicles of feelings lodged elsewhere, so many reflections, symptoms, and transpirations. They are the locus and machinery of the thing itself.

"[If] we hope," Rosaldo writes, with the groping awkwardness this sort of view tends to produce, given the ingrained Cartesianism of our psychological language, "to learn *how* songs, or slights, or killings, can stir human hearts we must inform interpretation with a grasp of the relationship between expressive forms and feelings, which themselves are culture-bound and which derive their significance from their place within the life experiences of particular people in particular societies." However resemblant their general aspect, and however useful it may be to compare them, the *mēnis*-wrath of Achilles and the *liget*-rage of Rosaldo's Philippine head-hunters draw their specific substance, she says, from "distinctive contexts and . . . distinctive form[s] of life." They are local "mode[s] of apprehension mediated by [local] cultural forms and social logics."[6]

From this general sort of platform, inquiry can move in a number of directions, most of which have been at least tentatively explored. There are "vocabulary of emotion" studies, designed to ferret out the sense of culturally specific terms for feelings, attitudes, and casts of mind, as Rosaldo does for the Ilongot *liget*. (In fact, this word is inadequately translated as "rage." It is closer to "energy" or "life-force," but even they won't do. One needs, as one does for *mēnis* in *The Iliad*, extended glosses, sample uses, contextual discriminations, behavioral implications, alternate terms.) A whole host of anthropologists, myself included, have performed similar services for words ethnocentrically, tendentiously, or merely lazily, translated from one language or another into English as those affective cliches "guilt" and "shame." The culturological linguist, Anna Wierzbicka, noting that Japanese words "such as *enryo* (roughly, 'interpersonal restraint'), *on* (roughly, 'debt of gratitude'), and *omoiyari* (roughly, 'benefactive empathy') . . . can lead us to the center of a whole complex of cultural values and attitudes . . . revealing a whole network of culture-specific . . . scripts," not only demonstrates the fact for Japanese, but for Russian (*toska*, "melancholy-cum-yearning"), for German (*Heimatliebe*, "love of native place"), and for what she calls "the great Australian adjective," *bloody*. Others have carried out comparable unpackings of Samoan *alofa* ("love or empathy . . . directed upward from status inferiors to status superiors"), Arabic *niya* ("intent" . . . "desire" . . . guileless" . . . "undiluted" . . . "sincere"), and Javanese *rasa* ("perception-feeling-taste-import-meaning").[7]

Beyond such vocabulary-system studies, there has been a wide range of other sorts of research designed to examine emotion meanings and, so far as such a thing is possible, map the conceptual space over which they extend. There are ethnomedical studies of indigenous concepts of disease, suffering, pain, cure, and well-being. There are ethnometaphorical studies of figural regimes—spirit possession, witchcraft, rites of passage—engraving feelings of . . . well, to reverse the usual Tarskian procedure, "possession," "witchery," and "passage." There are ethnopsychological studies of the importance of different emotions in different societies, and the way in which children learn how to feel them. And there are ethnoaesthetical studies of myth, music, art, and the tone and temper of everyday life. Each such study, or type of study, remains tentative and suggestive—difficult to pin down, hard to replicate. And some of them confuse more things than they clarify. But in their bulk, their variety, the range of materials upon which they touch, and especially their steadily increasing observational subtlety, the case for the cultural constitution of emotion seems, to me at least, fairly well made.

However that may be, the strongest, most developed challenges to culturalist, symbolic-action theories of emotion, feeling, and passion do not, in fact, come in the form of doubts about their empirical adequacy as such, which is, after all, but an interpretive issue only further, and more exact, observation can resolve. They come, rather, in the form of accusations of a more fundamental, more deeply crippling, even fatal deficiency: their supposed neglect of "intra-psychic" dynamics and thus their, also supposed, inattention to, and inability to deal with, agency, individuality, and personal subjectivity. Such accounts, the psychoanalyst Nancy Chodorow, who is particularly exercised in this regard, writes,

> are unable to conceive theoretically, even as they describe ethnographically, individual psychological processes of personal meaning creation. . . . [They] bypass the idiosyncratic, divergent ways in which emotions develop and are experienced. . . . Where, we might inquire, does the child gain the capacity, ability, or habit of "reading" cultural bodies in the first place if not in some internal or psychobiological parts of its being?[8]

As an analyst, and a fairly orthodox, Melanie Klein, Hans Loewald, D. S. Winnicott one, Chodorow has a strongly, down deep in the unconscious, "inner life" conception of how hallucinatory infants become fantasy driven adults. Besides the cultural and the biological, she says, there is "a third realm" which cannot be effectively understood (quoting Rosaldo, who, along with myself, is her main target here) "with reference to cultural scenarios and the associations they evoke" or "cultural scenes associated with particular emotions."

> What is missing [she writes] from the approach of doing things with emotion words is an understanding of what exists between universal human instinctuality or panhuman culture and universal cultural particularity, and how this in-between develops and is experienced in particular interpersonal and intrapsychic

settings to which projection and introjection, transference and counter-transference, give personal meaning. . . . [The] psychological [is] a separate register, [it is] sui generis.[9]

But it is not just in this notoriously self-contained and self-engrossed discipline, about whose claims for imperium and ultimacy, and whose peremptory way of putting things, even a sympathetic onlooker may reasonably have some reservations, that this sort of criticism arises. Anyone interested in individual development, from Jean Piaget and Lev Vygotsky to Jerome Bruner and Rom Harré, is likely to have similar concerns about any conception of the passions that does not inquire into their ontogenetic history. The issue is not that cultural analyses of emotions fail to account, as Chodorow seems to imply ("a separate register" . . . "this in-between" . . . "sui generis"), for how it really, really feels for someone actually, inside, in their heart of hearts, to have this one or that one. Put that way, the question is unanswerable; like pain (or "pain"), it feels as it feels. The issue is how, *mēnis*, *liget*, *wrath*, or *rage*, *toska* or *heimatliebe*, *on*, *enryo*, or *omoiyari* (or, for that matter, *bloody*), they come to have the force, the immediacy, and the consequence they have.

Again, recent research, mostly by developmental and comparative psychologists (Bruner, Janet Astington, David Premack), but on occasion by psychologically oriented linguists and anthropologists (George Lakoff, Carol Feldman, William Frawley, Roy D'Andrade) as well, has pushed forward with this matter with some rapidity.[10] Most notably, a seriously revised conception of the infant mind has emerged—not blooming, buzzing, confusion, not ravenous fantasy whirling helplessly about in blind desire, not ingenerate algorithms churning out syntactic categories and ready-to-wear concepts, but meaning making, meaning seeking, meaning preserving, meaning using; in a word, Nelson Goodman's word, world-constructing.[11] Studies of the ability and inclination of children to build models of society, of others, of nature, of self, of thought as such (and, of course, of feeling), and to use them to come to terms with what is going on round and about have proliferated and taken on a practical edge. Studies of autism as a failure (for whatever reasons) on the part of a child to develop a workable theory of "other minds," of reality-imagining and reality-instructing through narrative and storytelling, of self-construction and agency-attribution as a social enterprise, and of subjectivity as intersubjectively, thus contextually, thus culturally, achieved are giving us a picture of how our minds come to be in which "doing things with emotion words" and "personal meaning creation" do not much look like "separate registers." "The development of the child's thinking," Vygotsky, the godfather of this sort of work, wrote seventy years ago, "depends on his mastery of the social means of thinking. . . . The use of signs leads humans to a specific structure of behavior that breaks away from biological development and creates new forms of a culturally based psychological process."[12]

Thus it is that feelings happen: "between a literal lesion and a literary trope," as Richard Shweder has remarked, "there is a lot of room for a broken heart." But, as he also remarks, "frayed nerves, tired blood, splitting heads, and broken hearts [are] metonymies of suffering; they give . . . expression by means of body-part metaphors to forms of embodied suffering experience through the body parts used to express them. . . . [But] splitting heads do not split, broken hearts do not break, tired blood continues to circulate at the same rate, and frayed nerves show no structural pathology."[13]

Other emotional states, though, sometimes do; or at least involve observable (and perceptible) deformations in somatic processes. The recourse to body-part imagery to characterize not just suffering, but emotion generally (if hearts break with despair, they burst with joy) reminds us that, however they may be characterized, and however one comes to have them, feelings are *felt*. Faces flush hot and redden or they drain cold and pale, stomachs churn or sink, palms sweat, hands tremble, breath shortens, jaws drop, to say nothing of the complicated swellings and perturbations that eros brings on. Even literal lesions, if they are somebody's lesions, in somebody's brain, coloring somebody's life, and not extra-cultural gods from a cerebral machine, are worth looking at.

Neurologists have, of course, long investigated the implications for mental functioning of lesions located in one or another region of the brain. But, until recently, the bulk of this work has had to do with cognitive processing in the narrower, intellective sense—perceptional, linguistic, memory, or motor defects and deficits; Wer nicke failures to recognize, Broca failures to produce. Emotional alterations, perhaps because they are less definite in form and more difficult to measure (as well, perhaps, because they are not readily characterized in deficiency terms) have, from William James to Oliver Sacks, been more phenomenologically reported, albeit brilliantly, than somatically unpacked.

This, too, has now begun to change, in example of which fact, we may look, in hurried summary, at Antonio Damasio's *Descartes' Error: Emotion, Reason, and the Human Brain*, only one of a number of recent inquiries into what has come to be called "the embodied brain."[14] Damasio reports there on his work on persons—named, described, particularized, and culturally located persons—with frontal lobe injuries (a spike through the forehead, an excavated meningioma, a stroke, a leucotomy), and the inferences that can be drawn from their strugglings, their subjectivities, their personalities, and their fates concerning the role of feeling in the construction of a human existence: "Feelings let us catch a glimpse of the organism in full biological swing, a reflection of the mechanisms of life itself as they go about their business. Were it not for the possibility of sensing body states . . . there would be no suffering or bliss, no longing or mercy, no tragedy or glory in the human condition."[15]

And no meaning. The presenting condition of his frontal cases—a nineteenth-century New England railroad worker, a professional accountant, a stockbroker, a man damaged at birth and never recovered, a dozen or so in all—is a certain affectlessness, shallowness, detachment, and indecision, an irregularity of aim, an inability to choose a course, foresee consequences, or learn from mistakes, to follow convention, plan the future, respond appropriately to others; all this in the company of otherwise normal, even superior, motor, linguistic, perceptual, and intellectual abilities.

This "Gage matrix," as Damasio calls it after his type case, the unfortunate railroad worker with a hole in his forebrain—a certain Phineas P. Gage—is fundamentally an affective disorder, an attenuation of emotional capacity that cripples at once judgment, will, and social sensitivity:

> [Gage matrix] social behavior and decision-making defect [are] compatible with a normal social-knowledge base, and with pre-

served higher order neuro-psychological functions such as conventional memory, language, basic attention, basic working memory and basic reasoning . . . [but they are] accompanied by a reduction in emotional reactivity and feeling. . . . [And this reduction] in emotion and feeling [is] not an innocent bystander next to the defect in social behavior. . . . [The] cold-bloodedness of [Gage patients'] reasoning prevents [them] from assigning different values to different options, and [makes their] decision-making landscape hopelessly flat. . . . It . . . also [makes it] too shifty and unsustained for the time required to make response selections . . . a subtle rather than basic defect in working memory [that alters] the remainder of the reasoning process required for a decision to emerge.[16]

From this foundation, a parabolical syndrome teaching a conceptual lesson, Damasio goes on to develop an articulated theory of the way emotion functions in our mental life—somatic markers, recalled perceptions, dispositional body states, neural selves, and so on—which we cannot, and need not, follow out here (it is, in any case, appropriately tentative); save, perhaps, to note that Francis Bacon's laconical doctrine, "the intellect of man is no dry light," receives new and powerful empirical support. "Emotions and feelings [are] not intruders in the bastion of reason," Damasio sums up his studies and his point of view, "they [are] enmeshed in its networks for worse *and* for better."[17] The passions—love, pain, and the whole damn thing—can wreck our lives. But so, and as completely, can their loss or absence.

∽

So much, then, for my minature case in instructive point: emotion in culture, mind, and brain . . . brain, mind, and culture. It is, I trust, at least dimly apparent from these compacted, offhand accounts of differently imagined and differently pursued approaches to the study of feeling (though, I could, as well, have taken learning or memory, or perhaps even madness), how a restless, catch-as-catch-can movement of attention across counterpoised disciplinary matrices, an opportunistic shift of focus from one competing research program and community to another, can yield a sense of the general direction of things in a dispersed and distributed field of scientific inquiry.[18] Frontal assaults, massive drives toward conceptual unity and methodological agreement, have their place—now and then, and when the situation permits. So does ever-deepening technical specialization, insulated, purified, and border-patrolled fact-making, without which no science, even a social one, can advance. But they in themselves do not, and will not, produce the synoptical view of what it is we are severally after—the end, as we say, in mind.

In the present instance, what we are looking for and how we must look for it (as well as what we may achieve for ourselves and our lives in our looking) seems to me exactly, if tropologically, set out in Richard Wilbur's compendious little poem called . . . well, called . . .

Mind

Mind in its purest play is like some bat
That beats about in caverns all alone.
Contriving by a kind of senseless wit
Not to conclude against a wall of stone.

It has no need to falter or explore;
Darkly it knows what obstacles are there,
And so may weave and flitter, dip and soar
In perfect courses through the blackest air.

And has this simile a like perfection?
The mind is like a bat. Precisely. Save
That in the very happiest intellection
A graceful error may correct the cave.[19]

Notes

1. Clark, A., *Being There: Putting Brain, Body, and World Together Again*, Cambridge: MIT Press, 1997, p. 213.

2. B. Shore, *Culture in Mind, Cognition and the Problem of Meaning*, New York: Oxford University Press, 1996; J. Bruner, *Actual Minds, Possible Worlds*,

Cambridge: Harvard University Press, 1986; R. A. Shweder, *Thinking through Cultures: Expeditions in Cultural Psychology*, Cambridge: Harvard University Press, 1991; R. Harré, *The Discursive Mind*, Thousand Oaks, Calif.: Sage Publications, 1994; S. Toulmin, *The Inner Life: The Outer Mind*, Worcester, Mass.: Clark University Press, 1985; M. Douglas, *How Institutions Think*, Syracuse: Syracuse University Press, 1986; G. Bateson, *Steps toward an Ecology of Mind*, Novato, Calif.: Chandler, 1972; N. Goodman, *Ways of Worldmaking*, New York: Hackett, 1978.

3. M. Cole, *Cultural Psychology: The Once and Future Science*, Cambridge: Harvard University Press, 1996.

4. N. J. Chodorow, *The Power of Feelings, Personal Meaning in Psychoanalysis, Gender, and Culture*, New Haven: Yale University Press, 1999, p. 144.

5. M. Rosaldo, *Knowledge and Passion*, Cambridge: Cambridge University Press, 1980; C. Lutz, *Unnatural Emotions: Everyday Sentiments on a Micronesian Atoll and Their Challenge to Western Theory*, Chicago: University of Chicago Press, 1988; J. L. Briggs, *Never in Anger*, Cambridge: Harvard University Press, 1970; Shweder, *Thinking through Culture*; R. I. Levy, *Tahitians: Mind and Experience in the Society Islands*, Chicago: University of Chicago Press, 1973; A. Wierzbicka, *Understanding Cultures through Their Keywords*, Oxford: Oxford University Press, 1997.

6. Rosaldo, *Knowledge and Passion*, p. 222.

7. Wierzbicka, *Understanding Cultures*, pp. 16–17, 157, 218; Shore, *Culture in Mind*, pp. 301–302; L. Rosen, *Bargaining for Reality: The Construction of Social Relations in a Muslim Community*, Chicago: University of Chicago Press, 1984, p. 48; C. Geertz, *The Religion of Java*, Glencoe, Ill., The Free Press, 1960, pp. 238–241. For a succinct statement of this general approach, see, H. Geertz, "The Vocabulary of Emotion," *Psychiatry* 22 (1959):225–237.

8. Chodorow, *The Power of Feelings*, p. 161.

9. *Ibid.*, pp. 164, 166, 218.

10. J. Bruner, *Acts of Meaning*, Cambridge: Harvard University Press, 1990; J. W. Astington, *The Child's Discovery of the Mind*, Cambridge: Harvard University Press; 1993; D. Premack and G. Woodruff, "Does the Chimpanzee Have a Theory of Mind," *Behavioral and Brain Sciences*, 1 (1978):515–526; G. Lakoff, *Women, Fire, and Dangerous Things*, Chicago: University of Chicago Press, 1987; C. F. Feldman, *The Development of Adaptive Intelligence*, San Francisco: Jossey-Bass, 1974; Frawley, W., *Vygotsky and Cognitive Science, Language and the Unification of the Social and Computational Mind*, Cambridge: Harvard University Press, 1997; R. D'Andrade, "Cultural Cognition, "*Foundations of Cognitive Sciences*, in M. I. Posner, ed., Cambridge: MIT Press, pp. 745–830.

11. Goodman, *Ways of Worldmaking*; cf. J. Bruner, *The Culture of Education*, Cambridge: Harvard University Press, 1996.

12. Quoted in Frawley, *Vygotsky*, p. 143.

13. Shweder, *Thinking through Cultures*, p. 324.

14. A. R. Damasio, *Descartes' Error: Emotion, Reason, and the Human Brain*, New York: Putnam, 1994.

15. *Ibid.*, p. xv.

16. *Ibid.*, p. 51.

17. *Ibid.*, p. xii.

18. For a compelling discussion of schizophrenia in terms of cultural forms of sensibility, see L. A. Sass, *Madness and Modernism: Insanity in the Light of Modern Art, Literature, and Thought*, New York: Basic Books, 1992.

19. R. Wilbur, *New and Collected Poems*, New York: Harcourt Brace-Jovanovich, 1988, p. 240.

$\mathcal{XI}$ ∽

The World in Pieces:
Culture and Politics at the End
of the Century

To the memory of Edward Shils
. . . with whom I sometimes agreed

The World in Pieces

Political theory, which presents itself as addressing universal and abiding matters concerning power, obligation, justice, and government in general and unconditioned terms, the truth about things as at bottom they always and everywhere necessarily are, is in fact, and inevitably, a specific response to immediate circumstances. However cosmopolitan it may be in intent, it is, like religion, literature, historiography, or law, driven and animated by the demands of the moment: a guide to perplexities particular, pressing, local, and at hand.

This is clear enough from its history, especially now that that history is at last coming to be written, by Quentin Skinner, John Pocock, and others, in realistic terms—as a story of the engagements of intellectuals with the political situations that lie round and about them, rather than as an immaculate procession of doctrines moved along by the logic of ideas. It is, by now, hardly unrecognized that Plato's political idealism or Aristotle's political moralism had something to do with their reactions to the vicissitudes of the Greek city states, Machiavelli's realism with his involvement in the maneuverings of the Renaissance principalities, and Hobbes's absolutism with his horror of the rages of popular disorder in early modern Europe. Similarly for Rousseau and the passions of the Enlightenment, for Burke and those of the reaction to it, for balance of power *realpolitikers* and nineteenth-century nationalism and imperialism, for John Rawls, Ronald Dworkin, and the liberal rights theorists and the post-45 welfare states of North America and Western Europe, for Charles Taylor, Michael Sandel, and the so-called communitarians and the failure of those states to produce the life envisaged. The motive to general reflection about politics in general is radically ungeneral. It proceeds from a desire, a desperation even, to make sense of the play of power and aspiration one finds swirling about in this disrupted place, at that disjointed time.

Today, a decade after the fall of the Berlin Wall, it is clear that we are once more in such a place, at such a time. The world we have been living in since Teheran and Potsdam, indeed since Sedan and Port Arthur—a world of compact powers and contending blocs, the arrangements and rearrangements of macro-alliances—is no more. What there is instead, and how we ought to go about thinking about it, is, however, distinctly less clear.

A much more pluralistic pattern of relationships among the worlds's peoples seems to be emerging, but its form remains vague and irregular, scrappy, ominously indeterminate. The collapse of the Soviet Union and the fumblings of the Russia which has succeeded it (not the same one, even spatially, that preceded it) have brought in their wake a stream of obscure divisions and strange instabilities. So have the rekindling of nationalist passions in Central and Eastern Europe, the crosshatched anxieties that the reunification of Germany has stimulated in Western Europe, and the so-called American Withdrawal: the declining ability (and the declining willingness) of the United States to engage its power in distant parts of the world—the Balkans or East Africa, the Maghreb or the South China Sea. The growing domestic tensions in many countries arising from large-scale, culturally discordant migrations, the appearance of armed and impassioned religiopolitical movements in various parts of the world, and the emergence of new centers of wealth and power in the Middle East, in Latin America, and along the Asian edge of the Pacific Rim have but added to the general sense of motion and uncertainty. All of these developments, and others induced by them (ethnic civil wars, linguistic separatism, the "multiculturalization" of international capital), have not produced a sense of a new world order. They have produced a sense of dispersion, of particularity, of complexity, and of uncenteredness. The fearful symmetries of the postwar era have come unstuck, and we, it seems, are left with the pieces.

All large-scale, discontinuous changes of this sort, the sort that scholars and statesmen like to call "world historical," to excuse the fact that they did not see them coming, produce both new possibilities and novel dangers, unexpected gains, surprising losses. The disappearance, at least for the moment, of the threat of massive nuclear exchange, the freeing of a wide range of people from great power domination, and the relaxation of the ideological rigidities and forced choices of a bipolar world are positive developments from just about anybody's point of view. The recent advances toward peace and civility, fragile as they are, in South Africa, between the Israelis and the PLO, or, in a rather different way, in Northern Ireland, probably could not have occurred, and certainly not so quickly, if the distance between local dispute and global confrontation was still as short as it was before 1989. Nor, if it were, would Americans even be thinking of negotiating with Cubans, Russians with Japanese, Seoul with Pyongyang, Barak with Arafat.

On the other hand, the upheavals brought on by nationalist enmities previously held in check, if at enormous human cost, by powerful autocracies are hardly simply to be welcomed as the blessings of liberty. Neither are the falterings of European integration, now that the fear of Communism is relieved; the lessened ability of world powers to pressure client states to behave themselves, now that the rewards of clientship have lessened; nor the multiplication of candidates for regional domination, now that international politics have grown less constrained by global strategies. Superpower arms reduction and nuclear proliferation, political liberation and deepening parochialism, borderless capitalism and economic bucca-neering: it is difficult to draw a definite balance.

But perhaps the most fateful change is, again, the pervasive rag-gedness of the world with which, so suddenly, we now are faced. The shattering of larger coherences, or seeming such, into smaller ones, uncertainly connected one with another, has made relating local realities with overarching ones, "the world around here" (to adapt Hillary Putnam's lambent phrase) with the world overall, ex-tremely difficult. If the general is to be grasped at all, and new unities uncovered, it must, it seems, be grasped not directly, all at once, but via instances, differences, variations, particulars—piece-meal, case by case. In a splintered world, we must address the splinters.

And that is where theory, if there is to be any, comes in. In particular, where does this falling apart into parts—let us call it "disassembly"—leave the great, integrative, totalizing concepts we have so long been accustomed to using in organizing our ideas about world politics, and particularly about similarity and difference among peoples, societies, states, and cultures: concepts like "tradi-tion," "identity," "religion," "ideology," "values," "nation," indeed even "culture," "society," "state," or "people" themselves? Surely, we are not reduced, now that the stark opposition of "East" and "West" has been exposed as the ethnocentric formula it always was (the East is Moscow, the West is Washington, and every place else—Havana, Tokyo, Belgrade, Paris, Cairo, Beijing, Johannesburg—is derivatively located) to talking only about idiosyncratic details and immediate concerns, to thought-bites and the wandering attentions of the evening news? Some general notions, new or reconditioned, must be constructed if we are to penetrate the dazzle of the new heterogeneity and say something useful about its forms and its future.

There are, in fact, a fair number of proposals now being ad-vanced as to the direction that thinking about the emerging situa-tion ought to take: proposals about how to understand it, about how to live with it, about how to correct it, or, for there are always those (especially in Europe, where historical pessimism is so often taken for a mark of breeding and cultivation) who stoutly insist that nothing ever really changes in human affairs, because nothing ever changes in the human heart, about how to deny that it is actually emerging.

The most prominent of these proposals, or anyway the most celebrated, is, in at least one meaning of that manufactured and protean term, "postmodernism." In this view, the search for comprehensive patterns must simply be abandoned as a relic of the antiquated quest for the eternal, the real, the essential, and the absolute. There are, so it is said, no master narratives, about "identity," about "tradition," about "culture," or about anything else. There are just events, persons, and passing formulas, and those inconsonant. We must content ourselves with diverging tales in irreconcilable idioms, and not attempt to enfold them into synoptic visions. Such visions (this vision has it) are not to be had. Trying to achieve them leads only to illusion—to stereotype, prejudice, resentment, and conflict.

In full opposition to this neurasthenical skepticism about efforts to pull things together into encompassing accounts, *grands recits* with a plot and a moral, there are attempts not to discard large-scale, integrative, and totalizing concepts as vacuous and misleading, but rather to replace them by even more large-scale, integrative, and totalizing ones—"civilizations," or whatever. Attempts to tell stories even grander and more dramatic are beginning to appear, now that the older ones are wearing out, stories of the clash of uncommunicating societies, contradictory moralities, and incommensurable world views. "The great divisions among human kind and the dominating source of conflict [in the years immediately ahead]," the American political scientist Samuel Huntington has recently proclaimed, "will be cultural," not "primarily ideological or primarily economic."[1] "The clash of civilizations," he says, "will dominate global politics. The fault lines between civilizations [Christian and Islamic, Confucian and Hindu, American and Japanese, European and African] will be the battle lines of the future." "The next world war, if there is one," as he apparently thinks altogether likely, given these massive aggregations of religion, race, locality, and language, "will be a war between civilizations."

Faced with this choice between disabused skepticism that leaves us with little to say, save that difference is difference and there is no getting around it, and operatic word-painting that conjures up even more spectacular, war-of-the-worlds collisions than those we seem, just now, to have so narrowly avoided (as well as with various other implausible suggestions—that history has ended, that knowledge claims are but bids for power thinly disguised, that it all comes down to the fortunes of genes), those of us who are committed to sorting through concrete matters so as to develop circumstantial comparisons—specific inquiries into specific differences—may seem naive, quixotical, dissimulating, or behind the times. But if guidelines for navigating in a splintered, disassembled world are to be found, they will have to come from such patient, modest, close-in work. Neither cool scenes nor hot scenarios will really do. We need to find out how, rather exactly, the land lies.

But that, too, is much more difficult now that the way in which we have become accustomed to dividing up the cultural world—into small blocks (Indonesia, say, in my own case, or Morocco), grouped into larger ones (Southeast Asia or North Africa) and those into yet larger ones (Asia, the Middle East, the Third World, or whatever)—no longer works very well on any of its levels. Intensely focused studies (of Javanese music or Moroccan poetry, African kinship or Chinese bureaucracy, German law or English class structure) are no longer adequate, or even intelligible, as enclosed, free-standing inquiries unrelated to one another, to their setting and surroundings, or to the general developments of which they are a part. But at the same time, the lines along which such relationships might be traced, such settings described, and such developments defined are tangled, circuitous, and difficult to make out. The same dissolution of settled groupings and familiar divisions that has rendered the political world so angular and hard to fathom has made the analysis of culture, of how it is people see things, respond to them, imagine them, judge them, deal with them, a far more awkward enterprise than it was when we knew, or rather thought that we knew, what went with what and what did not.

In cultural terms, as in political, "Europe," say or "Russia," or "Vienna" must be understood not as a unity of spirit and value, set off against other such supposed unities—the Middle East, Africa, Asia, Latin America, the United States, or London—but as a conglomerate of differences, deep, radical, and resistant to summary. And the same is true of the various subparts we in one way or another mark off within these conglomerates—Protestant and Catholic, Islamic and Orthodox; Scandinavian, Latin, Germanic, Slavic; urban and rural, continental and insular, native and migrant. The disassembly of the political world has of course not caused this heterogeneity. It is history, careening and wayward, and riven with violence, that has done that. Disassembly has only made the hetero-geneity patent: plain, impossible to cover over with enormous ideas, impossible any longer not to see.

What we need, it seems, are not enormous ideas, nor the aban-donment of synthesizing notions altogether. What we need are ways of thinking that are responsive to particularities, to individualities, oddities, discontinuities, contrasts, and singularities, responsive to what Charles Taylor has called "deep diversity," a plurality of ways of belonging and being, and that yet can draw from them—from it—a sense of connectedness, a connectedness that is neither com-prehensive nor uniform, primal nor changeless, but nonetheless real.[2] Taylor's concern, facing ideologized separatism, the threatened de-parture of Quebec from Canada, is with political disassembly, with the belonging, citizenship side of identity in a splintered world: What is a country if it is not a nation? But the matter is the same on the being, selfhood side that is its mirrored and obverse face: What is a culture if it is not a consensus?

∞

A good deal of philosophical and social scientific thinking in Eu-rope and the United States is currently absorbed, not very effec-tively, with both of these questions, often, indeed, in ways which confuse them with one another, and with the far from identical and, to my mind, rather more awkward, flaccid, and overgeneralized, cer-tainly overused, notion of "nationalism." The coexistence, in most parts of the world, indeed in virtually all, of great cultural traditions, rich, distinctive, and historically deep (civilizations in the proper, not the polemical, sense of the term), with an endless progression of differences within differences, divisions within divisions, jumbles within jumbles, raises a question that cannot any longer be passed off as idle or inconsequent: how is it, in so multifold a world, that political, social, or cultural selfhood comes to be? If identity without unison is in fact the rule—in India or the United States, in Brazil or Nigeria, in Belgium or Guyana, or even in Japan, that supposed model of immanent like-mindedness and essentialized uniqueness—on what does it rest?

Here, too, however, the question is *mal posée* if it is interpreted as a general one looking for an invariant answer—the problem, again, in at least much of the writing on "nationalism" (or, for that matter, on "ethnicity" as well) that has become so popular in the last few years. For there are nearly as many ways in which such identities, fleeting or enduring, sweeping or intimate, cosmopolitan or closed-in, amiable or bloody-minded, are put together as there are materials with which to put them together and reasons for doing so. American Indian, Israeli, Bolivian, Muslim, Basque, Tamil, European, Black, Australian, Gypsy, Ulsterman, Arab, Maroon, Maronite, Hispanic, Flamand, Zulu, Jordanian, Cypriot, Bavarian, and Taiwanese—answers people sometimes give to the question, whether self-asked or asked by others, as to who (or, perhaps, more exactly, what) they are—simply do not form an orderly structure.

Nor a stable one. As the world becomes more thoroughly interconnected, economically and politically, as people move about in unforeseen, only partially controllable, and increasingly massive, ways, and as new lines are drawn and old ones erased, the catalogue of available identifications expands, contracts, changes shape, ramifies, involutes, and develops. A half century ago there were no Beurs or Bangladeshis, but there were Peranakans and Yugoslavians; Italy did not have a "Moroccan problem," Hong Kong did not have a Vietnamese one. (Nor Vancouver a Hong Kong one.) Even those identities that persist, as both Austrians and Americans have cause to know, as do Poles, Shi'is, Malays, and Ethiopians, alter in their bonds, their content, and their inner meaning.

Political theorists tend to operate at levels well above this thicket of characterizations, distinctions, particularities, and labelings that makes up the who-is-what world of collective identities, to float musefully over it as though in a Montgolfier balloon—perhaps for fear that descending into it will expose them to the sort of end-less, conflicting detail that so often overwhelms anthropologists; per-haps because the thicket as such seems somehow repellent: emo-tional, creaturely, irrational, dangerous; perhaps because it seems unreal or incidental, mere gloss, decor, and mystification. But if what we are in fact faced with is a world of pressed-together dissimilarities variously arranged, rather than all-of-a-piece nation-states grouped into blocs and superblocs (the sort of thing that is visible from a balloon), there is nothing for it but to get down to cases, whatever the cost to generality, certainty, or intellectual equilibrium.

But, in fact, the costs may not be so great as feared, and the benefits underestimated: abstraction from specifics is not the only form that theory takes. In the years immediately ahead, as China lumbers awkwardly and unevenly into the international economy, as Germany seeks to mend a half century of political division, as Russia tries to find some workable form in which to exist, as African societies try to contain multiple hatreds and intricate distinctions, as Japan, discovering or rediscovering its own variousness, seeks to define a place for itself in a region moving a half dozen directions at once, and as the United States, France, Mexico, or Algeria find themselves to rest on a good deal less commonality of mind than their public creeds proclaim them to have, approaches to political analysis that engage such matters in the fullness of their partic-ularity are likely to be more helpful to understanding than those that attempt to develop some overall, panoptical view.

It would seem, in short, that a number of serious adjustments in thought must occur if we, philosophers, anthropologists, historians, or whoever, are going to have something useful to say about the disassembled, or anyway disassembling, world of restless identities and uncertain connections. First, difference must be recognized, ex-plicitly and candidly, not obscured with offhand talk about the Confucian Ethic or the Western Tradition, the Latin Sensibility of the Muslim Mind Set, nor with wispy moralizings about universal values or dim banalities about underlying oneness: Rosie O'Grady and the Colonel's Lady. Second, and more important, difference must be seen *not* as the negation of similarity, its opposite, its con-trary, and its contradiction. It must be seen as comprising it: locating it, concretizing it, giving it form. The blocs being gone, and their hegemonies with them, we are facing an era of dispersed entanglements, each distinctive. What unity there is, and what identity, is going to have to be negotiated, produced out of difference.

Whatever originality and distinctiveness Malaysian and Chinese forms of life in Southeast Asia may have, for example, or English, Scottish, Welsh, or Irish in Britain, Indio and Latino in Nicaragua or Guatemala, Muslim and Christian in Nigeria, Muslim and Hindu in India, Sinhalese and Tamil in Sri Lanka, or Black and White in South Africa—and they clearly have a very great deal—it arises out of the ways in which the variety of the practices which make them up are positioned and composed. It is not, to adapt Wittgenstein's famous image of a rope, a single thread which runs all the way through them that defines them and makes them into some kind of a whole. It is the overlappings of differing threads, intersecting, entwined, one taking up where another breaks off, all of them posed in effective tensions with one another to form a composite body, a body locally disparate, globally integral. Teasing out those threads, locating those intersections, entwinements, connectings, and tensions, probing the very compositeness of the composite body, its deep diversity, is what the analysis of these sorts of countries and societies demands. There is no opposition between fine grained work, uncovering variousness, and general characterization, defining affinities. The trick is to get them to illuminate one another, and reveal thereby what identity is. And what it is not.

∞

To do this—to connect local landscapes, full of detail and incident, to the intricate topographies within which they are set—demands an alteration not only in the way in which we conceive of identity but of the way we write about it, the vocabulary we use to render it visible and measure its force. Political theory, so often in our times either synoptic musings about essentialized principles locked in a Manichaean death struggle—collectivism and individualism, objectivism and relativism, right and obligation, freedom and constraint—or ideological commitments dressed up to look like ineluctable deductions from inescapable premises, needs to get a firmer grip on the hard particularities of the present moment. But the language within which it is cast, a language of summings up rather than of sortings out, seriously inhibits most of it from doing so. The available genres of description and assessment are ill-fitted to a multiplex world, mixed, irregular, shifting, and discontinuous.

It would seem that something between, or perhaps combining in some fashion or other, philosophical reflections on the self, agency, will, and authenticity (or the questioning of these as ideological constructions or metaphysical illusions), historical tracings of the emergence of ethnicities, nations, states, and solidarities (or the imagining of these in the political rituals and cultural technologies of modern life), and ethnographical representations of mythologies, moralities, traditions, and world views (or, the excoriation of these as exoticizing, hegemonizing, neocolonialist reductions of a radically otherwise, put-upon other) would seem to be needed. But it is not very clear what that would be. Someone attempting, as I am here, to confront the confused and conflicted picture presented by a world no longer satisfactorily describable as either a distribution of peoples or a system of states, a catalogue of cultures or a typology of regimes, finds little to fall back upon in the received conceivings of the human sciences.

My tack here, improvisatory, opportunistic, and casually redirected as I go along, will be to focus in turn on the two questions I mentioned earlier as leading into the central interpretative issues raised up by the fractionation, the instability, and the uncenteredness of the post-Wall world: What is a Country if it is not a Nation? What is a Culture if it is not a Consensus? A few short years ago, when the chart of the world looked reasonably consolidated and its outlines more or less distinct, both of these questions would have seemed confused or senseless, because there was little, if anything seen to be separating the contrasted terms. Countries *were* nations—Hungary, France, Egypt, Brazil. Cultures *were* shared ways of life—Hungarian, French, Egyptian, Brazilian. To drive a wedge between the terms, and thus between the questions themselves, to disentangle them from one another and pursue them separately, would seem at best a pointless undertaking, and at worst a mischievous one.

It may be mischievous, or at least disequilibrating; but it is not pointless. There are very few countries any more, and perhaps there never were, that even approximately coincide with culturally solidary entities; Japan, Norway, possibly Uruguay, if you forget the Italians, maybe New Zealand, if you forget the Maoris. State forms—Mexican and German, Nigerian and Indian, Singaporean and Saudi Arabian—are so enormously various as hardly to be collected under a single term. The foundations of legitimacy of even immediate neighbors, the sorts of stories they tell themselves to account for their existence and justify its continuance—Israel and Jordan, Cambodia and Vietnam, Greece and Turkey, Sudan and Ethiopia—are contrastively phrased, scarcely translatable, in no way homologous. The illusion of a world paved from end to end with repeating units that is produced by the pictorial conventions of our political atlases, polygon cutouts in a fitted jigsaw, is just that—an illusion.

To take apart the political and the cultural aspects of the disassembled world, prior to relating them again to one another, at least permits us to uncover something of the maneuverings and cross-actions involved in the formation and interaction of collective personae, and some of the conundrums such maneuverings and cross-actions pose for the social orderings, the economies, the polities, and the day-to-day lives, in which they take place. We know at least something—not anywhere enough, but something—about how differences in power, wealth, status, luck, and ability are, for better or worse, composed in society, about how material interests are adjusted, reconciled, contained, or suppressed, and about how ideological conflicts are resolved or exacerbated, balanced or fought out, how they are managed. But in the face of social struggles phrased in terms of selfhood, of inbred feeling and primordial loyalty, of natural contrasts and immanent quiddities, we remain pretty much at sea. They seem to come like storms and evaporate with mere exhaustion or an unaccountable change in the weather, or else, and more often, persist like chronic irritants, smoldering, half-hidden, and merely lived (or died) with, not really understood, not really resolved.

An improvement upon this situation of mere witnessing, and mere deploring, is not easily come by. But surely the first move toward improving it is to look more carefully at just what, on the ground and in place, countries come to (or don't), as collective actors. And the second, surely, is to look at what it is (to the degree that it does) that makes them such.

Since 1945, we have gone from a situation in which there were perhaps fifty or so generally recognized countries, the rest of the world being distributed into colonies, protectorates, dependencies, and the like, to one in which there are nearly two hundred, and almost certainly more to come. The difference, of course, is the decolonization revolution that took place in Asia and Africa, and to some extent in the Pacific and the Caribbean, in the fifties and sixties, now reinforced by the breakup of the last of the transcultural empires (unless one considers China as such), the Soviet Union. This revolution has been generally understood, both by its leaders and its theorists, and by those against whom they were rebelling, as a liberation from foreign domination, and it was, consequently, rather quickly and easily assimilated to the nationalist movements in Europe and Latin America in the nineteenth century—as the last wave of a global thrust toward self-determination, the rule of like over like, the modernization of governance, the unification of state and culture, or whatever. But it was, as has become increasingly clear as time has passed and the more purely ideological ardors have cooled, something rather more profound than that. It was an alteration, a transformation even, of our whole sense of the relationships between history, place, and political belonging.

The realization that the appearance of a host of new countries, large, small, and medium sized, in Asia and Africa was something more than an imitative catching up on the part of the "undeveloped," or "backward," or "third" world to the so-called nation state pattern constructed in Europe from the seventeenth through the nineteenth centuries, that it was in many ways more of a challenge to that pattern than it was a reinforcement or a reincarnation of it, has been rather slow in coming. The diffusionist notion that the modern world was made in northern and western Europe and then seeped out like an oil slick to cover the rest of the world has obscured the fact (which should already have been apparent from developments in the United States and Latin America, leave aside Liberia, or Haiti, or Thailand, or Japan) that rather than converging toward a single pattern those entities called countries were ordering themselves in novel ways, ways that put European conceptions, not all that secure in any case, of what a country is, and what its basis is, under increasing pressure. The genuinely radical implications of the decolonization process are only just now coming to be recognized. For better or for worse, the dynamics of Western nation building are not being replicated. Something else is going on.

To find out what that might be involves, on the one side, an understanding of terms like "nation," "state," "people," and "society," the worn coinage of political analysis, that does not reduce them all to a common pattern, continuously reproduced, and, on the other, an understanding of terms like "identity," "tradition," "affiliation," and "coherence," the hardly less battered vocabulary of cultural description, that does not reduce them all to uniformity and like-mindedness, to a categorical mold. It is this enterprise I will take up, in a preliminary and exploratory manner, in the next two sections in the hope of illuminating the challenges and the imperilments, the terrors and the possibilities, of the world in pieces.

What Is a Country if It Is Not a Nation?

The words we use, these days, to refer to what we take to be the elementary building blocks of global political order—"nation," "state," "country," "society," "people"—have a disturbing ambiguity built into their range, intent, and definition. On the one hand, we use them interchangeably, as though they were synonyms. "France" or "Hungary," "China" or "Cambodia," "Mexico" or "Ethiopia," "Iran" or "Portugal" are all of these at once—nations, states, countries, societies, and peoples. On the other, we perceive them as leading us off, in their nuances and connotations, their resonances and their inward meanings, in rather different directions: toward blood, race, descent, and the mysteries and mystifications of biological alikeness; toward political and civic loyalty and the indivisibilities of law, obedience, force, and government; toward geographical aggregation, territorial demarcation, and the sense of origin, home, and habitat; toward interaction, companionship, and practical association, the encounter of persons and the play of interests; toward cultural, historical, linguistic, religious, or psychological affinity—a quiddity of spirit.

This ambiguity, persistent, stubborn, perhaps irremovable, has troubled the history of Europe and the Americas from at least the seventeenth century, and it now troubles, at least as relentlessly, Asia and Africa as well. The conception of the biological, the governmental, the territorial, the interactional, and the cultural as equivalent and substitutable expressions of the same reality, as folding into one another and converging toward some overall sum, and the sense that they so fold and converge only partially and incompletely, that they refer back to different realities, represent different sorts of solidarities and affiliations, grow out of different imaginings, different aspirations, and different fears, renders uncertain just what it is that is mapped on the political map of the world. What do we say when we say Mauritania? Slovakia? Bolivia? Australia?

If one browses through the relevant entries of the *The Oxford English Dictionary*, one sees this perplexity and its history, at least for Europe and for English (though I daresay about the same result would be obtained by wandering similarly through the *Grand Robert* or the *Deutsches Wörterbuch*), laid out before one. For each of the terms there is a sort of penumbral, ground bass meaning specific to it, surrounding it with a certain air and tonality, and what looks like a deliberate attempt, indeed a desperate one, to suppress this and force the word in toward a semantic coincidence with the others, to produce, whether as country, people, society, state, or nation, a generic unit of collective agency—bounded, nameable, single, and consistently defined; a historical self.

"Country," for example, said to come from the late Latin root from which we also get "contra" and "counter," moves from a so-called literal meaning, "that which lies opposite or fronting the view, the landscape spread out before one," through a series of definitions from the generalized "a tract or expanse of land of undefined extent; a region, a district," through the rather more specific "tract or district having more or less definite limits in relation to human occupation, e.g. owned by the same lord or proprietor, or inhabited by people of the same race, dialect, occupation, etc." and the "land of a person's birth, citizenship, residence etc.," to the wholly comprehensive "the territory or land of a nation; usually an independent state or a region once independent [this to deal with Scotland and Ireland] and still distinct in race, language, institutions, or historical memories" and, in culmination, the flat and simple "the people of a district or a state, the nation"—as in Macaulay's *History of England,* "The people had no love for their country or their king," which does not mean, I take it, that they disliked the landscape.[3]

"People," itself, follows a similar trajectory from a generalized and indistinct "populace," "multitude," or "commonality," through the rather more specific "persons in relation to a superior or someone to whom they belong" and "the whole body of . . . qualified citizens as a source of power," to, again, the unitary collective, "a body of persons composing a community, tribe, race, [folk], or nation"[4] So does "state," which comes of course, from roots for rank and standing, as in "estate" and "status," and moves semantically through "realm" and "commonwealth" to the more focused "the body of people occupying a defined territory and organized under a sovereign government . . . the territory occupied by such a body" and thence to the fully integral "the supreme civil power and government vested in a country or a nation." "The state is properly," Matthew Arnold wrote in *Democracy,*" . . . the nation in its collective and corporate capacity."[5]

The pattern repeats with "society" ("association with one's fellow men"; "intercourse with persons"; "the aggregate of persons living together in [an] orderly community"; "the system or mode of life adopted by a body of individuals for the purpose of harmonious coexistence"; "connexion . . . union . . . affinity").[6] But it is with the most radically consolidative term in this series, and the most elusive, "nation," that it comes to fullest expression, drawing all the others toward it like some semiotic strange attractor.

"Nation," which comes ultimately from Latin *nation-em,* "breed," "stock," "race," in turn derived from *nasci,* "to be born," has, or has had in the course of its evolution, a number of highly particular applications, such as "a family, a kindred," "an Irish clan," "the native population of a town or city," "a . . . class, kind, or race of persons," "a country, a kingdom," or "the whole people of a country . . . as opposed to some smaller or narrower body within it," the majority of which it has by now escaped into the magisterial capaciousness of what has become its central meaning: "An extensive aggregate of persons, so closely associated with each other by common descent, language, or history, as to form a distinct race or people, usually organized as a separate political state and occupying a definite territory." ("In early examples," the *Oxford English Dictionary* remarks, perhaps uneasy itself with the enormous reach and *pot-au-feu* quality the conception had by 1928 taken on, "the racial idea is usually stronger than the political; in recent use the notion of political unity . . . is more prominent," and gives two quotations, rather opposed in just this tendency, to compound the difficulty: Bright's pub-and-plough populist "the nation in every country dwells in the cottage," and Tennyson's sword-and-scepter hieratic "Let us bury the Great Duke [that is, Wellington] To the noise of the mourning of a mighty nation.")[7]

I bring all this up, not because I think words in themselves make the world go round (though, in fact, they have a lot to do with its works and workings), or because I think you can read political history off from the definitions in dictionaries (though, in fact, they are among the more sensitive, and underused, detectors we have for registering its subsurface tremors). I bring all this up because I think the tension between a convergent and a dispersive conception of collective agency, between the attempt to make the terms for such agency identic and interchangeable and the attempt to maintain their differences and separations, reflects, and indeed drives, a good deal of what is going on in the world these days as well as what philosophers, anthropologists, journalists, and ideologues have to say about what is going on.

Indeed, in the Europe between Napoleon and Hitler (to have a tendentious name for a tendentious period), the move toward the subordination of the various ways of thinking about the "what am I (or you, or we, or they)?" question to that of a comprehensive likeness of kind, difficult to specify, easy to feel, and impossible to eradicate, has been a central dynamic of political history; so much so that it has frequently been identified with the very process of modernization itself.[8] A relatively brief, as these things go, geographically highly localized, and in any case quite incomplete process has been taken as a general paradigm for political development overall and everywhere. It is this, as I would call it prejudice, that, first, the anticolonial revolutions, from India's in the late forties to Angola's in the early seventies, and now the disassembly of the bipolar world (aspects, as a matter of fact, of a single upheaval) have thrown into question.

So far as the anticolonial revolution (which in forty years has quadrupled the number of entities called countries, nations, states, or peoples—distinct societies with names and addresses) is concerned, it has been, as I remarked previously, simply assimilated, whole and entire, to the European development, or what is thought to have been the European development. Especially in its opening, declamatory phases, the Bandung days of the Nkrumahs, Nehrus, Hos, and Sukarnos (and the Maos and the Titos), it was seen as "the last wave" of a worldwide movement toward, to quote Benedict Anderson, the master-narrative theorist of all this, "nationness [as] virtually inseparable from political consciousness."[9] More recently, both the developments within those entities—Nigerian, Sri Lankan, and Algerian decomposition, Cambodian terror, Sudanese genocide, Yemeni civil war—and in their relationships with one another, have complicated the picture more than a bit. And so far as the disassembly of the bipolar world is concerned, the loss of a sense of analogous elements packed into a well-defined structure of power and importance, has rendered the notion that the world is composed of atomic nationalities, mighty and unmighty, sovereign and subaltern, hard to articulate and harder to defend. Resisting the coalescence of the dimensions of political community, keeping the various lines of affinity that turn abstract populations into public actors separate and visible, seems suddenly, once again, conceptually useful, morally imperative, politically realistic.

∞

In pursuit of this aim, one could of course simply run serially and routinely through the various pairs, people and society, society and state, state and nation, and so on, and lay out some of the mischief and misconceptions that result when they are kept insufficiently distinct. To an extent this has already been done, now and again and rather unsystematically, most especially for nation and state as the hyphen in the nation-state formula has begun at long last to be looked upon with a more critical eye and as the principle of national self-determination (any group should have a state that really wants one; any group that has a state is per se a nation) has come to be seen for the wisp or ideality, Tamilnad and Kurdistan, Surinam and Zaire, that it is. But I want to concentrate here on just one of these pairs, country and nation, and especially on freeing the first from the tentacles of the latter. Their fusion, or confusion, which amounts to the submergence of the idea of country almost altogether, not only obscures what is happening in this place or that. It prevents us from seeing very clearly how in fact our world nowadays is put together.

The easiest way to do this is, of course, simply to oppose them to one another. You can damn the one as "nationalism," something (to quote from the last American ambassador to integral Yugoslavia in an otherwise perceptive account of what happened there) "by nature uncivil, antidemocratic, and separatist, because it empowers one ethnic group over others," and praise the other as "patriotism," the decent and warming love of country—green valleys, sidewalk cafes, the call of the muezzin, Fuji in the mists, campos and piazzas, the scent of cloves. Or you can objectify them as classing expressions, irreconcilable sorts, the one bad, the other okay, of "nationalism" as such: "ethnic" vs. "civic," "official" vs. "popular," "divisive" vs. "unificatory," "Habsburg" (or "Eastern") vs. "Liberal" (or "Western") or whatever.[10] In either case, you get a manichaean picture which sets jealous provincialism and sanguineous xenophobia on the one side against honest pride and relaxed self-confidence on the other.

At some very general level, that view from the hovering balloon, this is plausible enough: the sort of nationalism associated with Hitler or Karadzic does seem in thoroughgoing contrast to the sort associated with Gandhi or Lincoln. But again, when we descend to cases, to the ethnicism (if that's what it is) of Israel or Bangladesh, Hungary or Singapore, or the patriotism (if that's what it is) of Castro or Solzhenitsyn, Enoch Powell or Jean-Marie Le Pen, things begin to grow rather less obvious. If one takes, for example, three countries beset right now, in ascending degrees of severity and danger, by nation-phrased collective identities resistant to their embrace, Canada, Sri Lanka, and (ex-) Yugoslavia, it is clear that the relationships between "country" and "nation" are so different from one to the next as to be as impossible to fold into a dichotomous opposition as they are into a promiscuous fusion. And if one moves on then, to Burundi or Nigeria, Afghanistan or Indonesia, Belgium or the United States (I leave aside Switzerland and Lebanon as almost too amenable cases), matters get more various yet. There is, again, nothing for it but a sort of political, or politico-economic, ethnography which can trace out the relationships between particular countries and the affinities and dissonances they are almost everywhere—no, not almost everywhere . . . everywhere—engaged with.

For, insofar as there is a distinction to be made between "country" and "nation," it lies not in the civility and unassertiveness of the one and the passion and clamorousness of the other, which is anyway (China, France, Morocco, Argentina) not always the case. It lies in the one as a political arena and the other as a political force: between a bordered, to some degree arbitrary, space within which the more immediate sorts of public struggle, the sort we unreflectively call domestic (the ordering of social encounters, the distribution of life chances, the utilization of productive resources) are supposed to be contained and regulated, brought into line, as against one of the central energies driving those struggles, the sense of whom one descends from, who one thinks, looks, talks, eats, prays, or moves like, and feels, in result, empathically bound to come what may.

If we take, briefly and with no serious attempt to unpack their histories, assess their prospects, or judge the rights and wrongs of things—a task I am, quite frankly, unprepared for—the three countries I just mentioned as undergoing varying degrees of nation-phrased tension, Canada, Sri Lanka, and the lingering shadow, not gone, not present, that is Yugoslavia, this interplay between the terrain of politics and their complexion is quite apparent. The arrangement and disarrangement of the rifts and solidarities that language, descent, race, religion, and so on generate and the spaces and edges within which those rifts and solidarities are so arranged and disarranged not only differ widely from one case to the next, the particularities of such difference deeply affect what, as we say, with perhaps more reason than we realize, takes place on the ground. A very large country, very unevenly occupied, a small, impacted island country, offshore from a continent, and an irregular cutout of mountain valleys, closed plains, incised rivers, and narrowed coasts, crowded round with jealous neighbors, provide ideational frames, specific and distinctive, for the clash of identities—historicized places that shape with some force the structure of the clash.

Canada, which has been described by the sardonic Toronto press lord, Conrad Black, as "historically (. . .) a collection of people who were not Americans: French-Canadians abandoned by France in 1763 after the British military victory; British Empire Loyalists who fled the American Revolution; immigrants and fugitives from Europe and recently other places, including the United States; Newfoundlanders who narrowly elected to become a Canadian province in 1949 after going bankrupt as an autonomous dominion," plus, though he, perhaps characteristically, forgets to mention them, a significant number of significantly different Amerindian groups, is surely one country in which the difference between the ideational space within which politics is framed and across which it ranges—ten million square kilometers between Detroit and the Artic Circle—and the collective identities that color those politics is impossible to miss.[11] The struggle there, so often seen (at least by outsiders) as a straightforward matter of French *fierté* and English bloody-mindedness, is in fact a multisided, "deep diversity" encounter played out over an immense, imperfectly known, uncertainly conceived, unevenly occupied, and unequally endowed territory. When perhaps 90 percent of the population is concentrated within three hundred kilometers of the U.S. border; when half the population lives in the Toronto to Montreal corridor alone and a quarter of it lives in Quebec, which is more than 80 percent French speaking; and when the other nine-tenths of the country, the more or less frozen north where the greater proportion of the natural resources of the country are located, is so thinly populated as to have an Amerindian majority in most places—merely to scratch the surface of the complexity here (a different sort of French minority in New Brunswick; Inuit Eskimos in the Northwest Territories; Ukrainians, Asians—a rapidly expanding group—and yet more Indians in the west; Métis, French and Indian mixed-bloods speaking a French and Indian Creole, in the forested center; wall-to-wall English in Newfoundland)—you obviously have a situation in which there is a good deal of room for maneuver between parts and wholes, however defined.

And the recent (though not only the recent) political history of the country has consisted of a whole series of such maneuverings, the majority of them abortive, or, to date, incomplete, indefinite, and of uncertain future. There have been attempts to revise constitutional arrangements, already among the most devolved in the world (only hollowed-out Belgium or burnt-out Lebanon seem further advanced), to devise new subunits of various sorts (the Yukon Council, Nunavut, the Métis Association), to adjust internal borders, to redistribute resources among regions and subgroups, and most especially to forestall, or, if that too fails, to prepare for the almost continuously threatened secession of Quebec. And all this while trying, in a country essentially defined by a single border, to maintain its integrity and self-direction vis-à-vis what its leaders usually carefully refer to as "our great neighbor to the south."

The result is at once fluid and oddly persistent—a chronic "Whither Canada?" debate in which language, religion, ethnicity, and regionalism seem continuously on the verge of altering the very shape of the country, redrawing its outlines and transforming the topography of the political landscape whole and entire, while not, so far anyway, managing actually to do so. How it will all play out of course remains to be seen. Will Quebec finally leave, half-leave ("a sovereign state within a sovereign state"), or merely go on endlessly threatening to leave? Whatever it does, what will its relations with the rest of Canada be, including, not unimportantly, with Indian tribes within its borders (Algonkians and Inuits, they comprise the majority in about half the territory claimed by it), with whom it is already embroiled concerning control over natural resources on Indian lands? ("The meek may inherit the earth," as J. Paul Getty is supposed to have said, "but they can forget about the mineral rights.") Will the resentments of the western provinces toward Ontario, which by now provides half the GDP (and in a Quebec-less Canada would provide an overwhelming proportion), or those of the English-speaking remnant in Montreal toward the French majority there, escalate into new fissures? How will the great, open north finally be organized, especially as European Canadians begin to move there? And so on, and on.

And so too with its relationship to its discomfiting neighbor. Black, himself a Quebec-born Anglophone who, like so many of his fellows (a hundred thousand since separatism got underway in 1976) has moved toward more congenerous surroundings, even projects a scenario (called, I trust ironically, "A More Perfect Union") in which, if the bicultural state dissolves, English Canada would form a federation with the United States, stabilizing the latter's "complicated demography" ("Geopolitically, America would be almost born again")—though it is unclear that even he is able to believe such a story.[12] What is clear is that Canada as a country is more a field of (culturally supposed) " 'breeds,' 'kinds' or 'stocks' of persons" than it is one in itself—something, of course, if anything even more true of the United States, "*voll*," as Herder said some time ago, "*von so viel kleinen nationen.*"

Sri Lanka, née Ceylon, is, just to look at it, hardly reminiscent of Canada. A tight little island, not a sprawling continental expanse, it is about a hundred-fiftieth its size. It is a hundred times more densely populated, with its inhabitants reasonably evenly distributed over the whole rather than packed in distinct concentrations set off from great emptinesses. It is a precipitate of a hundred and fifty years of direct colonial rule and more than a millennium of history, not a collection of peoples rather accidentally and rather recently thrown together. And it is tropical, Asian, and but weakly industrialized. That the internal tensions threatening to dismantle it, though, so far at least, much more severe, much more hate-filled, and much more marked with violence, are, nonetheless, in some ways, curiously resemblant of those threatening to dismantle Canada, gives some cause for reflection.[13] Here, too, the country is less itself a purported "stock" or a "kind" than an historicized terrain—a milieu and a place within which such stocks or kinds jostle and maneuver, mutually constructing themselves, their character, and their collective interests.

What seems, to an outsider in any case, most striking about Sri Lanka in terms of the identity-group tensions that have wracked it for the last four decades or so is not the fact that they are more starkly bipolar than is the rule in such cases these days (only Rwanda and Burundi, or perhaps Northern Ireland, seem to approach it in this regard; Nigeria, Yugoslavia, India, Canada, and the United States, multisided, wheels within wheels, are rather more the norm), or even that they are so severe, so chronic, and so resistant to difference splitting. What is most striking is that they involve a clash between two groups, both of which feel themselves to be in some way minorities, that they have arisen so recently as an almost direct result of the puzzlements of the "self" in "self-rule," and that they have taken place in a country that has been, in other respects, rather stable, progressive, and at least moderately successful —slowed population growth, contained inflation, improved education, a decent growth rate, and an infant mortality rate approaching Chile's or South Korea's, a life expectancy matching Hungary's or Argentina's.[14]

The two minorities situation is a result of the fact that the twelve million or so Sinhalese, most of whom are Buddhists and who speak an Indo-European language, are all of them there are in the world, while the three million or so Tamils, most of whom are Hindu and who speak a Dravidian language, are matched by thirty or forty million (the number is, characteristically, disputed) more of them just across the Palk Strait in southern India. Both, thus, can easily see themselves as being swallowed up by the other: the Sinhalese by Tamil expansionism, which has flared up periodically under the banner of a free and unified Tamilnad; the Tamils by Sinhala-only domination of Sri Lanka as such, a central theme in the political uproar that independence, itself a sedate and undramatic, almost *huis clos*, affair—no war, no revolution, not even all that much agitation—brought on.

The creation of a country, or more accurately, I suppose, the officialization of one where a colony had been before, is what set Sri Lanka's ethnical troubles in motion—not ancient grievances or long-nurtured fears. Before 1948, and for a few years after, a bicultural Anglicized elite, entrenched in Colombo, kept matters proceeding in a more or less orderly way; what group tensions existed were diffuse and local, kept in check by multiple differentiations, established accommodations, cross-cutting loyalties, and the practical intricacies of everyday life. But from the mid-fifties this delicate and somewhat artificial comity collapsed, replaced by a radical division of the population into "Sinhala" and "Tamil" (or "Buddhist" and "Hindu," or "Aryan" and "Dravidian") supercategories and an ascending curve of suspicion, jealousy, hatred, and violence that has not ended yet, despite a series of Canada-like constitutional proposals, a continuing shuffle of governments, and the reluctantly invited assistance, now terminated, of the Indian army.

What, in the space of a few short years, brought all this on— the coming to power of Sinhalese demagogues and the rejection of the English-speaking elite by the Sinhalese- and Tamil-speaking masses alike; the impassioned language battle, still unresolved, that followed from that; the transformation of Buddhism from a quietist religion into a militant creed under the leadership of revivalist monks and ayurvedic doctors; the growth of Tamil separatism, attraction toward south India, and movement back and forth across the Strait; the upsurge of internal migration, religious segregation, ethnic ingathering, and reciprocal terrorism; the recrudescence of a classical mythology of religious, racial, and communal warfare, Tamil conquests and Sinhalese explusions—can be here left aside. The details are obscure, in any case, and their weight more so. What is important is that, once again, the bounds of a country, celebrated and questioned, historically put together and historically takeable-apart, provide the frame within which identity conflicts crystallize: the stage—here, compact and congestive—on which, perforce, they work themselves out, or, of course, do not. It makes a difference where things happen.

It certainly does in the Balkans. In turning very briefly to Yugoslavia (or as we now must say, with a dying fall, "the former Yugoslavia"), it is not with the intention of sorting out what just about everyone else who has tried, even the skilled and desperate Messrs. Vance and Owen with their ten-ply restructuration of Bosnia-Hercegovina, has largely failed to sort out. Nor can I address the terrible issues of the morality and policy it has thrown up for a world unprepared to deal with them. I want only to conclude my short, illustrative, and quite arbitrary series (I could as well have taken Belgium, Nigeria, and Afghanistan; Brazil, Rwanda, and Czechoslovakia) of instructing cases: cases in which the discrimination of a country as a historicized place—a location, a name, and a rememberable past—from the affinitive, "who are we?" solidarities that support or trouble it is more helpful to reflection about a splintered world than is the fusion of the two into a one-size-fits-all, demonized "nationalism." Yugoslavia (I suppress "the former" henceforth, for the sake of style: it is to be taken as read, in its fullest irony) provides a case in which the sorts of tensions so far contained in Canada and at least, though the word doesn't seem quite right given the levels of violence involved, so far lived with in Sri Lanka, have, in a half-dozen years, overwhelmed the country: literally disassembled it; left it in pieces.[15]

The "virtue" (the word, of course, in the heaviest of shudder quotes) of the Yugoslav case is that the country came apart—that is, was taken apart—if not precisely in slow motion at least with a certain relentless, he who says "A" must say "B," deliberation in which the stages of disintegration are distinct, sharp, dramatic, and visible. There was Milosevic's speech in the capital of Kosovo on the six-hundredth anniversary of the famous lost battle against the Turks, finally demonstrating to even the most Yugoslavian of Yugoslavs (there were many still left then, and far from powerless) that the Serbian Question was back to stay. There was the almost furtive departure, via the confused and hesitant ten-day war, of Slovenia from the Federation in June of 1991, the coincident declaration of independence by Croatia, the recognition of both these events by a reuniting Germany, getting back into European politics as an unfettered actor, and the outbreak of war in Croatia as Belgrade moved to support its Serbian enclaves that immediately followed. There was the movement of the war to Bosnia-Herzegovina after its declaration of independence in mid-1992; the ill-fated

Vance-Owen cantonization plan in 1993—dismembering Bosnia in order to save it; the fragile and porous Sarajevo cease-fire, yet another cantonization plan; the fearful prospect of murder without end in 1994; and the trembling peace of the Dayton Accords. Each of these events, as well as a host of others—the shelling of Dubrovnik, the leveling of Vukovar, the siege of Sarajevo, the reduction of Mostar—are phases of a single process: the erasure of a country and the attempt to redelineate what then is left. (The more recent events in Kosovo are but another chapter in an unfinished—what is to become of Montenegro?—perhaps unfinishable, story.)

The country was, of course, never that firmly rooted; its history was short, vertiginous, interrupted, and violent. Assembled by the Great Powers after the Great War from some of the linguistic, religious, and tribal enclaves, that had been excited by the Balkan Wars and then left behind by the Austrian Empire, it was plagued from its birth by challenges to its integrity from both within and without—Croatian and Macedonian separatism, Hungarian and Bulgarian irredentisms—and passed from monarchy, to parliamentarianism, to Nazi occupation, to Communist dictatorship, and back to parliamentarianism in the space of some eighty years.

It seems rather a wonder that it took hold at all. But, at least in retrospect, it seems to have done so with considerable force, especially in the cities and towns, and it is not clear that its mental pull, the idea it projected, a North Balkan country with a multicultural population, has altogether dissipated yet, whatever the practical finality of its disappearance. The war that destroyed it went from being a Yugoslavian one, to being a Serbo-Croatian one, to being a Bosnian one—a succession of attempts, of ascending brutality and madness, to replace what had, almost accidentally, been lost: neither a state nor a people, a society nor a nation, none of which it had ever more than inchoatively been, but a country. Yugoslavia, or, one last time, "the former Yugoslavia," seems to be an almost pure case of the noncoincidence, in meaning and in fact, of these so often identified and interfused realities, and, in a negative way, the weight, the power, and the importance of the last.

"Zdravko Grebo [Misha Glenny writes of a friend of his, a law professor at Sarajevo University and a former politician] is a Bosnian who oozes humour and culture. His parents were Moslems from Mostar but he had been brought up in Belgrade and he continued to call himself a Yugoslav, even after he openly admitted that Yugoslavia no longer existed. 'What else can I call myself?' he mused, 'I can hardly start calling myself a Moslem or a Serb after all these years.' Bosnia (and Sarejevo especially) had the highest percentage of people who designated themselves Yugoslavs in the national census. When Yugoslavia was submerged in the blood of its own people, these Yugoslavs and the identity to which they still clung, were washed away into a river of poisoned history."[16]

The river of history need not, of course, have been so thoroughly poisoned. Lebanon aside, perhaps Liberia, perhaps Sudan, it has not been, so far anyway, in many countries, the overwhelming majority so far as mere numbers go, internally beset by cultural fault lines—Indonesia, the United States, India, Egypt, Kenya, Guatemala, Malaysia, Belgium. Canada still holds together, and if (as at the moment seems unlikely) it turns out to be unable to do so, it should be able to achieve the sort of velvet divorce that Czechoslovakia did, and before that Singapore and Malaysia did. Sri Lanka may yet contain its tensions within some sort of pliant and tractable constitutional structure as South Africa, a few short years ago surely the country thought least likely to succeed in such an effort and to descend into multi-sided chaos, is at least beginning to do. Even Yugoslavia might have avoided the worst if, as Glenny suggests, "the European Community and the United States [had guided] the inexperienced or opportunist leaders toward an agreed breakup of the country," and if the horror is not to spread to the southern Balkans, they will have to do so still.[17] Much depends upon how these things are managed.

We seem to be in need of a new variety of politics, a politics which does not regard ethnic, religious, racial, linguistic, or regional assertiveness as so much irrationality, archaic and ingenerate, to be suppressed or transcended, a madness decried or a darkness ignored, but, like any other social problem—inequality say, or the abuse of power—sees it as a reality to be faced, somehow dealt with, modulated, brought to terms.

The development of such a politics, which will vary from place to place as much as the situations it faces do, depends on a number of things. It depends on finding out the springs of identity-based differentiation and discord in this case or that. It depends on developing a less simplistically demonizing, blankly negative attitude toward it as a relic of savagery or some earlier stage of human existence. It depends on adapting the principles of liberalism and social democracy, still our best guides for law, government, and public deportment, to matters with respect to which they have been too often dismissive, reactive, or incomprehending; philosophically blind. But perhaps most important, it depends on our constructing a clearer, more circumstantial, less mechanical, stereotypic and cliché-ridden conception of what it consists in, what it *is*. That is, it depends on our gaining a better understanding of what culture, the frames of meaning within which people live and form their convictions, their selves, and their solidarities, comes to as an ordering force in human affairs.

And this, once more, means a critique of conceptions which reduce matters to uniformity, to homogeneity, to like-mindedness—to consensus. The vocabulary of cultural description and analysis, needs also to be opened up to divergence and multiplicity, to the noncoincidence of kinds and categories. No more than countries can the identities that color them, Muslim or Buddhist, French or Persian, Latin or Sinitic . . . Black or White, be grasped as seamless unities, unbroken wholes.

What Is a Culture if It Is Not a Consensus?

There is a paradox, occasionally noted but not very deeply reflected upon, concerning the present state of what we so casually refer to as "the world scene": it is growing both more global and more divided, more thoroughly interconnected and more intricately partitioned, at the same time. Cosmopolitanism and parochialism are no longer opposed; they are linked and reinforcing. As the one increases, so does the other.

The growth of technology, most particularly of communications technology, has knit the world into a single web of information and causality, such that, like the famous butterfly beating its wings in the

Pacific and bringing on a storm in the Iberian Peninsula, a change of conditions anyplace can induce disturbances anyplace else. We are all at the mercy of American money managers speculating in Mexican equities or British bankers in Singapore gambling on Tokyo derivatives. Kobe earthquakes or Dutch floods, Italian scandals or Saudi production targets, Chinese arms sales or Colombian drug smugglings, have near instant impacts, diffuse and magnified, far from their sources. CNN brings Bosnian slaughter, Somali starvation, or Rwandan refugee camps into the world's living rooms. Places normally quite obscure, provincial, and self-absorbed—Grozny, Dili, Ayodhya, or Cristobal de Las Casas; Kigali, Belfast, Monrovia, Tbilisi, Phnom Penh, or Port-au-Prince—momentarily challenge the great metropolises of the world for the world's attention. Capital is mobile and, as there is hardly a people, not even the Samoans, without a diaspora, so is labor. There are Japanese companies in the United States, German ones in Indonesia, American ones in Russia, Pakistani ones in Britain, Taiwanese ones in the Philippines. Turks and Kurds send money home from Berlin, Maghrebians and Vietnamese from Paris, Zairis and Tamils from Brussels, Palestinians and Filipinos from Kuwait City, Somalis from Rome, Moroccans from Spain, Japanese from Brazil, Mexicans from Los Angeles, a few Croats from Sweden, and just about everyone from New York. All this vast connection and intricate interdependence is sometimes referred to, after cultural studies sloganeers, as "the global village," or, after World Bank ones, as "borderless capitalism." But as it has neither solidarity nor tradition, neither edge nor focus, and lacks all wholeness, it is a poor sort of village. And as it is accompanied less by the loosening and reduction of cultural demarcations than by their reworking and multiplication, and, as I have pointed out above, often enough their intensification, it is hardly borderless.

Charting such demarcations, locating them and characterizing the populations they isolate, or at least set off, is at best an arbitrary business, inexactly accomplished. The discrimination of cultural breaks and cultural continuities, the drawing of lines around sets of individuals as following a more or less identifiable form of life as against different sets of individuals following more or less different forms of life—other voices in other rooms—is a good deal easier in theory than it is in practice.

Anthropology, one of whose vocations, at least, is to locate such demarcations, to discriminate such breaks and describe such continuities, has fumbled with the issue from the beginning, and fumbles with it still. But it is, nonetheless, not to be evaded with dim banalities about the humanness of humankind or underlying factors of likeness and commonality, if only because, "in nature," as the positivists used to like to say, people themselves make such contrasts and draw such lines: regard themselves, at some times, for some purposes, as French not English, Hindu not Buddhist, Hutu not Tutsi, Latino not Indio, Shi'i not Sunni, Hopi not Navajo, Black not White, Orange not Green. Whatever we might wish, or regard as enlightenment, the severalty of culture abides and proliferates, even amidst, indeed in response to, the powerfully connecting forces of modern manufacture, finance, travel, and trade. The more things come together, the more they remain apart: the uniform world is not much closer than the classless society.

Anthropology's awkwardness in dealing with all this, with the cultural organization of the modern world that ought, by rights, to be its proper subject, is in great part the result of the difficulties it has experienced, over the course of its vagrant and inward history, in discovering for itself how best to think about culture in the first place. In the nineteenth century and well into this one, culture was, before all else, taken to be a universal property of human social life, the techniques, customs, traditions, and technologies—religion and kinship, fire and language—that set it off from animal existence. Its opponent term was nature, and if it was to be divided into sorts and kinds, it was in terms of the distance one or another piece of it, monotheism or individualism, monogamy or the protection of private property, had, supposedly, moved away from nature, its progress toward the light. With the growth, after the First World War, of long-term, participatory fieldwork with particular groups—a lot of it on islands and Indian reservations, where breaks and edges were easier to discern and the notion that everything fit together easier to entertain—the generical conception began to be set aside, as diffuse and unwieldy, as well as self-serving, in favor of a configurational one. Instead of just culture as such one had cultures—bounded, coherent, cohesive, and self-standing: social organisms, semiotical crystals, microworlds. Culture was what peoples had and held in common, Greeks or Navajos, Maoris or Puerto Ricans, each its own.[18]

After, however, the Second World War, when even putative social isolates, jungle people, desert people, island people, arctic people, encapsulated people, grew fewer in number, and anthropologists turned their attention toward vaster, more mixed-up, iridescent objects, India, Japan, France, Brazil, Nigeria, the Soviet Union, the United States, the configurational view became, in turn, strained, imprecise, unwieldly, and hard to credit. One might plausibly regard the Nuer or the Amhara as an integral unit, at least if one blocked off internal variabilities and external involvements, as well as anything very much in the way of larger history, but that was difficult to do for Sudan or Ethiopia; for Africa, it was impossible, though a few have tried it. An Indonesian minority, such as the Chinese, a Moroccan one, such as the Jews, a Ugandan one, such as the Indians, or an American one, such as the Blacks, might show a certain character special to themselves, but they were hardly to be understood apart from the states and societies in which they were enclosed. Everything was motley, porous, interdigitated, dispersed; the search for totality an uncertain guide, a sense of closure unattainable.

A picture of the world as dotted by discriminate cultures, discontinuous blocks of thought and emotion—a sort of pointillist view of its spiritual composition—is no less misleading than the picture of it as tiled by repeating, reiterative nation-states, and for the same reason: the elements concerned, the dots or the tiles, are neither compact nor homogeneous, simple nor uniform. When you look into them, their solidity dissolves, and you are left not with a catalogue of well-defined entities to be arranged and classified, a Mendelian table of natural kinds, but with a tangle of differences and similarities only half sorted out. What makes Serbs Serbs, Sinhalese Sinhalese, or French Canadians French Canadians, or anybody anybody, is that they and the rest of the world have come, for the moment and to a degree, for certain purposes and in certain contexts, to view them as contrastive to what is around them.

Both the territorial compactness and the localized traditionalism that islands, Indian reservations, jungles, highland valleys, oases, and the like provided (or, anyway, supposedly provided, for even this was a bit of a myth) and the integral, configurational, it all goes together, notion of cultural identity—The Argonauts of the Western Pacific, The Cheyenne Way, The Forest People, The Mountain People, The Desert People—that such compactness and localization stimulated seem more and more beside the point as we turn toward the fragments and fragmentations of the contemporary world. The view of culture, *a* culture, this culture, as a consensus on fundamentals—shared conceptions, shared feelings, shared values— seems hardly viable in the face of so much dispersion and disassembly; it is the faults and fissures that seem to mark out the landscape of collective selfhood. Whatever it is that defines identity in borderless capitalism and the global village it is not deep-going agreements on deep-going matters, but something more like the recurrence of familiar divisions, persisting arguments, standing threats, the notion that whatever else may happen, the order of difference must be somehow maintained.

We do not know, really, how to handle this, how to deal with a world that is neither divided at the joints into ingredient sections nor a transcendent unity—economic, say, or psychological—obscured by surface contrasts, thin and concocted, and best set aside as inessential distractions. A scramble of differences in a field of connections presents us with a situation in which the frames of pride and those of hatred, culture fairs and ethnic cleansing, *survivance* and killing fields, sit side by side and pass with frightening ease from the one to the other. Political theories that both admit to this condition and have the will to confront it, to expose and interrogate the order of difference, rather than perfecting classroom visions of Hobbesian war or Kantian concord, only barely exist. Much depends upon their growth and development: you can't guide what you can't understand.

∞

In any case, if the elementalism of anthropology, its focus on consensus, type, and commonality—what has been called the cookiecutter concept of culture—is of doubtful use in promoting such growth and refinement, its cosmopolitanism, its determination to look beyond the familiar, the received, and the near at hand, is perhaps more valuable. The resolute undermining of all sorts of exceptionalisms, American, Western, European, Christian, and all sort of exoticisms, the primitive, the idolatrous, the antipodean, the quaint, forces comparison across the established realms of relevance and suitability—the considering together of what normally is not considered considerable together. In connection with the developments of the past half century, and most especially the past half dozen years that is our subject here, such ungrammatical comparison makes it possible to avoid the most pervasive misdescription of those developments: that they are divided into Western and non-western varieties and that the non-western variety is essentially recapitulative, a rerun of history the West has passed through, and more or less triumphed over, rather than, as is in fact the case, the edge of the new, premonitory and emblematic, of history to come.

This is particularly clear if one turns to the alterations of the political landscape in Asia, Africa, the Pacific, the Caribbean, and certain parts of Latin America after 1945. The dissolution of the great overseas empires—British, Dutch, Belgian, French, Portuguese, in a somewhat different way American, German, Italian, and Japanese (even Australia, after all, had a Protectorate, even if it had to inherit it from the Germans a bit late in the game)—made thoroughly plain that, despite the passionate solidarities of colonial revolt, the collective identities that drove that revolt and that suffuse the lives of the countries it created are ineradicably plural, compound, inconstant, and contested. The contribution of the Third World upheaval to the twentieth century's self-understanding lies less in its mimicries of European nationalism (which were in any case a good deal less intense in, say, Morocco, Uganda, Jordan, or Malaysia, than they were in, say, Algeria, Zaire, India, or Indonesia) than in its forcing into view the compositeness of culture such nationalism denies. We may come in time to see Asia's and Africa's political reconstruction as contributing more to transforming Euro-America's view of social selfhood than vice versa.

The reason for this is not that the nature of the countries formed out of the collapse of colonial empire is radically different in kind and construction from that of those which came into being earlier on in the West after similar collapses of similarly overstretched political, or politicocultural, imperia. It is that their nature is more open to view, less shrouded in buried history; like Bismarck's sausages, we have seen them made. More recent, as well as more rapidly and more deliberately established—countries aforethought—they have been born in the full light of history, the accidents and happenstances of their formation still plain and showing. The contingencies that produced them, and that virtually everywhere continue to maintain them, are not only evident, they are, in some ways, the most striking thing about them. France may seem, at least by now, a natural given. Even Italy may, or Denmark. It is hard to think that of Angola or Bangladesh.

The cultural make-up of the countries that emerged from the wreckage of what has come to be called, as though it were some sort of Enlightenment experiment conducted for the edification of political scientists, "the colonial project," is, of course, almost everywhere extremely heterogeneous, a collection of peoples, in many cases almost haphazard—the borders are where the ins-and-outs of European politics happened to place them. (Why are people who live in Abidjan Ivoiriens, people who live in Accra, a couple hundred miles along the same coast, Ghanaians? Why is half of New Guinea in Indonesia, half in the PNG? Burma a separate country, Bengal not? Why are some Yorubas Nigerian, some Benin? Some Thai Laotians? Some Afghans Pakistanis?) Language, religion, race, and custom meet at all sorts of angles, on all sorts of scales, at all sorts of levels, impossible for even the most passionate of nationalists to rationalize, obscure, or explain away as destined and inevitable.

It is not, however, the simple fact of cultural heterogeneity as such, and the great visibility of it, that is so instructive, but the enormous variety of levels at which such heterogeneity exists and has an effect; so many, indeed, that it is difficult to know how to organize a general picture, where to draw the lines and place the foci. As soon as you look into the details of the matter in any particular instance, the more obvious demarcations, the ones you can read about in the newspapers (Tamils and Sinhalese, Shi'is and

Sunnis, Hutus and Tutsis, Malays and Chinese, East Indians and Fijis) are almost overwhelmed by other demarcations, both those finer, more narrowly and exactly distinguishing, and those grosser, more broadly and generally so. It is difficult to find a commonality of outlook, form of life, behavioral style, material expression . . . whatever . . . that is not either itself further partitioned into smaller, infolding ones, boxes within boxes, or taken up whole and entire into larger, incorporative ones, selves laid on top of selves. There is, at least in most cases, and I suspect in all, no point at which one can say that this is where consensus either stops or starts. It all depends on the frame of comparison, the background against which identity is seen, and the play of interest which engages and animates it.

Indonesia, a country I have myself studied up close, and over an extended period of time (though most of it remains beyond my ken—encapsulated people and flung-out places, more heard about than known), demonstrates this difficult intricacy with particular force.[19] The country is, of course, one of the most complicated, culturally speaking, in the world, the product of an incredible stream of warring mind-sets—Portuguese, Spanish, Dutch, Indian, Chinese; Hindu, Buddhist, Confucian, Muslim, Christian; Capitalist, Communist, Imperial Administrative—carried by means of those great world-historical agencies, long-distance commodity trade, religious missionization, and colonial exploitation, into a vast, thousand-island archipelago occupied mainly (though not exclusively) by Malayo-Polynesians, speaking hundreds of languages, following hundreds of cults, and possessed of hundreds of moralities, laws, customs, and arts; hundreds of senses, subtly different or grossly, reasonably concordant or deeply opposed, of how life ought to go. Articulating its spiritual anatomy, determining how in identity terms it is put together and, so far anyway, holds together, indeed holds together surprisingly well given what it has to contend with, is a virtually impossible task. But it is one that anybody who has seriously to do with the place, either from within or without, is inevitably constrained somehow to attempt.

The usual way this is done, also whether from within or without, is by what might be called (indeed, in my still rather classificational, *âge classique*, discipline, is called) "peoples and cultures" discourse. The various "ethnic" or quasi-ethnic groups—the Javanese, the Batak, the Bugis, the Acehnese, the Balinese, and so on down to the smaller and more peripheral examples, the Bimans, the Dyaks, the Ambonese, or whoever—are named, characterized by some configuration of qualities or other; their subdivisions are outlined, their relations to one another defined, their position within the whole assessed. This yields again a pointillist view, or perhaps better here, given the indexical character of the ordering, a file card view, of the cultural compositeness of the country. It is seen as a set of "peoples," varying in importance, size, and character, and held within a common political and economic frame by an overarching story, historical, ideological, religious, or whatever, that provides the rationale for their being thus together, enclosed in a country. All the levels and dimensions of difference and integration, save two— the minimal consensual grouping called "a culture" or "an ethnic group" and the maximal one called "the nation" or "the state"— are occluded and washed out. Unfortunately, the matters that in the course of collective life actually work to align individuals in cooperative enterprises or to divide them from one another in clashing ones, the practices, the institutions, and the social occurrences within which difference is encountered and somehow dealt with, are occluded and washed out with them. The file cards are assembled, and the appropriate notations made. But they are not cross-indexed.

The fact is, however, that it is precisely in the cross-indexing that the various identities the cards isolate are formed and play against one another. They are not, these separated "cultures," or "peoples," or "ethnic groups," so many lumps of sameness marked out by the limits of consensus: they are various modes of involvement in a collective life that takes place on a dozen different levels, on a dozen different scales, and in a dozen different realms at once. The making and dissolving of village marriages and the governmental codification of family law, particular forms of worship and the officialized role of religion in the state, local patterns of sociality and overall approaches to government—these, and an enormous number of similar intersections of outlook, style, or disposition, are the bases on which cultural complexity is ordered into at least something of an irregular, rickety, and indefinite whole.

It is not possible to go into the details here—it is barely possible to go into the generalities; but the cultural variousness of Indonesia (which, so far as I can see, is as vast as ever, despite the supposedly homogenizing effects of television, rock, and high late capitalism) finds expression in the form of struggles over the nature of this whole. The way in which, and the degree to which, the contrasting aspects of the overall conglomerate are to be represented in the formulation of Indonesian identity is the heart of the matter. It is less consensus that is at issue than a viable way of doing without it.

So far as Indonesia is concerned, this has been achieved, to the degree, very partial, uneven, and incomplete, that it has been achieved, by developing a form of cultural politics within which sharply disparate conceptions of what sort of country the country should be, can be represented and blunted, celebrated and held in check, recognized and covered over, at the same time; what has well been called a working misunderstanding. It has not, of course, always worked. The 1965 massacres in Java, Bali, and parts of Sumatra, thousands dead, perhaps hundreds of thousands, was at base a movement of this multisided struggle for the country's soul to the level of violence. There have been ethnic revolts and religious ones, back-country upheavals and urban riots; as well as, as in East Timor or West New Guinea, the brute application of state power—consensus out of the barrel of a gun. But, so far, anyway, it has lumbered along, like India or Nigeria, a bundle of parochialisms that somehow adheres.

The grand particularities of the Indonesian case, admittedly a bit along toward the limit of things, aside, this overall picture of cultural identity as a field of differences confronting one another at every level from the family, the village, the neighborhood, and the region, to the countryside and beyond—no solidarity but that it is sustained against jealous internal divisions, no division but that it sustains itself against ravenous incorporative solidarities—is, I think, very close to general in the modern world; there is nothing "underdeveloped," "thirdworldish," or (that euphemism we have come to use to avoid saying "backward") "traditional" about it. It applies as fully to a France beset by tensions between *civism laique* and an inrush of Maghrebian immigrants who want to cook with cumin and wear headscarves in school, a Germany struggling to come to terms with the presence of Turks in a descent-defined *Heimatland*, an Italy regionalized into competing localisms only reinforced by modernity and uneven development, or a United States trying to remember itself in a multiethnic, multiracial, multireligious, multilinguistic . . . multicultural . . . whirl, as it does to such more brutally torn places as Liberia, Lebanon, Myanmar, Colombia, or the Republic of South Africa. The European (and American) exceptionalism that seemed, at least to Europeans (and Americans) so plausible before 1989—we have the nation-state, and they have not—has become increasingly implausible since. Yugoslavia, the former ex-, was, is, both the place where that idea seems to have died and —"the back porch of Europe is burning"—its last stand.

∞

By rights, political theory should be what I take it Aristotle wanted it to be, a school for judgment, not a replacement for it—not a matter of laying down the law for the less reflective to follow (Ronald Dworkin's judges, John Rawls's policy makers, Robert Nozick's utility seekers), but a way of looking at the horrors and confusions amidst which we all are living that may be of some help to us in surviving and quieting them, perhaps even occasionally in heading them off. If so, if that is in fact its vocation, it needs to devote a good deal more of its attention to the particularities of things, to what's happening, to how matters go. It needs to do this, not in order to turn itself into a running commentary on how awfully complicated everything is, and how intractable to logical ordering. That can be left to history and anthropology, the *complexicateurs terribles* of the human sciences. It needs to do it in order to participate in the construction of what is most needed now that the world is redistributing itself into increasingly various frameworks of difference, a practical politics of cultural conciliation.

Like any other politics, such politics will have to be targeted, tailored to circumstances, to times, and places, and personalities. But, like any other politics, it must develop, nonetheless, certain commonalities of diagnosis, of strategy and direction, a certain unity of intent. What it seeks in Diyabakar or Srinagar, it must seek as well in Trois Rivieres or South Los Angeles. Algerian *kulturkampf* must be juxtaposed to Irish; the velvet divorce of the Czechs and the Slovaks, to that, some years earlier, but oddly reminiscent, of Malaya and Singapore; the double pull, Germano/Latin, exerted upon Belgium to that, Graeco/Turanian, exerted upon Cyprus; the marginalization of America's Indians to that of Australia's Aborigines; the disassimilationism of Brazil to that of the United States. There is indeed a definable subject here. The trick is to define it, and having defined it, put it into some sort of order.

The central dynamic of this subject seems, as I have been saying, perhaps all too repetitively, to consist in two continuously opposing tendencies. On the one hand, there is the drive toward creating, or trying to create, *pur sang* droplets of culture and politics; the pointillist picture that both ethnic cleansing and the convergent conception of collective agency—"nation-ism"—aim to produce. On the other, there is the drive toward creating, or trying to create, an intricate, multiply ordered structure of difference within which cultural tensions that are not about to go away, or even to moderate, can be placed and negotiated—contained in a country. Such structures are, themselves, going to be different from one such country to another, the possibility of constructing them variously real. Positioning Muslims in France, Whites in South Africa, Arabs in Israel, or Koreans in Japan are not altogether the same sort of thing. But if political theory is going to be of any relevance at all in the splintered world, it will have to have something cogent to say about how, in the face of the drive toward a destructive integrity, such structures can be brought into being, how they can be sustained, and how they can be made to work.

This brings me to the final issue I want to address here, all too cursorily. This is the much discussed, but not much decided, capacity of liberalism (or more exactly, so that I am sorted with Isaiah Berlin and Michael Walzer and not with Friedrich von Hayek and

Robert Nozick, social democratic liberalism) to rise to this challenge, its ability to involve itself in the rancorous, explosive, and often enough murderous politics of cultural difference; indeed, to survive in its presence. The commitment of liberalism to state neutrality in matters of personal belief, its resolute individualism, its stress on liberty, on procedure, and on the universality of human rights, and, at least in the version to which I adhere, its concern with the equitable distribution of life chances is said to prevent it either from recognizing the force and durability of ties of religion, language, custom, locality, race, and descent in human affairs, or from regarding the entry of such considerations into civic life as other than pathological—primitive, backward, regressive, and irrational. I do not think this is the case. The development of a liberalism with both the courage and the capacity to engage itself with a differenced world, one in which its principles are neither well understood nor widely held, in which indeed it is, in most places, a minority creed, alien and suspect, is not only possible, it is necessary.

In the last few years, the years in which liberalism, of both the economistic, market utopian and the political, civil society sorts, has moved from being an ideological fortress for half the world to being a moral proposal to the whole of it, the degree to which it is, itself, a culturally specific phenomenon, born in the West and perfected there, has become, paradoxically, much more apparent. The very universalism to which it is committed and which it promotes, its cosmopolitan intent, has brought it into open conflict both with other universalisms with similar intent, most notably with that set forth by a revenant Islam, and with a large number of alternative visions of the good, the right, and the indubitable, Japanese, Indian, African, Singaporean, to which it looks like just one more attempt to impose Western values on the rest of the world—the continuation of colonialism by other means.

This fact, that the principles that animate liberalism are not so self-evident to others, even serious and reasonable others, as they are to liberals, is evident these days everywhere you look. In the resistance to a universal code of human rights as inapplicable to poor countries bent on development and indeed a device, mischievously contrived by the already rich, to hinder such development; in the father-knows-best moralism of a Lee Kuan Yew, paddling truants, journalists, and bumptious businessmen as insufficiently Confucian, or a Suharto, opposing free trade unions, free newspapers, and free elections as contrary to the spirit of Asian communalism; and in a broad range of discourses praising ritual, hierarchy, wholeness, and tribal wisdom, it is clear that Locke, Montesquieu, Jefferson, and Mill are particular voices of a particular history, not equally persuasive to all who hear them or their present-day champions.

Those who would therefore, promote the cause for which these names, and others more nearly contemporary—Dewey, Camus, Berlin, Kuron, Taylor—in their various ways variably stand (for "liberalism," too, is neither compact nor homogeneous, and it is certainly unfinished), need to recognize its culturally specific origins and its culturally specific character. They need . . . we need . . . most especially, to recognize that in attempting to advance it more broadly in the world, we will find ourselves confronting not just blindness and irrationality, the passions of ignorance (those we know well enough at home), but competing conceptions of how matters should be arranged and people related to one another, actions judged and society governed, that have a weight and moment, a rationale, of their own; something to be said for them. The issue is not one of "relativism," as it is often put by those who wish to insulate their beliefs against the force of difference. It is a matter of understanding that talking to others implies listening to them, and that in listening to them what one has to say is very unlikely, not at the close of this century, not in the opening of the next, to remain unshaken.

The argument that I set out at the beginning of this essay, that political theory is not, or anyway ought not to be, intensely generalized reflection on intensely generalized matters, an imagining of architectures in which no one could live, but should be, rather, an intellectual engagement, mobile, exact, and realistic, with present problems presently clamorous applies with particular force to liberalism, given as it sometimes has been to a certain indifference to the actuality of things, a certain taking of wish for accomplishment.

It must be reconceived, that is, its partisans must reconceive it, as a view not from nowhere but from the special somewhere of (a certain sort of) Western political experience, a statement (or, again, as it is no more unified than that experience has been, a set of statements reasonably consonant) about what we, who are the heirs of that experience, think we have learned about how people with differences can live among one another with some degree of comity. Faced with other heirs of other experiences who have drawn other lessons to other purposes, we can hardly avoid either pressing our own with whatever confidence we still feel in them and subjecting them to the risks of running up against these others and coming out at least somewhat, perhaps a good deal more than somewhat, banged about and in need of repair.

The prospect of a new synthesis—not that there ever really was an old one—seems to me quite remote. The disagreements and disjunctions will remain, even if they will not remain the same disagreements and disjunctions. Nor does the simple triumph of what that thoroughly English, quite disabused, and intransigently liberal, E. M. Forster, who did not expect it either, called love and the beloved republic look like much of possibility. We seem condemned, at least for the immediate future, and perhaps for a good while beyond it, to live at best in what someone, thinking perhaps of Yugoslavian truces, Irish ceasefires, African rescue operations, and Mideastern negotiations, has called a low-intensity peace—not the sort of environment in which liberalism has normally flourished. But it is the sort of environment in which it will have to operate if it is to persist and have an effect, and to maintain what seems to me its deepest and most central commitment: the moral obligation to hope.

Notes

1. S. Huntington "The Clash of Civilizations," *Foreign Affairs* (Summer 1993: 22–49. cf. S. Huntington, *The Clash of Civilizations and the Remaking of World Order*, New York: Simon and Schuster, 1996.

2. C. Taylor, "Shared and Divergent Values," in his *Reconciling the Solitudes: Essays on Canadian Federalism and Nationalism*, Montreal and Kingston: McGill-Queen's University Press, 1993, pp. 155–186.

3. *The Compact Edition of the Oxford English Dictionary*, Oxford: Oxford University Press, 1971 [1928], 1 :1078. For a more extensive and circumstantial discussion of vocabulary change in the English case, 1500–1650, see L. Greenfield, *Nationalism. Five Roads to Modernity*, Cambridge: Harvard University Press 1992, pp. 31–44.

4. *The Compact Edition of the Oxford English Dictionary*, 2: 661–662.

5. *Ibid.*, pp. 849–853.

6. *Ibid.*, pp. 359–360. All the terms reviewed here have, of course, allied meanings not directly involved in the semantic field I am describing —"people" denotes human beings as opposed to animals, "country" denotes rural ("the countryside") as opposed to urban, "society" denotes fashionable as in 'high society,' etc.—which would need to be taken into account in a full analysis.

7. *Ibid.*, 1: 30–31. The definitions given in *The American Heritage Dictionary of the English Language* (3rd ed., Boston: Houghton-Mifflin, 1992, p. 1203) present the crystallized, fully multiplex, modern consolidation: "1. A relatively large group of people organized under a single, usually independent government; a country. 2. The government of a sovereign state. 3. A people who share common customs, origins, history, and frequently language; a nationality. 4. A federation or tribe . . . 5. The territory occupied by such a federation or tribe."

8. See, for example, E. Gellner, *Nations and Nationalism*, Oxford, Oxford University Press, 1983, but the view is widespread.

9. B. Anderson, *Imagined Communities. Reflections on the Origin and Spread of Nationalism*, London: Verso, 1983, p. 123. Anderson's book is perhaps the strongest statement of the diffusionist, world-historical view "by which the nation came to be imagined, and once imagined, modelled, adapted and transformed" (p. 129), and, it might be added, in his view purified, in the independence movements of the fifties and sixties.

10. W. Zimmerman, "Origins of a Catastrophe: Memoirs of the Last American Ambassador to Yugoslavia," *Foreign Affairs* (March/April 1995): 7. For the "ethnic-civic" opposition, see M. Ignatief, *Blood and Belonging: Journeys into the New Nationalism*, New York: Farrar, Straus and Giroux, 1993; for "official-popular," B. Anderson, *Imagined Communities*; for "divisive-unificatory," "Habsburg-Liberal," "eastern-western"), E. Gellner, *Nations and Nationalism*. (The attempt to draw the bad nationalism/good nationalism line between Balkan "atavism" and West European "maturity," now much reinforced by the Yugoslavian tragedy and the failures of the European Union in the face of it, is part of the European exceptionalism view of things I shall discuss further below.)

11. C. Black, "Canada's Continuing Identity Crisis," *Foreign Affairs* (March/April 1995): 99–115, quotation at p. 101. In the following I am especially indebted to an unpublished paper (1995) by Russel Barsh, associate pro-

fessor of Native American Studies at the University of Lethbridge, Alberta, "Re-imagining Canada: Aboriginal Peoples and Quebec Competing for Legitimacy as Emergent Nations," and, *inter alia*, C. Taylor, *Reconciling the Solitudes*; M. Ignatief, *Blood and Belonging*, pp. 143–177; R. Handler, *Nationalism and the Politics of Culture in Quebec*, Madison: University of Wisconsin Press, 1988. For a review of the constitutional efforts to put Canada in order, see J. Tully, *Strange Multiplicity: Constitutionalism in an Age of Diversity*, Cambridge: Cambridge University Press, 1995. For an attempt to understand that multiplicity in terms of a contrast between "civilization" and "culture," see D. Verney, *Three Civilizations, Two Cultures, One State: Canada's Political Traditions*, Durham: Duke University Press, 1981. For French Canadian views, J. Letourneau, *Le question identaire au Canada Francophone*, Quebec: Pres Université Laval, 1997.

12. C. Black, "Canada's Continuing Identity Crisis," pp. 112–114; the figure for the outward migration of Anglophones from Quebec is from M. Ignatief, *Blood and Belonging*, p. 171. For Quebec, the (Cree) Indians, and the development of natural resources, *ibid*, pp. 163–167, and Barash, "Re-imagining Canada."

13. I depend here mainly on two books by S. J. Tambiah, *Sri Lanka, Ethnic Fratricide and the Dismantling of Democracy*, Chicago, 1986, and *Buddhism Betrayed? Religion, Politics, and Violence in Sri Lanka*, Chicago: University of Chicago Press, 1992, and on W. H. Wriggins, *Ceylon: Dilemmas of a New Nation* Princeton: Princeton University Press, 1960. I briefly reviewed the initial phases of, as it then was, Ceylon's ethnic conflict in C. Geertz, "The Integrative Revolution, Primordial Sentiments and Civil Politics in the New States," in C. Geertz, ed., *Old Societies and New States*, New York: The Free Press, 1963, pp. 105–157, esp. pp. 121–123. My statistics come from the above works, and from *World Development Report, 1992*, The International Bank for Reconstruction and Development, Oxford, 1992, and E. V. Daniel, *Charred Lullabies: Chapters in an Autobiography of Violence*, Princeton: Princeton University Press, 1996.

14. *World Development Report 1992*, 1992, op. cit., tables 1, 26, 28. Relative to some of its neighbors, Sri Lanka's advance has been somewhat less impressive in recent years, in part as a result of its communal troubles which have led to a significant diaspora to Europe, the Gulf, and the United States, but it still remains reasonably effective.

15. There has been so much in the world press over the last several years, as well as numerous books, articles, and commentaries, to say nothing of TV footage, that I need not cite sources here for what are in any case but generalized and quite unauthoritative remarks. I have relied heavily on Misha Glenny's detailed, insightful *The Fall of Yugoslavia: The Third Balkan War*, 2nd ed., New York: Penguin, 1994, to keep things straight factually and chronologically. Zimmerman, "Origins of a Catastrophe," has also been useful in this

regard. Ignatief, *Blood and Belonging*, pp. 19–56, though it deals only with Croatia and Serbia, invokes the devastation with great force, as does, for Bosnia-Hercegovina, D. Rieff, *Slaughterhouse: Bosnia and the Failure of the West*, New York: Simon and Schuster 1995, which also addresses the policy issues from a strongly interventionist standpoint.

16. Glenny, *The Fall of Yugoslavia*, p. 161.

17. *Ibid.*, p. 236.

18. There is, of course, a history of cultural configurationalism aside from and prior to ethnographical practice since Malinowksi or whomever, most especially that connected with Herder, the Humboldts, and the neo-Kantians, which had in fact a shaping impact on anthropology; for a good recent review, see S. Fleischacker, *The Ethics of Culture*, Ithaca: Cornell University Press, 1994, esp. chapter 5.

19. For a discussion of Indonesia's ethnic and religious composition, and the way in which it is being addressed, see my *After the Fact: Two Countries, Four Decades, One Anthropologist*, Cambridge: Harvard University Press, 1995, esp. chapters 1–3. I have not tried to include here the developments, most of which reinforce my arguments, that have followed upon the collapse of the rupiah, the resignation of Suharto, The Separation of East Timor, and the move, hesitant and confused, back toward popular government. See, also, my "'Ethnic Conflict': Three Alternative Terms," *Common Knowledge* 2, 3 (1992): 55–65.

Index ∞

agency: collective, 234, 257; and cultural theory of emotion, 210
agrarian reform, in new states, 25–28
Allport, Gordon, 8
American Council of Learned Societies, 7
American Psychological Association, 187
American Withdrawal, 219
Anderson, B., 261n.9
anthropologist: and otherness, 63–65; view of informants, 30–37; as writer-down, 126–127. *See also* fieldwork; Symbolic Construction of the State; *names of individuals*
anthropology: comparison in, 251; and cultural psychology, 192–193, 197–201; "Four Fields" ideology of, 90; "from the native's point of view," 76–78; and history, 118–123, 127–128, 132–133; and issue of culture and mind, 204, 207–211; "lost unity" of, 18; permanent identity crisis of, 89–91; tools of, 13–14; unity and diversity in, 97–98. *See also* social sciences
anthropology, cognitive, 136
anthropology, cultural, 90, 93–94; centrifugal movement in, 91, 120; disappearing subject, problem of, 91–92; in disassembled world, 248–250; divisions in, 97–98; lessons learned by author, 15–16; loss of research isolation in, 92–93; methodology of, 93, 110; moral issues of, 95–97; problematic of, 12–16; and relativism, 45; role of fieldwork in, 117–118; as social physics, 94–95, 145. *See also* fieldwork
anthropology, interpretive, 17

anthropology, physical, 90–91, 97
anthropology, psychological, 199
anthropology, symbolic, 17
anticolonial revolution, 230–231, 235; and cultural heterogeneity, 251–256
Antioch College, 5–7
antireductionism, 196
anti-relativism, 42–46; naturalist approach, 51–59; overheated presentation of, 46–51; rationalist approach, 59–63
Apter, David, 10
archaeology, 90–91, 97
argument, moral: and softening of cultural diversity, 78–82
Arnold, Matthew, 233
Astington, Janet, 211
asymmetry, moral: and cultural diversity, 79–82; of fieldwork, 29–37
Auster, Paul, 107

Bacon, Francis, 214
Bagehot, Walter, 128
Bali, author's fieldwork in, 9–10, 17
Barzun, Jacques, 22
Beckett, Samuel, 19
belief, "irrational," and anti-relativism, 60
Bellow, Saul, 193
Benedict, Ruth, 12, 44–45
Berlin, Isaiah, 257
biologism, 196
Black, Conrad, 238, 240
Boas, Franz, 12, 44
body-part imagery, to represent emotion, 212
Booth, Wayne, 43

boundaries, social/cultural, 79
Bourdieu, Pierre, 93
brain: embodied, 213; study of, 205–206. *See also* neurology
Braudel, Fernand, 120
Brenner, Suzanne, 179–184
Briggs, Jean, 208
Bruner, Jerome, 8, 211; and Cognitive Revolution, 188–190; and cultural psychology, 190–197
Burckhardt, Jakob, 128
Burma, Spiro's fieldwork in, 56

Callon, Michel, 159n.22
Canada, as "country" and "nation," 237–240, 245
Cannadine, David, 131
capitalism, borderless, 247, 250
caring, and scientific detachment, 40–41
Case of the Drunken Indian and the Kidney Machine, 79–82
Cavell, Stanley, 179
Center for Advanced Study in the Behavioral Sciences, 10
change: scientific, 160–166; world historical, 218–224
children. *See* early development, human
Chodorow, Nancy, 210–211
Chomsky, Noam, 206
Churchland, Patricia, 207
circumstantiality, and local knowledge, 137–138
civilization, 222, 224
Clark, Andy, 199, 204–205
Clastres, Pierre, 107–114, 116–118
Clendinnen, Inga, 123–125
Clifford, James, 108–110, 114–116, 118
Coase, Ronald, 10
Cobb, Richard, 120
Cognitive Revolution, 188–190
cognitive science, 61, 91, 151–152, 197, 203
cognitivism, 196
Cohn, Bernard, 130
Cole, Michael, 201–202n.14, 205
collage, society as, 85–88
colonialism, 95. *See also* anticolonial revolution
comparison: as characteristic of anthropology, 251; and local knowledge, 138
Conant, James Bryant, 166

consensus: and culture, 246–250, 252–255; universal, abandonment of hope for, 73
contact zones, Pratt's concept of, 108, 115–116
contextualism, 196
Cook, Captain James: debate over death of, 98–107
counterculture, Antioch College and, 5
country, 232–233; and culture, 228–231; and nation, 231–246
cultural anthropology. *See* anthropology, cultural
cultural deprivation hypothesis, 191–192
culture, 11–16; in anthropology and cultural psychology, 197–201; and consensus, 246–250, 254–255; and country, 228–231; and cultures, 248–250; and early development, 192; and mind, 203–207; and nature, 248
cultures, identifying, 247–248

Damasio, Antonio, 213–214
D'Andrade, Roy, 211
Danto, Arthur, 75, 77–78
data, anthropological: and relativism, 44–46
Davis, Natalie, 130
Dening, Greg, 123, 125–128
Dennett, Daniel, 207
detachment, scientific, 38–41
deviance, social: and anti-relativism, 57–60
Dewey, John, 21–22
difference, cultural: difference of, 177–178, 197–198, 200; recognition of, 226; and similarity, 226–227; understanding of, 102–107
Dilthey, Wilhelm, 145
"disappearing subject" problem, 91–92
disassembly, of bipolar world, 218–224, 235
disciplinary matrices, Kuhn's notion of, 206–207
diversity, cultural: and alternatives to us, 75–76; "deep," 224, 238–239; within a society, 79–82, 85–88, 177–178; softening of, 68–69, 78–82. *See also* ethnocentrism
diversity, in study of mind, 197–201
Douglas, Mary, 93, 120, 204
dress, women's, 179–184, 186n.10
DuBois, Cora, 9
Dumont, Louis, 93
Dworkin, Ronald, 219, 256

early development, human, 190–194, 211–212

Edelman, Gerald, 150–152, 206

Edgerton, Robert, 58

education: author's, 4–9; and Bruner's cultural psychology, 190–197; as example of touching faith problem, 32

educational reform, 192–194

Eggan, Fred, 10

Einstein, Albert, 49, 166

Eliade, Mircea, 128

emotion: culturalist theory of, 208–211; feeling of, 212; neurology and, 213–214; semiotic approach to, 208; vocabulary of, 208–209

Empson, William, 50

ethnicity, 225

ethnocentrism: author's views on, 74–75; future of, 69, 72, 86–88; Lévi-Strauss on, 70–72; Obeyesekere and, 105–106; revival of, 72–74; Sahlins and, 100, 105–106; trouble with, 75–78

ethnographer, 82–85

ethnography, 83–85

Evans-Pritchard, Edward, 128

"everything else hasn't worked" argument, 177

"evils of modernization" argument, 177–178

exceptionalism, European, 251, 256, 261n.10

experience, and religion, 170–171, 178–179, 182–184

favorite-cause analysis, and religion, 173

feelings. See emotion

Feldman, Carol, 211

Feyerabend, Paul, 162

Feynman, Richard, 153

fieldwork: and concept of culture, 14–16; as distinguishing methodology, 93, 110; as fusion of personal and professional spheres, 39–41; future of, 110, 117–118; and loss of research isolation, 92–93; moral asymmetry of, 29–37; role of detachment in, 39–41

fieldwork, author's: ethical dimensions of, 23–37; relinquishing of, 19; start in, 9; typewriter anecdote, 34–37. See also place names

"fieldwork habitus," Clifford's view of, 114–115

Fish, Stanley, 43

Fodor, Jerry, 62

Fogel, Robert, 19–20

Forster, E. M., 260

Fortes, Meyer, 10

Foucault, Michel, 120, 162

Frawley, William, 199, 211

Frazer, Sir James, 128

Freud, Sigmund, 49, 206

Frost, Robert, 20

Gadjah Mada (Indonesia), 9

Gage matrix, 213–214

Gass, William, 47–48

Geertz, Clifford, 93, 208, 210. See also fieldwork, author's

Geertz, Hildred, 7–9

Geiger, George, 7–8

Gellner, Ernest, 62, 93

generalizations, 134–136

Genovese, Eugene, 130

Getty, J. Paul, 240

G.I. Bill, 4

Gilbert, Felix, 130

Ginsburg, Carlo, 130

Glenny, Misha, 244–245

globalization, economic, 177

global village, 247, 250

Gödel, Kurt, 166

Goffman, Erving, 175

Goodman, Nelson, 211

Goody Jack, 93

Gorer, Geoffrey, 12

Grebo, Zdravko, 244–245

Greenberg, Joseph, 10

Guayaki, the, 107–108, 110–114

Hacking, Ian, 162

Handy, E. S. C., 127

Hanson, Norwood Russell, 162

Harris, Marvin, 93

Hartley, L. P., 120

Harvard: Center for Cognitive Studies, 189; Social Relations department, 7–9

Hawaiians, and death of Cook, 98–107

Head Start program, 190–192

Herodotus, 44

Herskovits, Melville, 44–45

Hesse, Mary, 162

heterogeneity, cultural: and anticolonial revolution, 251–256

psychology, cultural, 194–198, 207; and anthropology, 197–201; Bruner and, 190–197; and issue of culture and mind, 204–205

psychology, developmental/comparative, 211–212

psychology, evolutionary, 51

Putnam, Hillary, 221

Quebec, and Canada, 239–240

Quine, W. V. O., 10

quotation, use of, 109

rationality, practical: Obeyesekere and, 103–104

rationality debate, 61–63

Rawls, John, 219, 256

rebelliousness, as overpraised virtue, 18–19

Redfield, Robert, 12, 44

reductionism, 196

relativism, 164, 259. *See also* anti-relativism

religion: contemporary resurgence of, 172–178; and experience, 170–171, 178–179, 182–184; and favorite-cause analysis, 173; James and, 167–171, 184–185; Javanese, 15; subjectivism of, 170–171

religious change, communal dimension of, 178–179

religious struggle, 169–170

research, social scientific, 37–38

research isolation, loss of, 92–93

revolution of rising expectations, 32

Rorty, Richard, 59, 73–74, 77, 146, 150

Rosaldo, Michelle, 208, 210

Rosaldo, Renato, 137

Ruelle, David, 152–153

Sacks, Oliver, 213

Sahlins, Marshall, 93, 98–107, 206. *See also* Obeyesekere-Sahlins debate

Salkever, Stephen, 54–55

Sandel, Michael, 219

Sapir, Edward, 12

Scheffler, Israel, 43

Schneider, David, 8

Schorske, Carl, 120

science studies, 153–155, 164–165

scientism, 94–95, 136–137. *See also* naturalism

sentiment, James and, 168, 185

Shils, Edward, 10

Shore, B., 201–202n.14

Shweder, Richard, 208, 212

Sinhalese, the, 241–242

Skinner, B. F., 22

Skinner, Quentin, 218

social anthropology. *See* anthropology, cultural

social sciences, 138–140; cultural entrenchment of, 149–150; interpretation in, 143–144, 153–155; moral status of, 22–23, 37–41; and naturalism, 143–146, 156–157; scientism in, 136–137

social sciences, and natural sciences: "great divide" formulation, 150–153; and Kuhn's *Structure*, 160–166

society, 233; as collage, 85–88

sociobiology, 51

sociology of knowledge, 154, 161–162, 164–165

sociology of science, 154

Sorokin, Pitrim, 9

Soviet Union, breakup of, 230

Spanish, and Maya society: Clendinnen's study of, 124–125

Sperber, Dan, 62–63

Spiro, Melford, 10, 55–57, 93

Sri Lanka, as "country" and "nation," 237–238, 240–242, 245

state, 233; role of symbolic forms in, 128–132

state building, and communal conflict, 173–174

Stocking, George, 49

Stone, Lawrence, 120

Stouffer, Samuel, 8

structuralism, 107; Clastres and, 107, 112; Sahlins and, 103

subjectivism, of religion, 170–171

subjectivity, and cultural theory of emotion, 210

Sumatra, author's fieldwork in, 9–10

Symbolic Construction of the State, 128–132

symbolic domination, 129

Tamils, in Sri Lanka, 241–242

Taylor, Charles, 143–146, 156–157, 207, 219, 224

theory, anthropological: and notion of relativism, 44–46

Thomas, Hugh, 48